GW01091393

THE BBC MICROCOMPUTER FOR BEGINNERS

Seamus Dunn
Valerie Morgan
Lecturers in Education, New University of Ulster

Englewood Cliffs, New Jersey London New Delhi Rio de Janeiro
Singapore Sydney Tokyo Toronto Wellington

To LTS

Library of Congress Cataloging in Publication Data

Dunn, Seamus, 1939-
The BBC Microcomputer for beginners.

Bibliography: p.
Includes index.
Summary: Instructs the beginner in writing programs in the BASIC language and with facilities and characteristics of the BBC Microcomputer.
1. BBC Microcomputer—Programming—Juvenile literature.
2. Basic (Computer program language)—Juvenile literature.
[1. BBC Microcomputer—Programming. 2. Microcomputers—Programming. 3. Minicomputers—Programming. 4. Programming (Computers)] I. Morgan, Valerie, 1943-
II. Title. III. Title: BBC microcomputer for beginners.
QA76.8.B35D86 1983. 001.64'2 83-9494
ISBN 0-13-069328-6 (pbk.)

British Library Cataloging in Publication Data

Dunn, Seamus
The BBC microcomputer for beginners.
1. BBC microcomputer
I. Title II. Morgan, Valerie
001.64'04 QA76.8.B3
ISBN 0-13-069328-6

ISBN 0-13-069328-6

PRENTICE-HALL INTERNATIONAL, INC., *London*
PRENTICE-HALL OF AUSTRALIA PTY. Ltd., *Sydney*
PRENTICE-HALL CANADA, INC., *Toronto*
PRENTICE-HALL OF INDIA PRIVATE LIMITED, *New Delhi*
PRENTICE-HALL OF JAPAN, INC., *Tokyo*
PRENTICE-HALL OF SOUTHEAST ASIA PTE. LTD., *Singapore*
PRENTICE-HALL INC., *Englewood Cliffs, New Jersey*
PRENTICE-HALL DO BRASIL LTDA., *Rio de Janeiro*
WHITEHALL BOOKS LIMITED, *Wellington, N.Z.*

Printed in the United Kingdom
by A. Wheaton & Co Ltd., Exeter

10 9 8 7 6 5 4 3 2

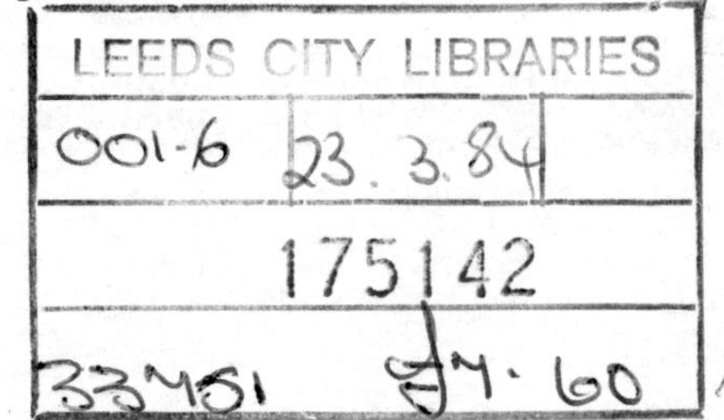

CONTENTS

PREFACE

This is a book with two purposes each of which supports and complements the other. The first is to teach the beginner how to write clear well-structured programs in the BASIC language; and the second is to ensure that the reader becomes familiar with all the facilities and characteristics of the BBC microcomputer.

The book emphasizes learning by doing. It should be read and used while sitting in front of the computer typing-in programs and instructions. It is not meant to be read by itself, independently. The contents have been tightly sequenced so that progress is made carefully and gradually with respect to each of the two purposes. However, any reader already familiar with the BASIC language could quickly use this knowledge to find out from this book how the various special characteristics of the BBC machine work.

Many books about BASIC are written either for large mainframe computers or are not designed for any particular machine or for any particular dialect of the BASIC language. This means that they can deal only with very general programming and are forced to leave out much that is specific and interesting. To some extent this means that the most important advantages of microcomputers are missed out. A machine like the BBC microcomputer allows the user not only the normal programming facilities but also a great variety of new sophisticated techniques, some of which arise from the way in which BASIC has been implemented, and some of which are to do with presentation, graphics, music and so on.

For these reasons, this book concentrates very carefully on bringing together the development of programming skills and the development of knowledge about the machine itself. In each chapter therefore new words and ideas related to programming and to some of the machine's special facilities (such as color, sound, graphics) are introduced and tried out.

The book has a total of fourteen chapters with exercises, and there are appendices containing summaries of data and information referred to in the book. Some of this information is hard to find elsewhere. The material can be used with either Model A or Model B of the machine.

CHAPTER 1
BEGINNING

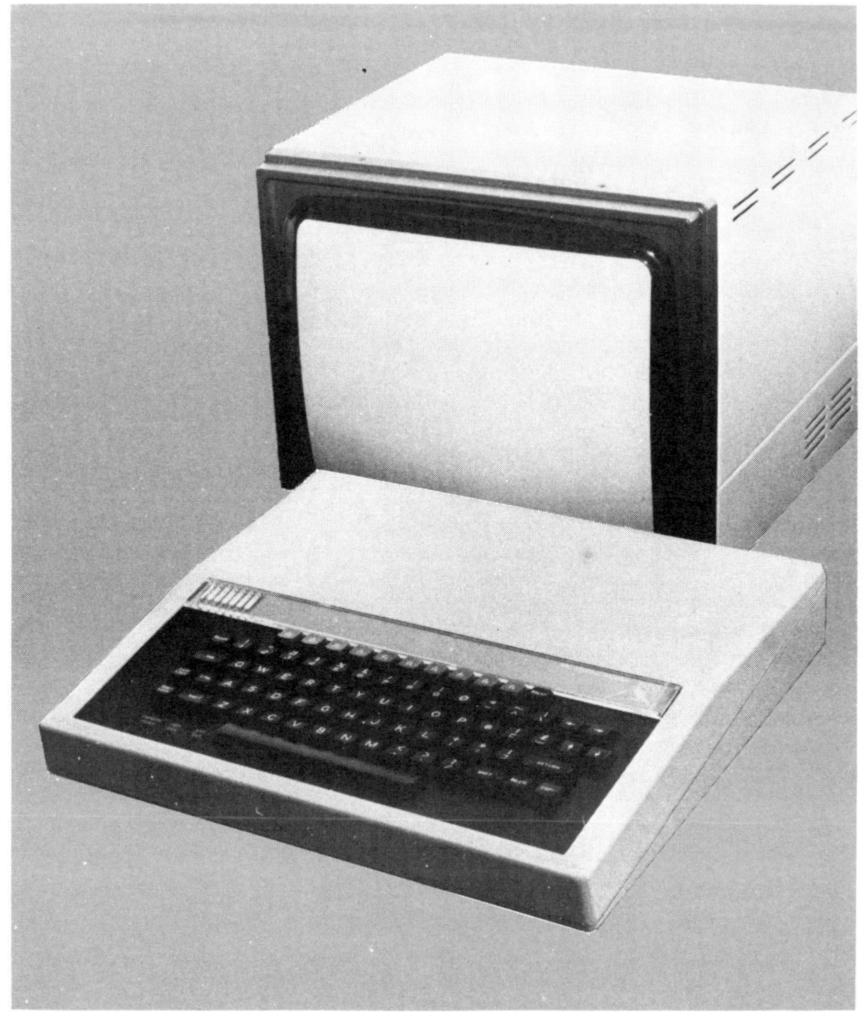

Getting started

The BBC microcomputer is a small cream-colored box, rather like a typewriter but with nowhere to put the paper. The keys are all black except for a row of 10 red keys along the top. Above the keyboard on the right are the words 'BBC Microcomputer' followed by a dotted 'owl' motif. On the bottom left there are three red warning lights, with the words 'cassette motor', 'caps lock' and 'shift lock' above them.

At the back (left) a power line is attached which should be connected to a plug in the usual way, and plugged into a normal power socket. There is a rocker switch beside this, but do not switch this on as yet.

You now need a monitor or a TV set, preferably one that allows color, although this is not essential. This must be connected to the computer using a cable, one end of which is attached to the normal aerial input on a TV (or the corresponding input on a monitor) and the other end of which is attached either to the socket marked 'UHF out' or to the socket marked 'video out'. Both of these are at the back (right) of the computer. If you are using a TV then an appropriate cable will have been supplied with the computer.

When this is attached (if you have difficulty see pages 7 and 8 of the User Guide supplied with the machine) turn on the TV and the computer, and wait for the TV to warm up a little. Notice that the computer makes a little bleep sound when it is switched on. If nothing appears on the screen except a bubbling white mass, then you will have to tune your TV. Press the button on any channel unlikely to be used for watching TV, such as channel 6 or 7, and turn the tuning button until the screen looks something like this. (On model B the 16 on the first line will be 32).

```
BBC Computer 16K

BASIC
>_
```

You are now ready to begin.

Typing on the screen

We will now try to make you familiar with the keyboard by performing a few simple exercises. When you press a key on the computer, the letter or number written on the key appears on the screen. You must press the key and then let it go at once. A little flashing dash (or thin rectangle) on the screen indicates where the letter on number will appear. This flashing rectangle is called the CURSOR. To demonstrate this, type in the word DOG. When you have done so, the screen will look like this:

```
BBC Computer 16K

BASIC

>DOG_
```

Nothing else happens because the computer does not know that you have finished. Now find the key with the word RETURN written on it. It is on the right side of the keyboard. Now press this key. The computer will respond, and the screen should look like this:

```
BBC Computer 16K

BASIC

>DOG

Mistake
>_
```

The key marked RETURN is the most important one on the computer. You must always press it when you wish to indicate that you have finished with your input and now wish the computer to do something. If you do not press it the computer will just sit there and do nothing.

In this case the response was the word Mistake which means that the computer did not recognize the word DOG as having any meaning for it. So the cursor has just moved onto the next line and is waiting for your next try at communication

You may now wish to go right back to the beginning and try all that again. One way to do this is to find the key on the top right with the word BREAK written on it. Press this, and the screen will now look almost exactly as it did when you first switched on. This is a very dangerous key and we mention it here mainly to make you aware of the danger. It has more or less the same effect as switching off and then switching on again. Obviously on most occasions it will not be wise to use this key.

Try typing in some other words, and remember to press RETURN after each. See if you can find a word which the computer recognizes. It is virtually impossible to damage the machine by pressing the keys.

Now try typing in a number. For example, when 45 is typed in, and the RETURN key pressed, the screen looks like this. (It does not exactly look like this, since we have been typing in other words, but we are just showing you the bit of the screen that we wish to talk about).

```
>45
>_
```

This time the word Mistake does not appear. The computer does not reject this number, but it does not do anything obvious with it either. Try other things with numbers. It may work like some calculators, so try something like 7-3 and then press RETURN. (The minus sign is on the top row).

Again there is no obvious answer and no Mistake message. We obviously need to learn the words that the computer understands and can respond to. It has a very limited vocabulary of about 120 words. The first of these to consider is the word PRINT.

The word PRINT

Type in the word PRINT followed by a number, like this: PRINT 48. Then press RETURN. The screen will look like this.

There are two things to notice about this. First, the computer has, for the first time, done exactly what we asked it to do. That is it has printed the number 48 on the next line. It has then gone on to the next line and is waiting for the next instruction.

The second thing to notice is that it has printed 48, not at the beginning of the line, but out about 10 columns. It will always do this with numbers. To demonstrate this, type in PRINT 3 and press RETURN. The 3 will be printed on the same column as the 8 of 48. This is the tenth column out from the left. The computer will print any number in such a way that its last digit appears on this tenth column. Check this by typing in some other numbers and pressing RETURN. Like this:

```
PRINT  1341          and press RETURN
PRINT 78932          and press RETURN
PRINT   134.6        and press RETURN
```

We now wish to use this word PRINT to get the computer to do some arithmetic. We will begin with addition, and suppose that we want the answer to 4+3.
Type in PRINT and then press the key with 4 on it. Then press the key with + on it. The result will be as follows:

That is the semicolon has appeared on the screen, instead of the plus. Notice that both the semicolon and the plus are written on the same key. When you simply press it, you get the semicolon. To get the plus you must use the SHIFT key. There are two of these, one on the left and one on the right of the bottom row of keys.

DELETE and SHIFT

First, however, we must get rid of the semicolon. To do this we use the DELETE key. This is on the bottom right side of the keyboard. Press it once. The result will be that the cursor moves back one place and wipes out the semicolon.

Now put one finger on the SHIFT key and hold it down. Then press the key with both the plus and the semicolon on it, and let go of both keys. This should produce a plus on the screen. If it does not, use the DELETE key and try again. Remember that you must HOLD the SHIFT key down while pressing the other one. Now press the 3 key and then press RETURN. The result is as follows:

```
>PRINT 4+3
         7
>-
```

To demonstrate this further, let us make some more mistakes. Suppose that we wished to type PRINT 13+4. Type in PRINT 13. Now type in 4567; so that the screen looks like this:

```
>PRINT 134567;_
```

Then press the DELETE key to remove the semicolon. Then press it again to get rid of the 7. Then press it again, and continue to press it until only PRINT 13 remains on the screen. Then hold the shift key and press + as before Then let go both keys. Then press 4 and then RETURN. The result will be 17.

These keys, the DELETE key and the two SHIFT keys, are very important. If at any time you make a mistake on the screen, you can always use the DELETE key to go back and correct it. When you wish to use any of the keys with two symbols, the top symbol can only be printed by holding one of the SHIFT keys.

Doing arithmetic

We now know how to do addition on the computer. Subtraction is done in exactly the same way. Try a few more examples like these. Remember to press the RETURN key when you want the answer.

```
PRINT 25 + 30
PRINT 17 - 11
PRINT 23 + 18 - 16
```

The multiplication sign is the star which is on the same key as the colon. To use it you must use the SHIFT key. Now try some multiplication problems, like these:

```
PRINT 5 * 7
PRINT 8 * 3 - 5
PRINT 3 * (8 + 4)
```

Notice that, in this last one we used the brackets to enclose the sum of 8 and 4. This means that we are multiplying together 3 and 12, so the answer should be 36. There are two mistakes you might make here. First, you might leave out the brackets. Type it in, as follows:

```
PRINT 3 * 8 + 4
```

and press RETURN. This time the answer is 28. That is, three and eight are multiplied together, and four is added to the result. The other mistake is to leave out the multiplication sign, that is the star. Type this in:

```
PRINT 3(8 + 4)
```

and press RETURN. The screen looks like this:

```
>PRINT 3(8 + 4)
          3      12
>_
```

That is, the computer has treated this as two problems. First PRINT 3 and then PRINT 8+4. So it is most important not to leave out the multiplication sign.

The sign for division is the slash line on the same key as the question mark. It looks like this /. Try some examples; remember to press RETURN after each.

```
PRINT 12/3
PRINT 20/4
PRINT 17/8
```

Finally, try some more complicated problems using a variety of operations. Remember that if you wish to ensure that a particular operation is done first, put brackets round it. Here is an example:

```
PRINT 3 + 5 * (6 - 2)
```

The computer will calculate 6-2 first, to get 4. It will then multiply this by 5 to get 20, because multiplication is done before addition. Finally, it will add 3 to get 23. To summarise this the symbols used in arithmetic are:

```
+  add
-  subtract
*  multiply
/  divide
```

The order in which these are performed is:

(a) Any operations put inside brackets are done first.
(b) If there are brackets within brackets, the inside ones are cleared first.
(c) The arithmetical operations are then performed in this order: multiplication and division first, then addition and subtraction.

The red keys

Later on in this book there will be a section on the ten red special-function keys along the top of the keyboard. We will, however, use one of them now just to demonstrate the idea. They are labelled f0, f1, and so on up to f9. We will use the first one labelled f0. (f is short for function).

The first word in the computer's vocabulary that we have met is the word PRINT. Since we have to use this a great deal it would be handy if we could type it by just pressing a single key. Type in the following line carefully. Don't worry for the moment about what it means. The symbol 0 after the word KEY represents the numeral zero and is on the second row of the keyboard. There it appears with a stroke across it. It must not be confused with the letter O which is just below it on the keyboard.

```
* KEY 0 PRINT
```

Now press the key marked RETURN. The red key f0 has now been programmed. We can now use it as follows. Suppose that we wished to type in

    PRINT 35 * 4

First, press the red key f0. Immediately the word PRINT will appear on the screen. Then type in the rest of calculation and press RETURN. This means that each time you wish to use the word print, just press the key f0.

Look at the line again. The star and the word KEY tell the computer that we are about to 'program' one of the special-function f keys. The zero, in this case, tells it which of the f keys we are referring to. The word after this is the statement or command that will now be associated with that key.

If you switch the machine off and then on again, you will have lost this facility and will have to type it in again. However, using the BREAK key does not remove it.

PRINT with words

We now know how to use PRINT with numbers to do calculations. We must now try to print letters and words. Type in PRINT A. (Remember to use your f0 key). Now press RETURN. The result is as follows:

```
> PRINT A

No such variable
>_
```

Try some other letters, or even words. For example, try PRINT PRINT by pressing f0 twice and then pressing RETURN. The same message, 'No such variable', will appear each time. This is because nearly all letters or words represent variables for the computer. You can think of a variable as the name or the title of a unit of memory inside the machine. This unit of memory is then used to store a number in. The variable does not exist until it has a number stored in it, and so, in this case we get this message "No such variable". (There will be much more about variables and their meaning later on Page 32).

Now try this again, only this time put quotation marks around the word or letter that you wish to print. Here is an example. It shows what happens when you type in PRINT "BBC" and press RETURN.

```
>PRINT "BBC"
BBC
>_
```

So, the computer will print exactly what it finds inside quotation marks. Try a line containing some of the other symbols as well as letters:

```
>PRINT "* & 6 ARE SYMBOLS"
* ! & 6 ARE SYMBOLS
>
```

Notice also that, unlike numbers, material inside quotation marks is printed starting on the column on the extreme left of the screen. If you type in a long sentence you will, after forty characters, reach the edge of the screen. You can however keep on typing in material onto the next line and the computer will accept both lines as one.

You can now combine material of this kind with number calculations. Here is an example:

```
>PRINT "THE SUM OF 3 AND 4 IS" 3+4
THE SUM OF 3 AND 4 IS          7

 _
```

Notice that the words and numbers inside the quotation marks appear in the result exactly as printed; but the actual calculation of 3+4 is left outside the quotation marks and so this is performed and becomes 7. You could get further insight into this by typing in the following, and pressing RETURN.

```
PRINT "THE SUM OF 3 AND 4 IS 3+4"
```

This time everything is put inside quotation marks, and so the actual calculation is not performed. Do some more examples like this and think about the difference.

Drawing and color

The BBC microcomputer has very good drawing and color facilities. We will develop these ideas a little at a time as we go through the book without always going into a lot of detail especially at the beginning.

First type in MODE 5 and press the RETURN key. The screen will clear and the cursor will appear at the top left hand corner of the screen. The computer has 8 possible modes each with a different combination of color, graphics and text facilities. (Model A of the computer has only enough memory to support 4 of these modes). When it is switched on the machine is in MODE 7 automatically, and you could now get back to this mode simply by typing in MODE 7 and pressing RETURN.

There are essentially two differences between modes 5 and 7. We can demonstrate the first at once. Press the f0 key to put PRINT on the screen and then press RETURN. Now look at the actual letters in the word. They look different and are in fact twice as broad as letters in mode 7. This means that you can only have 20 letters or symbols on one row across the screen. When in mode 7 it is possible to have 40 letters or symbols across the screen.

The second difference is that in mode 5 we can use some new words to draw line pictures on the screen in what are called high resolution graphics. These words will not work in mode 7 and would just be ignored. The first word we will use is DRAW. Type in this and then press RETURN:

```
DRAW 500,600
```

The screen will now look something like this:

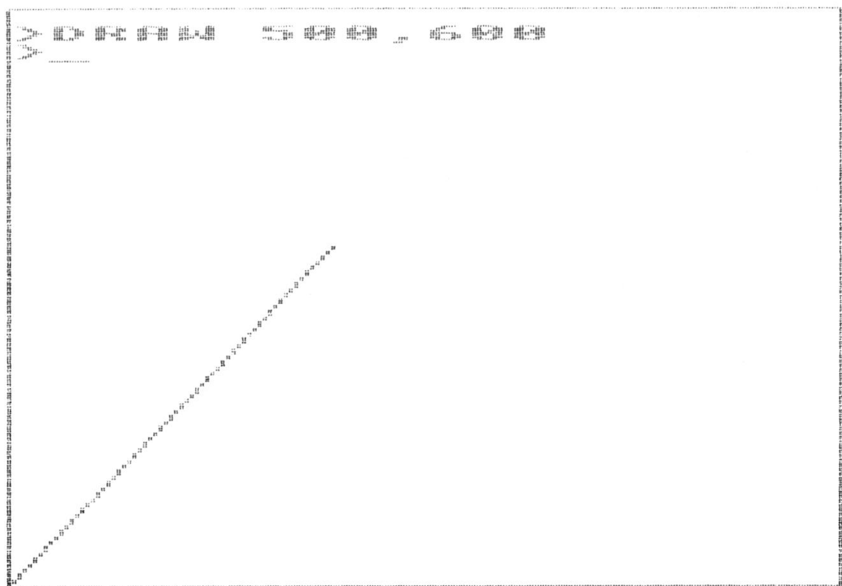

When using DRAW the screen must be thought of as being numbered like this:

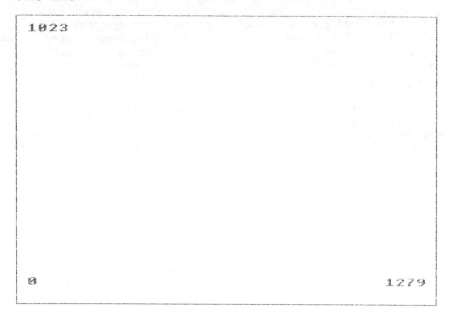

If you move along the bottom of the screen 500 points and then move up the screen 600 points, you will have reached the point 500,600. So the instruction "DRAW 500,600" resulted in a line being drawn from the point (0,0), that is the bottom left hand corner, to this point 500,600.

Now type in DRAW 900,300 and press RETURN. This time the screen must be thought of as looking like this:

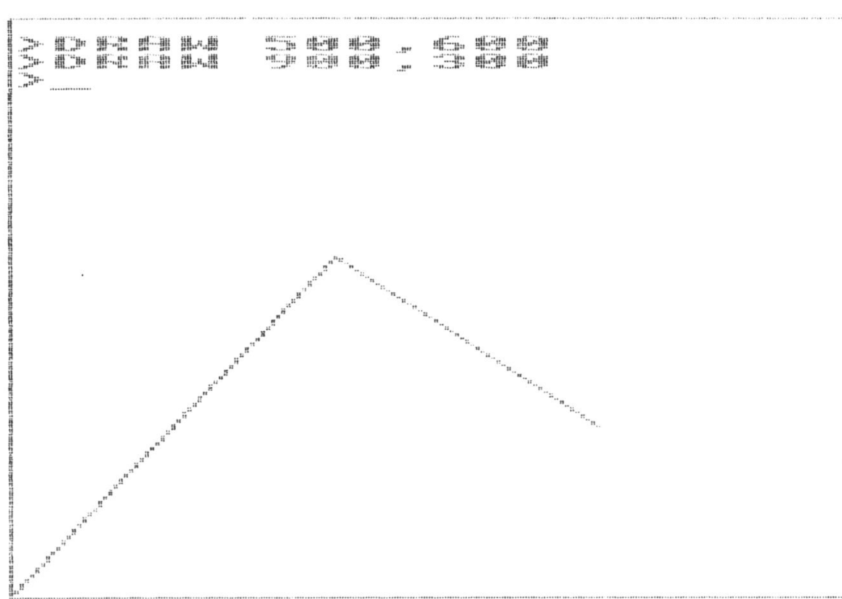

So the word DRAW means that the line will begin at the last point reached (in this case 500,600) and will be joined to the new point (in this case 900,300). Only the first line starts at the point (0,0). Now complete the triangle by typing in DRAW 0,0.

Suppose that we now wished to draw a rectangle in the middle of the screen, like this:

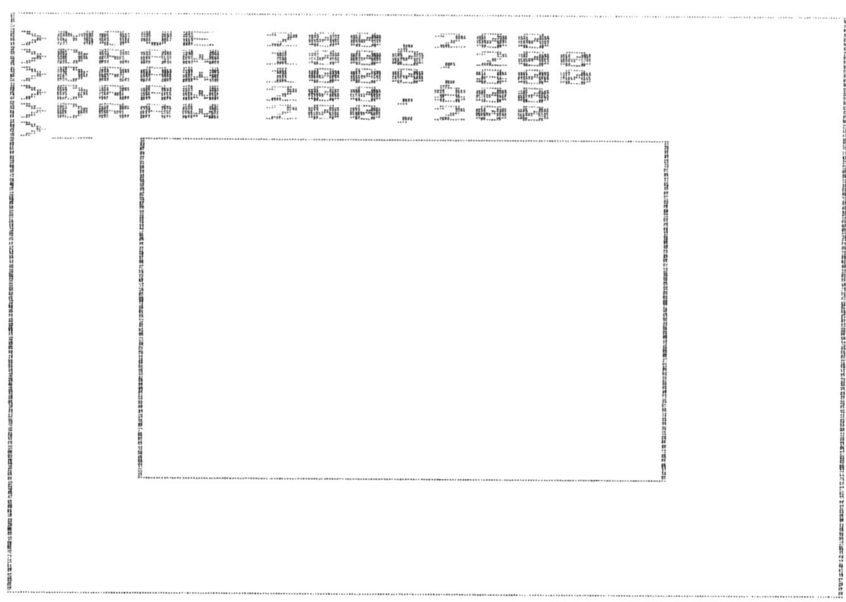

First type in MODE 5 and press RETURN. This clears the screen and returns the computer to its original state. This means that if you now use the word DRAW, a line will be drawn from the bottom left-hand corner, and we do not want this. So we introduce a new word, that is MOVE. Type in

```
MOVE 200,200
```

and press RETURN. Nothing obvious happens, but the computer has moved the starting-point for drawing to the point (200,200). Now type in

```
DRAW 1000,200
```

and press RETURN. The result is that the bottom line of the rectangle is drawn. To complete the rectangle type in the next three statements, and press RETURN after each:

```
DRAW 1000,800
DRAW  200,800
DRAW  200,200
```

You should now have completed the full rectangle.

In mode 5 we can write and draw using four different colours, that is Black, Red, Yellow and White. If you are using a Black and White TV set these will appear as shades of gray. In the discussion that follows we will assume that you are using a color set. As usual, type in MODE 5 and press RETURN. Now type in COLOUR 1 and press RETURN. (Notice that the machine uses the British spelling of color, i.e. colour). Now type in this line:

```
PRINT "WRITING IS NOW IN RED"
```

and press RETURN. All letters should now be appearing in red. If they are not try tuning your set.

Now type in COLOUR 2, and press RETURN. Now type in some message and again press RETURN. This time the writing will be in yellow. Then try COLOUR 3, and this time the writing will be in white. Finally, type in COLOUR 0, and press RETURN. The color of letters will now be black, but since the screen is also black they cannot be seen at all. To recover from this situation type in COLOUR 3 and press RETURN.

You can experiment with these colors, using numbers other than 0,1,2, or 3, to see what happens. A summary of the colors and their numbers is given below:

```
BLACK     0
RED       1
YELLOW    2
WHITE     3
```

Now type in CLS and press RETURN. The effect is to clear the screen completely. CLS is short for Clear Screen. Now type in MODE 7 and press RETURN.

More communication

When we were dealing with numbers and letters we met PRINT, the first word of the computer's vocabulary. Then when we looked at graphics we met the set of words MODE, DRAW, MOVE, COLOUR and CLS. The next word to be considered is LET. Oddly enough the word LET is not necessary and later on will be left out. But it is useful at this stage because it helps to demonstrate a particular point.

Type in these two lines: (At the end of each we have put the word RET. This is short for RETURN, and is there to remind you to press the RETURN key. We will use this signal from now on. When you see it, just press the RETURN key. Do not type in RET).

```
LET A = 3    RET
PRINT A      RET
```

The result is that the number 3 is printed as shown.

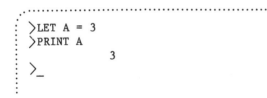

```
>LET A = 3
>PRINT A
          3
>_
```

To explain this we must try to understand what happens inside the computer. The first line LET A = 3 chooses a unit of memory, labels it A, and stores the number 3 inside it. We must imagine a box like this:

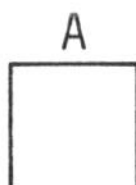

It is labelled A, and the number that is placed in this box called A can be changed to any other number at any time. That is the contents of A can vary. For this reason A is called a variable. However the actual number that is placed in A at any time is called a constant. So, in this case the variable A contains the constant 3.

Typing in a line like LET A = 3 enters it on the screen only; but pressing the RETURN key enters the line into the computer's memory. The next line, which is a request to PRINT A, makes the computer take the number that is stored in the unit of memory called A (that is, the number 3) and print it on the screen.

Now type in the following. Remember that RET means press the RETURN key.

```
LET A = 5     RET
LET B = 4     RET
LET C = A*B   RET
PRINT C       RET
```

The result will be 20. It is possible to shorten this a little by putting all these statements on one line, separated by full colons.

```
LET A = 5 : LET B = 4 : LET C = A*B : PRINT C   RET
```

Notice that the RETURN key needs only to be pressed once, at the end of the line. The colon is interpreted by the computer as meaning the end of a statement, as though the RETURN key had been pressed. Finally the word LET can be left out, if it is desired, so the last example could be shortened further to:

```
A = 5 : B = 4 : C = A*B : PRINT C    RET
```

Strings

When any letters or symbols which are not simply numbers to be calculated with are being used the computer treats these as, what are called, strings. This means that even numbers, if put in quotation marks, are considered by the computer as strings. For example 32 is a number to the computer but "32" is a string. Similarly PC32 is a string simply by not being a number. (Unless of course it is a variable name). The following are all examples of strings. They are always placed inside quotation marks.

(a) "MICROCOMPUTER"
(b) "BBC TV"
(c) "A/O*$"

Any letter or number or string that the computer can use is called a character; and any collection of characters represents a string. This means that a string can be a recognizable word, although it need not be, and it can include numbers, symbols, spaces. Type in some of these and put a PRINT in front. Like this:

```
PRINT "Z4K9 IS NOT A WORD"    RET
```

Now try this:

```
LET A$ = "HELLO"       RET
```

Now type in PRINT A$ and press RETURN. As with numbers it is possible to choose a unit of memory to store strings in, but the letter used must be followed by a dollar sign as above. This is read "A-STRING" and the unit of memory labelled A$ has the word (or string) HELLO stored inside it. So the screen should look like this:

```
>LET A$ = "HELLO"
>PRINT A$
HELLO
>_
```

Labels like A$ are called STRING VARIABLES because they can be used to represent any string. That is to say the store labelled A$ can be made to contain any string. So A$ is the variable and the word stored in it, in this case HELLO, is a constant. Try the following. Remember that RET means press the RETURN key.

```
A$ = "ACORN" : PRINT A$              RET
B$ = "MICRO COMPUTER" : PRINT B$     RET
C$ = "RUBBISH" : PRINT C$            RET
```

Strings can be 'added' together to make longer strings using an ordinary plus sign.

```
A$ = "COM" : B$ = "PUTER" : C$ = A$+B$ : PRINT C$      RET
```

The result is as follows:

```
>A$ = "COM" : B$ = "PUTER" : C$ = A$+B$ : PRINT C$
COMPUTER
>_
```

Notice that there is no space left between the two strings "COM" and "PUTER" when they are added together. If you wished to have a space there are three ways to do it.

```
A$ = "DONALD" : B$ = " " : C$ = "DUCK"   RET
PRINT A$+B$+C$                          RET
```

The result is DONALD DUCK. B$ is produced by leaving a single space between the two quotation marks. The second way to do it is as follows:

```
A$ = "DONALD" : B$ = "DUCK"   RET
PRINT A$+" "+B$               RET
```

The third way to do it is simply to leave a space between the last D of Donald and the quotation marks.

All of the work so far has involved you in direct communication with the computer. You have not yet begun to write programs. This non-programming kind of interaction is called being in COMMAND mode, or IMMEDIATE mode. In the next chapter we will begin to learn how to make the computer act in PROGRAMMING mode.

Problems

1. Use the computer as a calculator, with the word "PRINT" to do some arithmetic problems, like the following:

(a) 4.27 + 31.28 + 173.1
(b) My annual salary is $13452. How much do I get monthly?
(c) What is 6¢% of 73216?
(d) What is the new price caused by a mark-up of 11% on 12345?
(e) If I spend $1.34, $1.78 and $0.69, how much change do I get from $5?

2. To begin with a bill was $172. Therefore, on the computer I write: A = 172 and press RETURN. $13 is added to this each week, so on the computer I write B = 13 and press RETURN. I pay off $27 each week, so again, I write C = 27 and press RETURN. After one week, I still owe:

```
D = A + B - C : PRINT D         RET
```

and the next week, I still owe:

```
D = D + B - C : PRINT D         RET
```

and I keep repeating this last line. Try it and see.

Use the computer to solve this similar problem. A debt of $650 is increased by 2% each week and is decreased by $71 each week.

Use the computer to write the debt on the screen each week until it is paid off.

3. Try this. Type in line 1:

```
A$ = "A" : PRINT A$            RET
```

Then type in line 2:

```
A$ = A$ + A$ : PRINT A$        RET
```

Repeat this line a few times. Begin again with:

```
A$ = "12345" : PRINT A$        RET
```

(Remember that RET means press the RETURN key).

4. Type in a sequence of lines which will draw a five-pointed star on the screen like this:

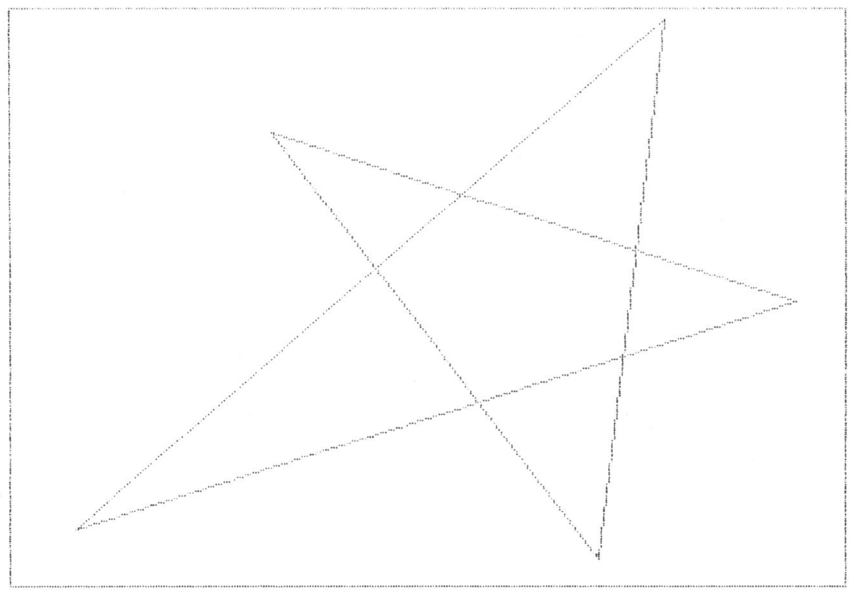

CHAPTER 2
PROGRAMMING

Using BASIC

The BBC microcomputer uses the programming language BASIC. This is built into the machine and is available to be used as soon as the computer is switched on. You cannot harm or destroy the language because it is stored in read-only-memory chips, called ROM chips. As the name suggests these can be read from but cannot be written to. So, although you can access or make use of this language, you cannot change the way it functions.

Of course BASIC is not the only programming language that can be used on the computer, but it is the most simple and the one most easily available. BASIC stands for 'Beginners All-purpose Symbolic Instruction Code'. It has the great advantage that it is an interactive language. That is, you use it and learn about it by sitting at the machine, typing in statements and commands, and getting an immediate response. You don't have to learn it all in a book or write it all down first. You can do a little of all of these as you go along.

Storing in memory

We have already, in Chapter 1, found out how to get a response from the computer by typing in a line like this:

```
PRINT "IMMEDIATE RESPONSE"    RET
```

Remember that RET means press the key marked RETURN. Do this now just to remind yourself about what happens. Now suppose we wished to do this again or something similar. We would have to type it all in again, or use the COPY key. (This is described later on page 37). We have not held onto the instruction or stored it for later use. The instruction to PRINT is used the moment you press RETURN, and cannot be used again without retyping the whole line.

If we wished to write an instruction into the computer in such a way that we could use it again and again, we must start off by giving it a number. This is called PROGRAMMING. Here is an example. Type it in now.

```
1  PRINT "MEMO TO FRED"                              RET
2  PRINT "REMEMBER TO SEND ME A COPY OF"             RET
3  PRINT "FIGURES FROM LAST YEAR.  PLEASE."          RET
4  PRINT "           SEAMUS."                        RET
5  PRINT "P.S. THE ADDRESS IS"                       RET
6  PRINT "COLERAINE, NORTHERN IRELAND."              RET
```

It is very important to remember to press the RETURN key at the end of each line. If you make a mistake remember that you can use the DELETE key.

Notice that, because you have put a line number at the beginning of each line, the computer has not (yet) responded by doing what you have asked it to. It has not printed "MEMO TO FRED" or any of the other parts of the message. Compare this with a direct instruction like this:

```
PRINT "THIS PRINTS AT ONCE"                RET
```

In this case, the computer does respond at once. However the material in the lines numbered 1 to 6 which you have typed in is still in the computer's memory waiting to be used. To demonstrate this, type in the word LIST and press RETURN. Do this a number of times and convince yourself that the program typed in above is still there. You can list it as often as you wish.

So a program is a store of instructions in the form of a set of numbered lines. It is retained in memory waiting to be used. The word it is waiting for is RUN. Type this in and press RETURN. The result will be as follows:

```
MEMO TO FRED
REMEMBER TO SEND ME A COPY OF
FIGURES FROM LAST YEAR.  PLEASE.
           SEAMUS.
P.S. THE ADDRESS IS
COLERAINE, NORTHERN IRELAND.
>_
```

Now type in LIST and press RETURN. Then type in RUN again and press RETURN. Think about the difference between the two responses. When you type in LIST, the program with line numbers is printed on the screen. But when you type in RUN the program is actually used. The computer goes to the line numbered 1 and prints, MEMO TO FRED. It then goes to line 2 and prints the message there; then to line 3, and so on.

Changing line numbers

We may decide that we wish to change this program by putting in an extra line between the lines numbered 1 and 2. Suppose, in this case, we wish to put today's date in after "MEMO TO FRED". At the moment this is not possible. So we need to change the numbering.

You should now do three things. First, type in LIST and press RETURN. Then type in RENUMBER and press RETURN. Finally type in LIST again and press RETURN. Now compare the two listings carefully. The first shows the program exactly as you typed it, with the lines numbered 1,2,3,4,5,6. The second shows the program with the lines numbered 10,20,30,40,50,60. Everything else is the same. So, the effect of the command RENUMBER is to change the line numbers so that the first line number is 10, the second is 20, and so on.

We can now insert the extra line for the date between lines 10 and 20, as follows:

```
15 PRINT "TUESDAY 14th SEPT."              RET
```

Type this in, remember to press RETURN, and then LIST the program again. The computer will have put the lines in the correct numerical order, even though this line numbered 15 was put in last. Now RUN the program again. That is, type in RUN and press RETURN.

Because of this kind of difficulty it is not normal to begin numbering a program with 1,2,3, and so on. You can decide for yourself where to begin and what size of gap to leave between lines. Many programmers like to begin with 10 and go up in jumps of 10, and RENUMBER by itself will do this. Others begin at 100 and go up in jumps of 20. To do this you type in RENUMBER 100,20 and press RETURN. The decision is your own. In this book all program examples will normally begin at 100 and go up in 20's. The largest possible line number is 32767.

However, no matter how you begin to number the lines the RENUMBER command allows you to tidy it all up whenever you wish. To demonstrate this, suppose we now wished to have this program numbered from 1000 with gaps of 200 between line numbers. To do this, type in:

```
RENUMBER 1000,200                RET
```

Now list the program to see if it has worked. Remember that using RENUMBER by itself always has the effect of making the first line number 10, with gaps of 10 between line numbers. (For an interesting response from the computer try typing in RENUMBER 1000,1000).

Removing a program

There are a number of ways of changing a program, removing part of a program from memory, or removing all of a program from memory. Suppose in this case that we had changed our mind and wished to remove the line with the date on it. It is now numbered 1200. So, just type in this number, by itself, and press RETURN. Now LIST again and check that this line has been removed. So to remove any single line just type in its line number and press RETURN.

Now suppose that we wished to send this memo to KEITH rather than to FRED. This means we must change the line numbered 1000. Type in the new line as follows:

```
1000 PRINT "MEMO TO KEITH"        RET
```

Now type in LIST and look at line 1000. The new version of this line simply replaces the old one.

To remove more than one line of a program we use the word DELETE. (This is not to be confused with the key marked DELETE). Suppose that we wished to remove the lines numbered 1400, 1600 and 1800. Type in this

```
DELETE 1400,1800                  RET
```

Now LIST the program to make sure that these lines have been removed. Finally, it may be desirable to remove all of a program. The word used to do this is NEW. Type it in and press RETURN. Now try to LIST the program to make sure that it has been removed. Now suppose that you change your mind again and decide that you had made an awful mistake and really wanted this program after all. It can still be recovered using the word OLD. Type this in now and press RETURN. Then type in LIST and the program should have returned. Notice that OLD does not bring back the lines removed using DELETE. Also, if you type in a program line after using NEW, then OLD will not recover the program.

AUTO and ESCAPE

First type in NEW to remove the current program. Now we wish to type in a short program with line numbers beginning at 100 and going up in 20's, so type in the following:

AUTO 100,20 RET

Immediately the screen looks like this:

```
> AUTO 100,20
  100 _
>
```

In other words, the command AUTO has meant that the computer actually prints the line numbers for you. So now type in:

PRINT "THIS IS AN EXAMPLE" RET

The screen will now look like this:

```
> AUTO 100,20
  100 PRINT "THIS IS AN EXAMPLE"
  120 _
```

This time as soon as you press RETURN the next line number, 120, appears and is waiting for the rest of the line. Type in:

PRINT "OF HOW TO USE AUTO" RET

When you press RETURN, 140 will appear; and the problem now is, how do we stop line numbers appearing automatically. To do this, press the key marked ESCAPE on the top left of the keyboard. The result will look like this:

```
>AUTO 100,20
  100 PRINT "THIS IS AN EXAMPLE"
  120 PRINT "OF HOW TO USE AUTO"
  140
ESCAPE
>_
```

If you type in AUTO by itself and press RETURN the first line number will be 10 and the line numbers will go up in tens, so that the next one will be 20, and the next one 30, and so on. But if you wish to specify what the first line number should be and the amount by which line numbers should increase each time then you must put those numbers after the word AUTO before pressing RETURN. The above example demonstrates this with 100 and 20.

The ESCAPE key can be used in many other situations to get out of difficulties, especially when running programs. If at any time you get stuck and don't know what to do, or if the screen cursor disappears, just press ESCAPE and the computer returns to direct mode. It is much less dangerous than pressing the BREAK key which returns the computer to its original state. (However even after using BREAK the command OLD will restore a program). Now type in LIST and press RETURN to check if the program is still there.

INPUT

Later in this chapter we will rewrite the MEMO program just described, but this time we will write it in such a way that we can change the name of the person to whom it is being sent, the date, and the reason for sending it. This sort of information changes each time we wish to send a memo, and so the program will begin by asking the user to feed this information in as the program is being run. To do this we will use the word INPUT. But, before we do this we need to discuss how the statement INPUT works. First type in NEW and then this program, and we will then discuss what it is doing.

```
100 INPUT A                      RET
120 B = 4 * A                    RET
140 PRINT B                      RET
```

An attempt is being made in the diagram that follows to picture the process that is now described, so keep your eye on this. On the left it shows the program; in the middle it shows what is happening inside the computer's memory; and on the right it shows what should appear on the screen.

Program	Inside Memory	Computer Screen
100 INPUT A	A [ ]	?_
		the user inputs 9
	A [9]	?9
120 B=4*A	A [9] B [36]	?9
140 PRINT B	A [9] B [36]	?9

First type in RUN and press RETURN. The computer will now go to the first line, that is line 100. The instruction there is INPUT A. This means, label a unit of memory A and then invite the person using the computer to put a number on the screen and press RETURN. The computer does this by printing a question mark on the screen and stopping there. So, at this moment there should be a question mark on the screen, which means that the computer is waiting for you.

Type in 9 (or any number) and press RETURN. The computer now stores this 9 in the memory unit labelled A, and then goes on to the next program line numbered 120. It now labels a new unit of memory as B, and stores in this a number which is 4 times the number in A, that is 4 times 9 or 36. It then moves on to line 140 and obeys the instruction there, which is to print on the screen the number stored in B. All of this happens very quickly indeed.

Now RUN the program again, and this time respond to the question mark with a different number, say 5. Try it a few times with different numbers. Now add this line to the program:

```
 90 PRINT "PUT IN ANY NUMBER"                RET
```

Now run the program again. This time the program actually tells us what to do. The introduction of the statement in line 90 has made the program a little bit more understandable to anyone trying to use it. Later on we will consider at length how to write a program so that it is presented on the screen in a sensible easily understood way.

Screen format

Keep the same program, but add the new lines 130 and 135, and change line 140. The new program should look like this:

```
 90 PRINT "PUT IN ANY NUMBER"
100 INPUT A
120 B = 4*A
130 C = 5*A
135 D = 6*A
140 PRINT A,B,C,D
```

Now run the program, and when the question mark appears on the screen, put in 2 for A and press RETURN. The computer responds as shown. (The row of numbers along the top will not appear on the screen. They are there just to show you the spacing).

```
1234567890123456789012345678901234567890
         2         8        10        12
>_
```

First notice that in mode 7 (which is the normal mode) the screen is 40 columns wide. Then notice that each number is printed with its last digit just below one of the 0 digits. In fact the first number, that is 2, appears on the tenth column; the second number that is 8, appears on the twentieth column; the third number, that is 10, is written so that its last digit 0 appears on the thirtieth column (so the 1 of 10 appears on the twenty-ninth column.) Finally the fourth number, that is 12, appears with its digits on the thirty-ninth and fortieth columns. This spacing is caused by the commas. In programs which involve printing numbers on the screen, using commas will always produce this kind of format.

Now rewrite 140 as follows. (Remember that, when we type in a new line numbered 140, it simply replaces the old one):

```
140 PRINT A;B;C;D                RET
```

That is, replace the commas by semicolons. Now run the program again, and when the question mark appears, put in 2 again for A and press RETURN. The response is shown below where, again, numbers are written across the top to show the spacing.

```
1234567890123456789012345678901234567890
         281012
>_
```

Once again the first number, that is 2, is placed in the tenth column. The others are now placed beside 2 without any spaces. The use of semicolons always pushes the written responses together in this way.

If you wish to know more about how to format numbers using commas and semicolons, try some experiments. For example, try replacing line 140 by each of these in turn. Run the program each time before trying the next version of line 140.

```
140 PRINT; A,B,C,D               RET
140 PRINT; A;B;C;D               RET
140 PRINT; A,;B;C;D              RET
140 PRINT; A,;B,;C,;D            RET
```

Finally, this line makes use of the single quotation mark or the apostrophe. This is on the same key as 7 on the keyboard:

```
140 PRINT A'B'C'D                RET
```

The result of this is to print these four numbers 2,8,10,12, all on separate lines.

Screen format with strings

Remove the last program by typing in NEW. Now copy this program.

```
100 A$ = "ALEX"                                  RET
120 B$ = "BILL"                                  RET
140 C$ = "CECIL"                                 RET
160 PRINT A$,B$,C$                               RET
```

Now RUN this program. The screen will look like this, where again we have used the row of reference numbers along the top.

```
1234567890123456789012345678901234567890
ALEX      BILL      CECIL
>_
```

Notice that, once again, the screen is divided across into bands that are 10 columns wide. But this time the first letter of each word appears on the column headed by a 1: that is in columns 1, 11 and 21. This spacing was caused by the commas. Now replace line 160 as follows:

```
160 PRINT A$; B$; C$                             RET
```

When we run the program the screen looks like this:

```
ALEXBILLCECIL
>_
```

This time no spaces are left at all. If we wished to have a space between each name this should be put in beside each name when it is declared in lines 100, 120 and 140. For example change line 100 to:

```
100 A$ = "ALEX "                                 RET
```

A space has been left between the X of ALEX and the closing quotation mark. Now run your program again.

INPUT with a string

We will return to the MEMO program to look at how it might be made more general. First type in NEW and press RETURN. We want the program, at its beginning, to ask the user to input three pieces of information:

(a) the name of the person to whom the memo is being sent;
(b) today's date;
(c) the reason why the memo is being sent.

Begin as follows, with an instruction using PRINT and then an INPUT.

```
100 PRINT "WHO IS RECEIVING THIS MEMO?"    RET
120 INPUT A$                               RET
```

This means that the name of the person receiving the memo is being stored in the variable A$. The program continues in the same way:

```
140 PRINT "WHAT IS TODAY'S DATE?"         RET
160 INPUT B$                              RET
180 PRINT "REASON FOR MEMO?"              RET
200 INPUT C$                              RET
```

This is the first half of the program. The second half uses this information to write the memo. Type this in, and remember to press RETURN at the end of each line.

```
220 PRINT:PRINT:PRINT                            RET
240 PRINT "MEMO TO "A$                           RET
260 PRINT B$                                     RET
280 PRINT "THIS IS A MEMO TO REMIND YOU ABOUT"   RET
300 PRINT C$
```

There are three points about this part of the program.

1. Line 220 uses the word PRINT by itself, repeated 3 times, to make a space which separates the two parts of the program.

2. In line 240 the word PRINT refers both to the words MEMO TO and to the variable A$, which is the label of the unit of memory containing the name of the person receiving the letter. That is both the two words and the names are printed. (There is a space between MEMO TO and the quotation marks).

3. Do not use a comma as part of any of the inputs for A$, B$, C$. If you do the computer will only accept the material up to but not including the comma. If you really need a

comma, put quotation marks at the beginning and at the end of the expression.

Now type in RUN and press RETURN. The computer will print on the screen the message WHO IS RECEIVING THIS MEMO? Respond by typing DAVID JENKINS, or any other name you wish. Then press RETURN. The computer will then print, WHAT IS TODAY'S DATE? You can put this in whatever way you like, so long as you do not include a comma. For example, THURSDAY 12th JUNE, and press RETURN. The computer will now print REASON FOR MEMO. Type in, COMMITTEE MEETING TODAY AT 2.00 P.M. and press RETURN. The screen will then look like this:

```
MEMO TO DAVID JENKINS
THURSDAY 12th JUNE
THIS IS A MEMO TO REMIND YOU ABOUT
COMMITTEE MEETING TODAY AT 2.00 P.M
>_
```

Try it again and put in a variety of responses. Try to think of ways of improving the program so that it produces a greater variety of memo types. At this stage the memo only appears on the screen, but if you have a printer attached then proceed as follows. First make sure that the printer is switched on. Then hold the key marked CTRL and press the letter B. Then press the RETURN key. The printer should make some sort of response to this. Then RUN the program again. This time the output will go to the printer. To switch the printer off, simply use CTRL and C and then press RETURN. There is more detail about the use of the CTRL key on page 142.

INPUT with graphics

We will now make use again of some of the graphics statements that we met in Chapter 1. This time we will use them within a program, and we will use the word INPUT to allow us to specify the points to be used in drawing lines. We will produce a program that allows us to draw any triangle that we wish on the screen. In order to specify the first corner of this shape, we need to know how far over from the bottom left to go, and how far up from the bottom left. We will use the variable names A,B for these. Here are the first three lines of the program. Type them in, and remember to press RETURN at the end of each line. Remember also that CLS clears the screen.

```
100 CLS
120 PRINT "ENTER 2 NUMBERS SEPARATED BY A COMMA"
140 INPUT A,B
```

In a similar way we will use C,D and E,F for the other two points. So the program continues like this:

```
160 PRINT "NOW 2 MORE NUMBERS FOR THE NEXT POINT"
180 INPUT C,D
200 PRINT "NOW THE LAST POINT"
220 INPUT E,F
```

We now need a routine which actually draws the triangle. To begin with, we need to go into MODE 5, which is one of the possible graphics modes. Then we need to MOVE, without drawing a line, to the first corner. The following lines will do this:

```
240 MODE 5
260 MOVE A,B
```

Finally, we need three DRAW statements to produce the three triangle sides.

```
280 DRAW C,D
300 DRAW E,F
320 DRAW A,B
```

Type these all in, and then RUN the program a few times to make sure that it can be used to draw triangles. Remember that the screen is numbered across from 0 to 1279, and up from 0 to 1023.

REM

If you wished to make this program easy to read and understand when listed, you could now add some REM lines. REM is short for REMARK and it allows you to annotate or write explanatory comments into a program. This is because the computer ignores all lines beginning with REM when it is running a program in BASIC. It acknowledges their existence only when listing a program. Here are some examples of REM statements attached to the memo program just completed:

```
 90 REM MEMO PROGRAM
 95 REM FIRST PART
210 REM SECOND PART
```

Upper and lower case

So far we have used only capital or upper case letters to write programs, and to respond to input commands. But the computer does allow you to use lower case letters on certain occasions.

When the machine is first switched on, the red light below the caps lock sign on the bottom left side of the keyboard is also on. This means that when you press any of the letter keys, these appear on the screen in CAPITALS. When you hold the SHIFT key and press these again, they will still be in CAPITALS. Try this by typing in COMPUTER, first directly and then holding the SHIFT key. There will be no difference. Now press the key with 4 on it. This makes 4 appear on the screen. Then hold the SHIFT key and press this same key. This time the dollar sign appears on the screen. Now try a few more keys and make sure that you know what will happen.

Now press the CAPS LOCK key once. This will make the red light go off. Press it again and it will go on; and then once again to turn it off. Now type in the word computer directly and this time it appears in lower case. But the keys with two symbols like 4 have not changed. Now hold the SHIFT key and type in COMPUTER, and this time it appears in upper case again. When the keyboard is like this it behaves like a normal typewriter.

Finally press the SHIFT LOCK key once and the red light below the words shift lock will go on. Now try typing with letter keys and with other keys which have two symbols. Do this both directly and holding the SHIFT key. In all cases only upper case letters are possible, or the upper symbols on the keys.

So, clearly if you wish to use both lower and upper case you must, at the beginning, press the CAPS LOCK key once to turn off all red lights and then use the keyboard like a normal typewriter.

However, when using any of the special words in the computer's vocabulary these must always be put in capital letters. That is words like PRINT and INPUT and RUN. If you put them in lower case the computer will not recognize them.

Variable names

So far we have used single letters like A, B or C to represent variables, and A$, B$, C$ to represent string variables. However we can use any name we wish for a variable, and it can be as long as we wish and it can be in upper case or lower case or even a mixture of these. There are four rules or restrictions about variable names and we will now demonstrate each in turn.

1. All variable names must begin with a letter of the alphabet, and not a number. First type in this line, and press RETURN:

```
NUMBERS = 4 : PRINT NUMBERS                    RET
```

The computer accepts the word NUMBERS as a variable name. But now try a variable name beginning with a number.

```
34TH NAME = 17 : PRINT 34TH NAME               RET
```

In this case, there is no response at all. Can you see why? Try typing in LIST followed by RETURN. You will find that the computer has treated the 34 as the line number of a program. Now try the same thing in another way:

```
17STONE = 91                                   RET
PRINT 17STONE                                  RET
```

This time, in response to the statement PRINT 17STONE, the compute prints the 17 and then says, No such variable. In other words it does not recognize the word STONE. So, the rule is, don't begin a variable name with a number.

2. Don't leave any spaces in a variable name. First try this. (Note that we are using lower case this time for the variable name, but not for the word PRINT):

```
bank balance = 53: PRINT bank balance          RET
```

The response to this is the word Mistake. Now try it again like this:

```
bankbalance=53 : PRINT bankbalance             RET
```

This time it should actually print 53. If you get the error message Mistake, make sure that you have put PRINT in capitals. Remember that all the words in the computer vocabulary must be in capitals. For this reason it is a good idea always to use lower case for variable names and we will always do so in the rest of the book. It means that we can usually see at a glance what words are being used for variables.

3. Don't use any of the other symbols such as the question mark or the star within variable names.

4. Variable names should not begin with any word from the computer's vocabulary. This is only a problem if you allow yourself to write variable names in upper case. For example, you might wish to use a word like TOTAL for a

variable. The computer will reject this because TO is a reserved word. But it will quite happily accept total as a variable. The fact that this computer allows you to use full words for variables means that programs are much easier to read and to understand. We will demonstrate this in the next section.

READ, DATA and RESTORE

We have looked earlier at how we can use the word INPUT to feed numbers and words into a program while it is actually running. But sometimes there will be a set of numbers or words that are constant in that we use them over and over again within a program.

In this example we will find the average of a set of 3 numbers. They are 16, 83, 51. First of all we put this set of numbers in what is called a DATA statement. (Remember to press RETURN after each line).

```
100 DATA 16,83,51
```

Then we declare a variable 'total' to hold the sum of all these numbers. To begin with it is zero:

```
120 total = 0
```

Then we read the first number from the data list:

```
140 READ first
```

This means that the variable first is now equal to 16, which is the first number on the data list on line 100. Then we add this to the variable total which acts as a sort of accumulator:

```
160 total = total + first
```

Remember what this means. On the line 120 total was put equal to zero. Now on line 160 total becomes what it was, that is zero, plus the first piece of data, that is first (or 16). Then READ the next piece of data:

```
180 READ second
```

And add this to the accumulator:

```
200 total = total + second
```

At this stage total is equal to 16+83. Then READ the third and last piece of data, and add this to the accumulator:

```
220 READ third
240 total = total + third
```

Finally, calculate the average and PRINT both the total and the average:

```
260 average = total/3
280 PRINT total, average
```

The complete program now looks like this. LIST your version and compare it. Remember that the most usual mistake is to forget to use capitals for key-words like DATA, READ, PRINT:

```
100 DATA 16,83,51
120 total = 0
140 READ first
160 total = total + first
180 READ second
200 total = total + second
220 READ third
240 total = total + third
260 average = total/3
280 PRINT total,average
```

Now type in RUN and press RETURN. The response will be:

That is, the sum or total is 150 and the average is 50. There are a number of points to make about this program.

1. The words used as variable names like first, second, third, average, were chosen by us.

2. The use of words like these makes the whole program much easier to read and understand.

3. Certain statements are used repeatedly in this program, for example lines 140, 180 and 220. This kind of repetition can be avoided by using certain programming techniques called loops which we will come to later.

We will now develop a program that uses both numerical data statements and string data statements. This program reads the names of the months of the year into string variables which we call month1$, month2$, and so on. It then reads the numbers representing the number of days in these months into number variables which we call days1, days2, and so on. Since this is just an illustration we have only used the first three months. First the data statements:

```
100 DATA January, February, March
120 DATA 31, 28, 31
```

Now some lines to read these into the variables:

```
140 READ month1$
160 READ month2$
180 READ month3$
200 READ days1
220 READ days2
240 READ days3
```

Note that we could have put all 6 of these READ statements in one line using the word READ once and separating the variables with commas. Like this:

```
140 READ month1$,month2$,month3$,days1,days2,days3
```

Now a set of PRINT statements to set this data out in neat columns. Line 260 make a 3-line space:

```
260 PRINT : PRINT : PRINT
280 PRINT month1$, days1
300 PRINT month2$, days2
320 PRINT month3$, days3
```

Now suppose that, later on in this program, we wished to READ this DATA again for some other purpose. If we simply use another READ statement the machine will respond with 'out of DATA'. So we must RESTORE the DATA before we can use it again. Add these lines to the program:

```
340 RESTORE
360 READ first$
380 PRINT "The first month is " first$
```

Now RUN the program to see if it works. Then remove line 340 and RUN it again. (Of course this is a very unreal example since we already have the data January stored in the variable month$). Now put in line 340 again as follows:

```
340 RESTORE 120
```

This means that the first piece of DATA will be READ from line 120. RUN this to check that this is so.

More graphics

In an earlier section (page 30) we used the word INPUT to allow us to draw triangles on the screen. This meant that we could draw a different triangle each time we used the program. However, there will be occasions when the position of the triangle will be fixed, so we can use the words READ and DATA. Suppose, for example, the corners were at the points (100,100), (900,300) and (400,700). We can put these numbers in a DATA statement and then READ them into the variables (over1,up1), (over2,up2) and (over3,up3). This is done in lines 100 and 120.

```
100 DATA 100, 100, 900, 300, 400, 700
120 READ over1, up1, over2, up2, over3, up3
```

The rest of the program is much the same as on page 25 except that we use, for the first time, the word GCOL. In this case this makes the sides of the triangle appear as red.

```
140 MODE 5
160 GCOL 0,1
180 MOVE over1,up1
200 DRAW over2,up2
220 DRAW over3,up3
240 DRAW over1,up1
```

If we had wished to make the triangle sides yellow we could change line 160 to GCOL 0,2. There will be more about this later.

The COPY key and screen editing

On the bottom row of the keyboard, on the extreme right, there is a key with the word COPY written on it. This is used to change and edit lines on the screen. It is used in association with the four arrowed keys on the top right of the keyboard. These are used to move the cursor around the screen. The best way to get to know how to use these keys is to practise with them, but we will now show two examples of how they might be used. (Remember to type in NEW to get rid of the last program).

First suppose we have typed in a line with a mistake on it. Here is an example. Type it in and press RETURN.

```
300 PRINT "This is a misteak."
```

If the line with a mistake is part of a long program the quickest way to change it is to list the line first so that it is available near the bottom of the screen. In this case there is no problem as it is the only line. Press once the key with the arrow pointing upwards. The small thin cursor will move up below the 3 of the number 300. It will also leave behind a second cursor which is a full white block. Now press the copy key once and look carefully at what has happened. Then press it again a few times. If you hold it with your finger it will run across the screen quite quickly. But stop when it gets to the 't' of the wrong misteak. Then type in the rest of the word correctly; i.e. type in 'ake'. You can then either continue to type in a full stop and quotation marks, and press RETURN; or use the arrow right key to move the cursor to the full stop and then copy the last two symbols, and then press RETURN. Either way the effect is to EDIT the mistake.

The second example uses the COPY key when a program contains a number of lines that are almost identical. Suppose we wished to type in the following three lines. (First type in NEW and press RETURN).

```
100 PRINT "What is the first number "; : INPUT one
120 PRINT "What is the second number "; : INPUT two
140 PRINT "What is the third number "; : INPUT three
```

Begin by typing in the first line as shown, and then press RETURN. Then type in 120 and then move the cursor up below the P of the word PRINT. Then press the COPY key and copy the line up to the end of the word first . Then use the DELETE key to remove first, type in second, and then use the COPY key again until the word INPUT has been copied. Then type in two and press RETURN. This reads as though it is very complicated, but it is really very easy in practice. Now type in 140 and copy line 120 in more or less the same way.

You should now experiment with the four arrow keys and the COPY key so that you know how they work, and you should then use them every time you think they might be useful. Certainly screen editing is a great deal easier when they are used.

Shorthand and repeating

We noticed in the last section that when the COPY key was held down the cursor moved across the screen from left to right. This is true of any key including the arrow keys, and there are occasions when this facility can be very useful. Suppose for example we wanted to separate two messages on the screen with a row of stars. We could do this by typing in a line like this.

```
500 PRINT "********************"
```

Begin to type this in but when you get to the first star just hold your finger on the key and it will repeat the stars across the screen. Try this with other keys.

Another useful feature is the way in which various keywords can be shortened. This can be a great time-saver. In most cases the shorthand involves using the first or the first few letters of the word followed by a full stop. First of all an example. Type this in exactly as shown and press RETURN: (Type in NEW and press RETURN; then

```
100 P. : I. "This is an example " one
```

Now type in L. and press RETURN. The result is:

```
100 PRINT : INPUT "This is an example "one
```

This means that L. is a shorthand for the word LIST, P. is a shorthand for the word PRINT and I. is a shorthand for the word INPUT. Notice that, even when we type in a shorthand version of a word, it is immediately translated by the computer into a longhand version.

Almost all the words that form the BASIC language used by this machine have shorthand versions, and a full list is given in The User Guide, Pages 483-484. However some of the words are already quite small and a shorthand version is not really very much of a time saver. A list of some of the more useful ones is given below, in alphabetical order.

```
DATA..........D.
DELETE........DEL.
INPUT.........I.
LIST..........L.
PRINT.........P.
RENUMBER......REN.
RESTORE.......RES.
```

Problems

1. Write a program that allows you to enter a set of six names and an amount of money for each name. It should be written in such a way that:

(a) The computer invites you, with a message on the screen, to put in the information.
(b) When it has all been entered, the computer lists the names and amounts on the screen.

Use the words PRINT, INPUT and REM.

2. Write a program which prints on the screen a price list containing six items of clothing and their corresponding prices. The names of the items and their prices should be placed in data statements, and the program should use the words READ and DATA.

3. This problem is quite similar to problem one. The program should allow you to enter a set of four names and addresses where each address is to be three lines long. That is, a total of 16 inputs will be demanded. The program should be written so that:

(a) The computer invites you to put in the information.
(b) When it has all been entered, the computer displays the names and addresses on the screen.

Use the words PRINT, INPUT and REM and use A1$, A2$, A3$ and A4$ for the names. Similarly, use B1$ to B4$ for the first lines of the addresses. Then use C1$ to C4$, and D1$ to D4$ for the other two lines.

4. Use the sort of techniques developed for the memo program on page 21 to produce a standard letter to a client, as shown below. The words in capitals, however, will change with each run of the program and these should be input at the beginning of the program. So the program should begin by inviting the input of the following data:

(a) Today's date (Use date$).
(b) Person to whom the letter is addressed (B$). (person$).
(c) Reason for meeting (C$). (reason$).
(d) Date when writer will be available (D$). (date2$).
(e) Time when writer will be available (E$). (time$).
(f) Where the writer will be available (F$). (where$).

```
1st Feb.

Dear MR. EVANS,

              I would like to arrange a meeting to discuss:

                    YOUR RECENT ORDER

I would be available on MONDAY 14TH JAN. in MY OFFICE at
HALF PAST TWO.

I would be grateful if you could come at this time.

                    Yours sincerely,

                    Fergal Dunn.
```

CHAPTER 3
PROGRAM PRESENTATION

Introduction

When a program has been typed in to the computer, or put in from tape or disk, and you need to use it, you then type in RUN and press RETURN. If the program has been carefully written it ought then to be completly clear what the program is about, and what it wants you to do. This level of well-organized explanation and presentation needs to be maintained all the way through the program, so that the user is never placed in the position of not knowing what to do next, or what the results mean.

This chapter is about this kind of presentation and structure. The techniques used are very simple and easy to adapt. It begins with a short five-line program, and adds to this repeatedly until it ends up as a quite long but well-documented final program. It is absolutely essential that, at each stage in what follows, you type in the new lines, list the program to check its accuracy, and run it to see what it now does. Indeed the two commands LIST and RUN should be used often when writing programs as they allow you to get instant feedback about what is going on.

User presentation

We begin by typing in a short five-line program as shown. It is carrying out a simple arithmetical calculation involving two multiplications and one division. However, don't worry if, to begin with, you do not understand what it is doing. Type it in, in the usual way, remembering to press the RETURN key after each line. The unusual line numbers are because this is going to be part of a longer program. The rest will be added as we go along. If you have already been using the machine, remember to type in NEW.

```
420 INPUT rate
460 INPUT time
500 INPUT money
540 interest = money*rate*time/1200
560 PRINT interest
```

Now type in RUN and then press RETURN. The computer goes to the first line, 420, and because it is an input, responds with ? It has now labelled a unit of memory rate and is waiting for you to tell it what number to store in it. That is, it needs an input from you. Press 5 and then the RETURN key. The computer responds with another question mark This is its response to line 460. It has labelled a unit of memory time and is waiting for an input from you. Press 24 and then the RETURN key. Another question-mark appears in response to line 500. This time type in 200 and then RETURN. The screen now looks like this:

```
?5
?24
?200
             20
>_
```

If this does not work, check your program by typing in LIST, and pressing RETURN.

All of this will be easy to do, but it will be difficult to understand what is going on. No attempt has been made to make the program understand-able to the user in the way it appears on the screen when you type RUN. We will now try to improve this presentation so that it is self-explanatory and can be used by anyone.

Purpose of program

The object of this program is to provide a simple method of calculating simple interest on a sum of money at a given rate for a given number of months . The word 'rate' on line 420 stands for the rate of interest. The word time on line 460 stands for the number of months involved, and the word money on line 500 stands for the amount of money. These lines invite you to tell the machine what rate, time and money are to be on one particular occasion. We entered 5 for the interest rate, and 24 for the number of months - that is 2 years, and finally 200 for the amount of money involved.

Line 540 does the calculation. That is, it multiplies together the amount of money, the interest rate and the time in months, and divides this by 1200: that is, by 12 to change months into years, and by 100 for the percentage. It calls the result interest. Line 540 prints this result on the screen.

LIST

It is helpful to be able to look at the program, or any part of it, on the screen whenever it is wished. This is done by typing in LIST and then pressing RETURN. This will produce a display of the whole program, but there are also four variations on this which can be used when only part of a program is wanted. These make use of the comma, and this symbol can be thought of in this context as meaning to .

Example 1	LIST 460, 560 This lists all lines from 460 to 560.
Example 2	LIST, 540 This lists all lines from the beginning to line 540.
Example 3	LIST 460, This lists all lines from 460 to the end of the program.
Example 4	LIST 560 This lists line 560 only.

Try all of these. Remember to use the shorthand for LIST, i.e. L.

Clear screen and title

If you have been trying some of the things described above, the chances are that your screen is covered with statements and print. The result is that when you input RUN followed by RETURN the question mark appears at the bottom of all this, scarcely visible. Now type in this new line and press RETURN.

```
100 CLS
```

This means that you have programmed the clear screen command. As soon as the machine comes to line 100 after RUN has been typed in, it will clear the screen and go on to the next line. Try it now and see. Type in RUN and press RETURN. The screen should clear and a question mark with a flashing cursor should appear alone at the top. Now press the Escape key to get out of the program.

It always helps to put a title on your programs. This can be done very simply, but it can also be worked on and made very impressive. First, a simple version:

```
140 PRINT "                SIMPLE INTEREST"
```

Type in this line and RUN the program. Remember that, if you wish to center the title, there are 40 spaces across the screen.

One simple way to do this is to use the TAB function. This word is dealt with in detail on page 192, but a simple example of one of its uses can be inserted here. Rewrite line 140 as follows:

```
140 PRINT TAB(12,1); "SIMPLE INTEREST"
```

Now type in RUN again and press RETURN and look at the result. Line 140 now has the effect of moving or tabbing the cursor over 12 spaces from the left and down one line from the top. This means that the first letter of SIMPLE INTEREST, that is the S, is printed, on the 13th space from the left and on the second row of the screen.

Reverse field

Letters and symbols are normally printed on the screen as white lines against a black background. It is possible to reverse this with words and lines so that they become black lines against a white background. This helps to draw attention to particular words and commands and is especially suitable for the title. The way to do this is now demonstrated. It makes use of two ideas that have already been mentioned in Chapter 1. These are to do with the words MODE and COLOUR. In chapter 1 we used MODE 5 because it allowed us to use four colors. This time we will use MODE 6 which uses only two colors on the screen at one time. These are initially black and white. In this mode the word COLOUR then allows for the following four possibilities:

COLOUR 0. This means that printing on the screen is in black letters. Since the screen itself is normally black, the effect is that you cannot see what is being printed.

COLOUR 1. This means that printing on the screen is in white letters, and this is the normal situation.

COLOUR 128. This changes the screen background to black. Since it is normally black, this will have no effect unless the screen background color has previously been changed.

COLOUR 129. This changes the screen background to white.

There are now four possible combinations:

COLOUR 0, with COLOUR 128. This means black letters on a black background, which cannot be read.

COLOUR 0, with COLOUR 129. This means black letters on a white background. This is sometimes called reverse field.

COLOUR 1, with COLOUR 128. This means white letters on a black background. This is the normal (sometimes called default) situation.

COLOUR 1, with COLOUR 129. This means white letters on white background, which cannot be read.

These possibilities are summarized in the following table:

	COLOUR 0	COLOUR 1
COLOUR 128	Black on black	White on black or normal
COLOUR 129	Black on white or reverse field	White on white

We now wish to put our title into reverse field. First we must go into MODE 6. This itself has the effect of clearing the screen, so we will replace line 100 by this:

```
100 MODE 6
```

We then need a line to turn on reverse field. Type this in, and press RETURN.

```
120 COLOUR 0: COLOUR 129
```

Now type in RUN and press RETURN. The title should now be in reverse field, The problem is that everything that follows is also in reverse field. So we must turn it off again. Type in this line:

```
180 COLOUR 1 : COLOUR 128
```

Now run the program again, and everything should work properly. We will want to use this reverse field capacity again in the program so we will put it in what is called a PROCEDURE and then use this procedure each time we need it. Later on there is a full chapter on the use of these procedures, but we will introduce the idea here and then develop it in full later.

A procedure is a very simple and useful idea. We take a subprogram that we may need to use more than once within a program and instead of typing it in each time, we place it in a separate isolated part of the program and then call it up whenever we need it. This means it need only be typed in once.

In this case we are dealing with a routine for turning on reverse field. We will put the procedure at line number 780:

```
780 COLOUR 0 : COLOUR 129
```

We then need an introductory or defining line, with a name for the procedure, like this:

```
760 DEF PROCrevfieldon
```

Notice that the title 'revfieldon' is chosen by us and we have put it in lower case. The two words DEF and PROC must be used and must be in upper case, and there must be no space between PROC and the name and no spaces within the name. Finally we need an end line and it must always be of the form ENDPROC, with no spaces, like this:

```
800 ENDPROC
```

So, the complete procedure looks like this:

```
760 DEF PROCrevfieldon
780 COLOUR 0 : COLOUR 129
800 ENDPROC
```

We must now call this procedure from an appropriate point within the main program. To do this we change line 120 as follows:

```
120 PROCrevfieldon
```

That is to say, in order to call up a procedure we need only use the word PROC followed immediately (with no spaces) by the procedure name.

We also wish to put the routine for turning reverse field off into a procedure, and then call it. This procedure looks like this:

```
820 DEF PROCrevfieldoff
840 COLOUR 1 : COLOUR 128
860 ENDPROC
```

We then call the procedure as follows:

```
160 PROCrevfieldoff
```

We now do not need line 180, so remove this. This means that the first lines of the program, excluding the procedures, now look like this:

```
100 MODE 6
120 PROCrevfieldon
140 PRINT TAB (12,1); "SIMPLE INTEREST"
160 PROCrevfieldoff
```

One of the advantages of using procedures is that the names chosen for them can suggest very clearly exactly what they are doing. So a line like PROCrevfieldon can be read as meaning 'turn on reverse field'. This means that the whole program becomes easier to read, and the logic is easier to follow. For example if we look again at the first four lines of this program we can read it as meaning:

1. Go into mode 6.
2. Turn on reverse field.
3. Print simple interest in the middle of the first line.
4. Turn off reverse field.

Finally we need an END line to separate the main body of the program from the procedures. Put this in as follows:

```
740 END
```

Description

The program has now been titled but there is still no attempt to tell the user what is going on or how he should interact with the computer. So we need a description of the program's intentions.

```
200 PRINT "This program allows you to calculate"
220 PRINT "simple interest.  It invites you to"
240 PRINT "put in three pieces of information:-"
260 PRINT"     1.  The annual percentage rate of interest."
280 PRINT"     2.  The time in months."
300 PRINT"     3.  The sum of money involved."
```

Try typing this in and running the program.

There are two problems now: (a) the instructions are very crowded; and (b) we are still not told exactly how to respond to the ? sign that is printed after them. So we must consider SPACING and further INSTRUCTIONS TO USER.

Spacing

1. A single line space can be made by putting in an extra line containing just the word, PRINT. For example, type this in, press RETURN and RUN the program.

```
180 PRINT
```

There will be an extra line space, that is a line will be printed with nothing on it, as a result of the instruction in line 180. It is also possible to put an extra PRINT with a colon at the beginning or end of the appropriate existing lines. However, the quickest and most simple way to make an extra space is to use the apostrophe sign after the word PRINT or at the end of the PRINT line outside the quotation marks. We can demonstrate this using line 200 and the COPY key. First list line 200 as follows:

```
200 PRINT "This program allows you to calculate"
```

Then use the key with an arrow pointing upwards on it to move the cursor up one line to the beginning of line 200. Then press the COPY key a few times until it reaches the end of the word PRINT. Then use the SHIFT key to type in an apostrophe (it is on the same key as 7). Then use the COPY key to copy the rest of the line exactly as it is. The result will be:

```
200 PRINT' "This program allows you to calculate"
```

Repeat this process for each of the lines 220 to 300. Also remember to remove the extra line 180 put in earlier as a demonstration.

2. Large spaces. Obviously a larger space than one line will sometimes be needed. This can be done using a line like this:

```
180 PRINT : PRINT : PRINT : PRINT
```

In most programs such a spacing is used quite often and is therefore best to put into a procedure, like this:

```
880 DEF PROCspace
900 PRINT : PRINT : PRINT : PRINT
960 ENDPROC
```

Then we can use this procedure whenever we wish to have a larger space between chunks of writing on the screen. For example, now type in this line:

```
180 PROCspace
```

and RUN the program. There will now be a quite large space between the Title and the first line of explanation.

However, we can make even better use of the procedure facility in this case in that we have the facility to vary the size of the space as we wish. To do this we change the procedure as follows. First retype line 880

```
880 DEF PROCspace(number)
```

The word number here is a variable which, when we have finished changing the procedure, will allow us to decide what size of space we want. For example we can then change line 180 as follows:

```
180 PROCspace(3)
```

This will then make a three line space. In other parts of the program when we call this procedure again we can change the variable to other numbers instead of 3. The next part of this new version of the procedure uses a routine known as a loop. There is a full chapter on this sort of routine beginning on page 000, but its meaning here is fairly clear. First type it in.

```
900 FOR count = 1 TO number
920 PRINT
940 NEXT count
```

We could of course have put all three of these statements on one line separated by full colons. The procedure now means that a single line space caused by line 920, is repeated by the loop. The loop is caused by a combination of lines 900 and 940, up to whatever number is entered within the program for the variable number . For example in line 180 we use the number 3, so there will be a 3 line space. The full procedure now looks like this:

```
880 DEF PROCspace(number)
900 FOR count = 1 TO number
920 PRINT
940 NEXT count
960 ENDPROC
```

and we have called it once, at line 180. We will also call it at line 380 as follows:

```
380 PROCspace(2)
```

The complete program so far is now listed and annotated. You should list your program, add any new lines, and make sure that yours is exactly like this one.

```
A       100 MODE 6

B       120 PROCrevfieldon
        140 PRINT TAB(12,1); "SIMPLE INTEREST"
        160 PROCrevfieldoff

C       180 PROCspace(3)

D       200 PRINT' "This program allows you to calculate"
        220 PRINT' "simple interest.  It invites you to "
        240 PRINT' "put in three pieces of information:-"
        260 PRINT' "     1.  The annual percentage rate of
            interest."
        280 PRINT' "     2.  The time in months."
        300 PRINT' "     3.  The sum of money involved."

E       380 PROCspace(2)

F       420 INPUT rate
        460 INPUT time
        500 INPUT money
        540 interest = money*rate*time/1200
        560 PRINT interest
        740 END

G       760 DEF PROCrevfieldon
        780 COLOUR 0 : COLOUR 129
        800 ENDPROC
        820 DEF PROCrevfieldoff
        840 COLOUR 1 : COLOUR 128
        860 ENDPROC
        880 DEF PROCspace(number)
        900 FOR count = 1 TO number
        920 PRINT
        940 NEXT count
        960 ENDPROC
```

Part A   This puts the computer in MODE 6 and clears the screen.

Part B This creates the title in reverse field.

Part C This makes a three-line space.

Part D This describes the program.

Part E This makes a two-line space.

Part F This solves the problem and prints the result.

Part G Three procedures.

Instructions to user

When this program is now run, the screen looks like this:

```
      Simple Interest


 This program allows you to calculate

 simple interest.  It invites you to

 put in three pieces of information:-

     1.  The annual percentage rate of interest.

     2.  The time in months.

     3.  The sum of money involved.


     ?-
```

We must now consider the second problem mentioned above. That is, we have not yet given explicit instructions about what we want the user to input. This is done as follows. Type in these lines:

```
340 PRINT "Enter each of these in turn and then"
360 PRINT' "press the RETURN key."
400 PRINT "First put in the annual percentage rate of
           interest."
440 PRINT' "Now the time in months."
480 PRINT' "Now the amount of money."
```

Now RUN the program again. This immediately presents another problem. This time there is too much material for the screen and the title is pushed off the top. The next section shows you how to stop this happening.

Press the space-bar

This technique allows the computer to present information in chunks. This means that you can read some of instructions or messages on the screen, and then by pressing a key, usually the space-bar, bring up the next chunk of information. Once again we will put this technique in a procedure since we will be using it more than once.

Here is a first attempt at writing the routine. Copy it in and we will then discuss its meaning.

```
 980 DEF PROCholdscreen
1020 PRINT TAB(12,21); "Press space bar"
1080 Z = GET
1100 ENDPROC
```

On line 980 the procedure is defined with the title 'holdscreen'. Line 1020 prints the message 'Press space bar' on the 21st row of the screen, and 12 spaces in from the left. In other words, down near the bottom of the screen. Line 1080 used a new word. The statement is Z = GET. This tells the computer to expect an input of one single character from the keyboard. Until a key is pressed, the computer waits at this line. But as soon as (almost) any key is pressed it moves on to the next line of the routine, which is ENDPROC. So, although the message on line 1020 refers to the space bar, almost any other key would do instead.

However, it would look much better if the words 'Press the space bar' were in reverse field. So, we can call up the procedures for doing this as follows:

```
1000 PROCrevfieldon
1040 PROCrevfieldoff
```

Finally we can improve it even further with a better spacing, so we call up the space procedure as follows:

```
1060 PROCspace(2)
```

Notice that we have called procedures from within a procedure. This is an interesting idea. In fact it is possible to call a procedure from within itself. This is called 'recursion' and is discussed on page 161.

The complete holdscreen procedure now looks like this:

```
 980 DEFPROCholdscreen
1000 PROCrevfieldon
1020 PRINT TAB(12,21); "Press space bar"
1040 PROCrevfieldoff
1060 PROCspace(2)
1080 Z = GET
1100 ENDPROC
```

Now call this procedure so as to stop the title being pushed off the screen.

```
320 PROCholdscreen
```

Now RUN the program and see what happens

Explaining the answers

The response from the machine when the numbers have been put in is to print the answer on the next line and stop. Some further lines of explanation, and some further changes in spacing would improve its legibility further. Type in the following lines:

```
520 PROCspace(4)
560 PRINT "The interest is      " interest
580 PROCspace(3)
```

Line 520 and 580 make large spaces on each side of the important message on line 560, which now describes the variable as well as printing its value.

Finally it is useful to put some instructions at the end about what the user may wish to do next. Put in the lines shown.

```
600 PRINT "Do you wish to do another one?"'
620 INPUT answer$
640 IF answer$ = "yes" OR answer$ = "YES" THEN 100
660 PROCspace(3)
680 PRINT "Thank you.  If you wish to start again"
700 PRINT' "type in RUN and press RETURN."
720 PRINT' "Goodbye for now."
```

The computer responds to line 620 by printing a question mark on the screen and waiting for you to type in a word and press RETURN. This word is stored in a variable answer$. If the word is yes or YES (in capitals) then line 640 sends the computer back to line 100, that is the beginning of the program. If the response is any other word then the computer goes on the next line, that is line 660. This makes a large space, and then the final message is printed by lines 680 to 720.

The complete program now follows. Check yours against this and try running it a few times.

```
100 MODE 6
120 PROCrevfieldon
140 PRINT TAB(12,1); "SIMPLE INTEREST"
160 PROCrevfieldoff
180 PROCspace(3)
200 PRINT "This program allows you to calculate"
220 PRINT' "simple interest.  It invites you to"
240 PRINT' "put in three pieces of information:-"
260 PRINT' "     1.  The annual percentage rate of
           interest."
280 PRINT' "     2.  The time in months."
300 PRINT' "     3.  The sum of money involved."
320 PROCholdscreen
340 PRINT "Enter each of these in turn and then"
360 PRINT' "press the RETURN key."
380 PROCspace(2)
400 PRINT "First put in the annual percentage rate of
          interest."
420 INPUT rate
440 PRINT' "Now the time in months."
460 INPUT time
480 PRINT' "Now the amount of money."
500 INPUT money
520 PROCspace(4)
540 interest = money*rate*time/1200
560 PRINT "The interest is   "interest
580 PROCspace(3)
600 PRINT "Do you wish to do another one?"'
620 INPUT answer$
640 If answer$ = "yes" OR answer$ = "YES" then 100
660 PROCspace(3)
680 PRINT "Thank you.  If you wish to start again"
700 PRINT' "type in RUN and press RETURN."
720 PRINT' "Goodbye for now."
740 END
760 DEF PROCrevfieldon
780 COLOUR 0 : COLOUR 129
800 ENDPROC
820 DEF PROCrevfieldoff
840 COLOUR 1: COLOUR 128
860 ENDPROC
880 DEF PROCspace(number)
900 FOR count = 1 TO number
920 PRINT
940 NEXT count
960 ENDPROC
```

```
 980 DEF PROCholdscreen
1000 PROCrevfieldon
1020 PRINT TAB(12,21); "Press space bar"
1040 PROCrevfieldoff
1060 PROCspace(2)
1080 Z = GET
1100 ENDPROC
```

Problems

1. This is a short program which translates pounds weight into grams.

```
200 INPUT pounds
210 grams = pounds * 453.593
230 PRINT pounds,grams
```

Type this in and then add as many other lines as are necessary to turn this into a self-explanatory, easily used conversion program. Try to use as many of the techniques discussed in Chapter 3 as possible.

2. Write another program of this sort which invites the user to put in a small set of numbers one at a time. The program then calculates and presents the average of these. Again try to make sure the program is self-explanatory and easy to use.

3. Write a program which will convert any sum of money from one currency into four other currencies. The program should invite you to put in the names of the four other currencies and their current exchange rates. It will then calculate the exchange values and print all four of these on the screen.

CHAPTER 4
CONDITIONALS

An Introduction to IF and THEN

Very often within a program we have to instruct the computer to make a decision about what to do next, and this decision is usually dependent on the value of a number, or the choice of a word, or on what results come from a particular kind of calculation. Suppose, for example, we had just used a formula to do some calculation and the computer had produced an answer which was stored in the variable 'answer'. (In order to avoid having to type in a big procedure for this example we can simulate the problem simply by using INPUT). So we can begin the program like this:

```
100 INPUT number
```

Now suppose that we wish to check whether this number is positive or negative. If it is negative we wish to change it to positive. However, if it is positive, we will not change it at all. So we need a line like this, which uses two new words, that is IF and THEN.

```
120 IF number < 0 THEN number = -number
```

(The sign $<$ means smaller than, or is less than). This line works as follows. If the number is smaller than zero then it is negative, that is it has a minus sign in front of it. So line 120 tests for this, and if it finds that the number is less than zero then it puts a second minus sign in front of it, and the two minuses together become a plus sign. However, if the number is not less than zero, then the computer goes on directly to the next line.

We then need a third line to let us know whether the process has worked correctly or not. This line simply prints out the number so we can tell if we have succeeded in making it positive.

```
140 PRINT "The number is "number
```

Type in these lines and then type in RUN and press RETURN. When the question mark appears on the screen, type in -3 and press RETURN. The computer will print 3 on the screen. That is to say, it will change the -3 into 3. Now RUN it again, and this time respond with 3. Again, the computer will type 3 on the screen. So, whether you respond with -3 or 3, the computer treats it as 3, which is what we wanted. The complete program looks like this:

```
100 INPUT number
120 IF number<0 THEN number = -number
140 PRINT "The number is "number
```

Here is another example. Suppose we wanted only to use the units digit from any number. There are a number of more-or-less complicated ways to do this, but we will use IF and THEN as follows. First we need only change line 120 to begin with.

```
120 IF number >9 THEN number = number - 10
```

(The sign > means greater than). RUN this a few times and respond to the question mark with some single-digit number like 7 or 4. Then respond with some numbers like 13 or 19. In these last cases the computer will print 3 and 9 as a result of line 120.

However the program is still not complete in that it will not work for numbers greater than 19. To solve this we need an extra line as follows.

```
110 IF number > 19 THEN PRINT "TOO BIG" : GOTO 100
```

The logic of this can be explained as follows. There are two possibilities.

(a) The number is not greater than 19. In this case the computer goes on immediately to the next line, that is line 120.

(b) The number is indeed greater than 19. In this case the computer continues along line 110, prints the message TOO BIG on the screen, and then continues to the statement GOTO 100 after the colon. This means go to line 100. The meaning of the GOTO is fairly clear. It is always followed by a line number (or by a variable representing a line number). It is a word that ought not to be used very often in computing as it can lead to confusion. There is more about this on page 74. (It must be written as one word with no space between GO and TO that is GOTO).

The complete program now looks like this. Type it in and RUN it a few times to make sure that it works and to make sure that you know how it works.

```
100 INPUT number
110 IF number >19 THEN PRINT "TOO BIG" : GOTO 100
120 IF number >9 THEN number = number - 10
140 PRINT "The number is  "number
```

Using INPUT for PRINT

It is possible to use the word INPUT so that it combines the facilities of both PRINT and INPUT. For example first type in NEW and press RETURN, and then type in these two lines.

```
100 PRINT "Input the number you have chosen."
120 INPUT number
```

These two lines can be combined into one line as follows. Type in NEW and then this line.

```
100 INPUT "Input the number you have chosen  "number
```

Run this and see what happens. The result should look like this:

```
Input the number you have chosen  -
```

That is to say the request to the user and the flashing cursor now appear on the same line. Notice that we left two spaces between the word 'chosen' and the quotation marks. If the message that you wish to put on the screen is a question, then change the format slightly as follows.

```
100 INPUT "Do you wish to repeat this (Y/N)  ", answer$
```

Now RUN this and notice that there is now a question mark on the screen just in front of the cursor. This is caused by the comma after the quotation marks on line 100.

In fact we can use INPUT in very much the same way as we use PRINT. For example we could have a line like this. (Type in NEW first).

```
200 INPUT'' "Put in a number  "A'' "Now another number  "B
```

The effect of this will be to make two line spaces caused by the two apostrophes after INPUT. Then 'Put in a number' will be printed. So, press 4 and then RETURN. The two apostrophes after A will make two more line spaces and then 'Now another number' will appear on the screen. Try it and see.

This makes the INPUT statement a very useful one. However there are some situations where it has limitations. Suppose for example we were writing a program and wished to invite the user to put in his address, one line at a time. The program line might look like line 120. (Type in NEW first).

```
100 CLS
120 INPUT "Next address line  ",address$
140 PRINT address$
```

Now the first line of my address is

```
14, "THE SHRUBBERY"
```

The quotation marks are there because this is a very special name locally. So RUN the program and respond to line 120 with this line of address. Line 140 prints what the computer actually stores in address$. It accepts only the material up to the comma, and nothing after it. That is, in this case only the 14 is accepted.

To get round this we need a new word called INPUTLINE. This accepts everything that is typed on the screen, including commas and quotation marks. So we can change line 120 to :

```
120 INPUTLINE "Next address line  ",address$
```

Now RUN it again and respond with 14, "THE SHRUBBERY". This time the computer accepts everything.

IF and THEN with strings

The next example shows how to make similar decisions using strings instead of numbers. Very often in a program we want to ask the person using the machine a question. An example occurs at the beginning of a game, where we might want to say something like: "Do you want instructions? Answer YES or NO." The corresponding program would look like this:

```
100 INPUT "Do you want instructions.  YES OR NO  ", answer$
```

We now want to examine the response made to the question on line 100. This response is held by the string variable answer$. If it is equal to the word YES then we will direct the program to the procedure containing instructions. If it is not equal to the word YES then it will simply go on to the next line of the program, that is line 160. The next line looks like this:

```
140 IF answer$ = "YES" THEN PROCinstructions
160 PRINT "Next line of program."
180 END
```

Line 140 uses IF THEN to test the response. Line 160 is just a dummy line representing the rest of the program. Line 180 is there because we are now going to enter a dummy procedure in order to test the program.

```
500 DEF PROCinstructions
520 PRINT "These are dummy instructions."
540 ENDPROC
```

When you have typed this in, RUN the program a few times and respond with both YES and NO to see what happens. One final addition to this could be used to avoid a possible problem. If you respond with YES, but use lower-case letters the computer reads it as no, since line 140 checks only for the word YES in upper case. To solve this we can change line 140 as follows, using the new word OR in a way whose meaning is fairly obvious.

```
140 IF answer$ = "YES" OR answer$ = "yes" THEN
                   PROCinstructions
```

This line will check both for YES in capitals and yes in lower case. RUN it again and try each of these ways of writing yes.

IF, THEN and ELSE

Now suppose that we have a double choice to make a decision about. That is to say we want to look at a condition, for example the value of a number. IF the number is equal to 37 (for example) THEN we will do one thing. IF it is not equal to 37, THEN we will do something different. The new word to be used in this situation is ELSE. So the program looks like this. (First type in NEW).

```
100 INPUT number
120 IF number = 37 THEN PRINT "YES" ELSE PRINT "NO"
```

RUN this a few times and respond each time to the question mark with a number that is not equal to 37. The response each time will be NO. Then put in 37 and this time the answer will be YES.

Sometimes, within a program, we must make a decision about which of two different and, perhaps, long processes we wish to go on and perform next. These two processes will be written as procedures and we must use IF THEN ELSE to direct the computer to these different procedures. Suppose for example we were writing a program to calculate the total cost of a number of footballs. These footballs can be bought singly at $50 each, or they can be bought in boxes of 10 at $450 each box. If you buy less than ten you pay the dearer price, that is $50 each. If you buy more than ten you pay $450 for each box of ten, and then $50 for each single football, which of course is cheaper. The program begins like this. Type in NEW and then copy each line as we come to it.

```
100 CLS
120 INPUT'' "How many footballs do you wish to buy  ",qty
```

These two lines clear the screen (line 100), ask the question about the number of footballs (line 120), and store the response in the variable 'qty' which is short for quantity. We now need a decision line which determines whether the number being bought is less than ten and therefore dear, or greater than or equal to ten and therefore cheap. We will then write two procedures to calculate the total in each case. We will call these PROCcheap and PROCdear. So the decision line looks like line 160. Then we can finish using line 180.

```
160 IF qty >= 10 THEN PROCcheap ELSE PROCdear
180 END
```

Now we need the two procedures. We will first deal with PROCdear.

```
200 DEF PROCdear
220 cost = 50 * qty
240 PRINT' "The total cost is  "cost
260 ENDPROC
```

Since in this case the footballs are priced at 50 each, the total will simply be the quantity multiplied by 50. This is done in line 220 and the variable used to hold the total is 'cost'.

We will now deal with PROCcheap.

```
280 DEF PROCcheap
300 tens = qty DIV 10
320 units = qty - 10 * tens
340 cost = 450 * tens + 50 * units
360 PRINT' "The total cost is  "cost
380 ENDPROC
```

In this case the calculations are slightly more complicated. Suppose for example the quantity was 23. Then we need to know how many tens there are. To do this we use the new word DIV. This has the effect of dividing the number 'qty' by 10 (in this case) and ignoring the remainder. So 23 DIV 10 becomes 2. This is done in line 300, where the number of tens is stored, appropriately, in a variable called tens. If we now multiply this variable, tens, by 10 and subtract this from the original number, we will get the number of units in the number. Use the example 23 again. In this case tens = 2. So 10 * tens = 20. So 23 - 10 * tens is 3.

We store the number of units in the variable called units, and this is done in line 320. The calculation to find the cost is then done on line 340, and the rest follows. The complete program is shown below. Type it in and try it. For example the number 23 should produce the answer 1050.

```
100 CLS
120 INPUT'' "How many footballs do you wish to buy.  ",qty
160 IF qty >= 10 THEN PROCcheap ELSE PROCdear
180 END
200 DEF PROCdear
220 cost = 50*qty
240 PRINT' "The total cost is  "cost
260 ENDPROC
280 DEF PROCcheap
300 tens = qty DIV 10
320 units = qty - 10 * tens
340 cost = 450 * tens + 50 * units
360 PRINT' "The total cost is  "cost
380 ENDPROC
```

More than one choice each

There is one further complication that can arise. When in any situation the choice is made using IF THEN ELSE, it may be that there are two things to be done in each case. First, a simple example without too much explanation. Suppose we have two variables called first and second. We input a number to a program. If this number is negative (that is, less than zero) then we wish both variables, i.e. first and second to be zero. However, if the number that has been input is positive (or zero) we want the variable first to be equal to 3, and second to be equal to 5. In other words:

```
IF number < 0 THEN first = 0 and second = 0
IF number >= 0 THEN first = 3 and second = 5
```

The sign < means greater than; and >= means greater than or equal to. Now type in NEW and then the first line of the program as follows:

```
100 INPUT number
```

We might then want to try a line like those above. For example we might try:

```
IF number < 0 THEN first = 0 AND second = 0
```

Unfortunately the machine will not accept this use of the word AND so this will not work. One way to do it is to use two lines like this one:

```
120 IF number < 0 THEN first = 0 ELSE first = 3
```

This takes care of the variable 'first'. Then use an almost identical line to take care of the variable second.

```
140 IF number < 0 THEN second = 0 ELSE second = 5
160 PRINT number, first, second
```

Line 160 prints the results on the screen so that you can check whether or not the logic is working. RUN the program a few times and check that when you put in a negative number like - 4, the result is - 4 0 0 Then check that when you put in a positive number like 4, the result is 4, 3, 5.

One last point about this. The word THEN in these lines can often be left out. So that the program just completed can look like this with the word THEN missing.

```
100 INPUT number
120 IF number < 0 first = 0 ELSE first = 3
140 IF number < 0 second = 0 ELSE second = 5
160 PRINT number,first,second
```

Multiple choices and the word ON

Sometimes there are a number of options to choose from. That is the person using the program is presented with a MENU or list of options, chooses one of them by pressing an appropriate key, and then the program must use this choice to determine which procedure to use. Suppose for example we had to make a choice within a program about whether to:

(a) begin the whole process (whatever it is) all over again;

(b) go on with the current process without changing;.

(c) end the use of the program completely.

To set this up we might begin with a screen MENU like this:

```
   Choose one of the following:-

      1......Begin again.

      2......Go on as before.

      3......End for now.
?-
```

The program which accomplishes this looks like the following. Type it in and try it.

```
100 CLS
120 PRINT''' "Choose one of the following:-"
140 PRINT' "   1....Begin again."
160 PRINT' "   2....Go on as before."
180 PRINT' "   3....End for now."
200 INPUT "Now choose a number  ",number
```

Whatever number we choose is stored in the variable 'number'. We could now use a series of lines beginning with the word IF, one for each choice on the MENU. Like these:

```
240 IF number = 1 THEN PRINT "You have chosen one." : GOTO
    300
260 IF number = 2 THEN PRINT "You have chosen two." : GOTO
    320
280 IF number = 3 THEN PRINT "You have chosen three." :
    GOTO 340
```

This means that, if the number 1 is chosen, a message declaring this appears on the screen. The program is then sent to line 300 (using the statement GOTO 300) to deal with this choice. Similarly when the numbers 2 or 3 are chosen. At each of the lines 300,320 and 340 it would then be possible to place appropriate routines. We will do no more here than put in a memo line in each case. However, when the routine is completed it is normally necessary to direct control of the program back to the MENU. The exception is when 3 is chosen. In that case the program ends. The lines that follow are meant simply to illustrate the process:

```
300 PRINT "This is the BEGIN AGAIN ROUTINE." : GOTO 120
320 PRINT "This is the GO ON AS BEFORE ROUTINE." : GOTO 120
340 PRINT "This is the END routine."
360 END
```

There is one other problem to be taken care of immediately after the menu choice. Suppose the person using the program presses 4 or 5 or 0 by mistake, instead of 1,2 or 3. We need a line that traps this mistake, as follows.

```
220 IF number < 1 OR number > 3 PRINT "Number out of range." : GOTO 200
```

Notice that, at the end of this line the program is returned to the INPUT line, that is line 200. RUN the program a few times and check that it works by pressing various numbers. Now LIST the program and look at it. The lines 240, 260, 280 are all alike in that they begin with IF. Indeed if the MENU had 20 choices, there would have to be 20 such lines. This seems a bit cumbersome and uneconomical and there is a more precise way of doing it. Remove lines 240, 260 and 280 and then type in this new version of 240.

```
240 ON number GOTO 300,320,340
```

The effect of this is exactly the same as the three lines just removed. That is, when the variable number is 1, then the program is directed to line 300: when the number is 2 to 320: and when the number is 3 to 340. Try it and see.

This problem of multiple choices can lead to a complicated and confusing program. In the one that we have just written we made some attempt to keep it organised, but even so the number of GOTO statements can make it difficult to follow the reasoning at every stage. Ideally we should use Procedures for each menu choice but it is not possible to use a line like:

```
ON number PROCbegin, PROCgo, PROCend
```

So in this case we would have to use a number of GOTO statements to direct the program to the appropriate procedure, and back from it.

It is possible, however, to use the words GOSUB and RETURN and these give some level of structure and flow to the program. We will now rewrite this last program using these words.

GOSUB RETURN

In the last program all the lines up to the end of the menu, that is up to and including line 200, can be retained. So type in DELETE 220, 340 to get rid of the others. Now type in the two new lines numbered 220 and 240 and LIST the program so that it looks like this:

```
100 CLS
120 PRINT''' "Choose one of the following:-"
140 PRINT' "   1....Begin again."
160 PRINT' "   2....Go on as before."
180 PRINT' "   3....End for now."
200 INPUT' "Now choose a number  "number
220 ON number GOSUB 260, 300, 340
240 GOTO 120
```

Line 220 uses the word ON in exactly the same way as before. That is when the variable number is equal to 1, then the statement GOSUB 260 is used: when it is equal to 2, then GOSUB 300 is used: when it is equal to 3, then GOSUB 340 is used. Finally, if anything other than these three numbers is chosen, line 240 sends the program back to the Menu. This line contains the only GOTO in the program.

The statement GOSUB 260 means go to the subroutine which begins at line 260. We will now write this subroutine and examine it. Once again we simply use a PRINT statement to illustrate the process:

```
260 PRINT' "This is the BEGIN AGAIN ROUTINE."
280 RETURN
```

The word RETURN on line 280 signals the end of the subroutine and this means that the computer automatically goes back to the line immediately after the line on which the statement GOSUB 260 appeared. That is to line 240. In other words it does not need a GOTO statement. So the order in which the computer executes the program lines is as follows. (This is when number equals 1).

```
220 ON number GOSUB 260, 300, 340
260 PRINT' "This is the BEGIN AGAIN ROUTINE."
280 RETURN
240 GOTO 120
```

The second subroutine, when number equals 2, is almost identical to this in its structure:

```
300 PRINT' "This is the GO ON AS BEFORE ROUTINE."
320 RETURN
```

Finally the END subroutine is a bit different since it marks the end of the program.

```
340 PRINT' "This is the END ROUTINE."
360 END
```

The completed program now looks like this:

```
100 CLS
120 PRINT''' "Choose one of the following:-"
140 PRINT' "   1....Begin again."
160 PRINT' "   2....Go on as before."
180 PRINT' "   3....End for now."
200 INPUT' "Now choose a number  "number
220 ON number GOSUB 260, 300, 340
240 GOTO 120
260 PRINT' "This is the BEGIN AGAIN ROUTINE."
280 RETURN
300 PRINT' "This is the GO ON AS BEFORE ROUTINE."
320 RETURN
340 PRINT' "This is the END ROUTINE."
360 END
```

This is tidier and easier to read than before. It is possible to improve this even more using REM statements to highlight the beginning of each subroutine. For example, a group of lines like this could be used for each

```
250 REM ************
252 REM    BEGIN
254 REM ************
```

There is a further example using GOSUB and RETURN with a Menu on page 104, chapter 6.

Symbols for comparison

When using IF and its related words (like THEN, ELSE, ON) symbols denoting relationships are usually needed. There are essentially only three of these, as follows:

(a) = The symbol for Equality as in 12 = 3x4

(b) The symbol for Less than as in 9 < 10. (This symbol is easy to remember since it looks like an L which is the first letter of less).

(c) The symbol for Greater than, as in 12 > 3.

There are three other relations that use combinations of these symbols, as follows:

(d) < = This means Less than or Equal to.

(e) > = This means Greater than or Equal to.

(f) < > This means Not Equal to.

We have used most of these at some stage in this chapter and there are many examples in other parts of the book.

Boolean operators

The four words AND, OR, EOR and NOT are called Boolean operators and they are normally used in conditional statements, that is in IF THEN statements. We have already used OR on page 65, but we will now try to explain what these words mean in programming. To do this we will use a short program which begins as follows:

```
100 INPUT one$
120 INPUT two$
```

We are going to input two words or strings in response to these two lines. The correct responses, as far as the computer is concerned, are TOM and JERRY. We now have two sentences that we want to use as responses to these two inputs. They are:

```
140 note1$ = "At least one of these is correct."
160 note2$ = "Neither of these two is correct."
```

Finally we come to the important line which decides, on the basis of the two inputs, in lines 100 and 120, which of these responses or notes to print. We use the Boolean operator OR in this case.

```
180 IF one$ = "TOM" OR two$ = "JERRY" THEN PRINT note1$
    ELSE PRINT note2$
```

Now RUN this program four times. Each time respond as shown below and check that the computer's response is also as shown.

1. Type in TOM and then JERRY. These are both correct, and the computer's response will be 'note1$', that is 'At least one of these is correct."

2. Type in TOM and DICK. This time the second is wrong, but the computer's response will be the same.

3. Type in TIM and JERRY. This time the first is wrong, but the computer's response will be the same once more.

4. Type in TIM and DICK. Now both are wrong and the response will be 'note2$', that is 'Neither of these two is correct.'

So, in line 180, the word OR means if either of the two inputs is correct or if both are correct then it will print note1$. If both are incorrect then and only then will it print note2$.

Now change the last three lines of the program as follows. In particular notice that we have changed OR to AND on line 180.

```
140 note1$ = "Both of these are correct."
160 note2$ = "At least one of these is wrong."
180 IF one$ = "TOM" AND two$ = "JERRY" THEN PRINT note1$
    ELSE PRINT note2$
```

Now RUN this program four times as before and look at the the results. In this case both of the inputs have to be correct to get note1$ printed. If either or both are wrong then note2$ is printed.

Think about the difference between OR and AND as a result of these two programs and then consider this situation. A man is in debt and needs $35,000. So he is trying to sell a house and a car at the same time. Ideally he would like to get $30,000 for the house and $5,000 for the car, but he realizes that he might not be offered this much. Among others there are two possible decisions that he can make. (a) He will not sell unless he is offered the price he wants for both of them. (b) He will sell if he is offered the price he wants for either of them.

Here is a list of possible situations:

	House	Car	Description
Case 1	30000	5000	Both correct
Case 2	30000	4000	Car too little
Case 3	29000	5000	House too little
Case 4	29000	4000	Both too little

We will now write a short program to illustrate these examples. First type in NEW and then the following two lines:

```
100 INPUT hp
120 INPUT cp
```

We have called the house price hp and the car price is called cp. Then the conditional line using IF THEN ELSE would take one of the two forms. In the situation where he will sell only where case 1 prevails we would write:

```
140 IF hp > = 30000 AND cp > = 5000 THEN PRINT "Sell" ELSE
    PRINT "Do not sell".
```

In other words we must use the Boolean AND in this case. Notice that we have also used the symbols >= meaning 'greater than or equal to'. Now RUN this program and test it by putting in the above combinations of prices.

In the other situation described, that is where he will sell if cases 1, 2 and 3 prevail, then we would write:

```
140 IF hp > = 30000 OR cp > = 5000 THEN PRINT "Sell" ELSE
    PRINT "Do not sell.
```

We now come to the Boolean NOT. This is used to invert the meanings normally attached to OR and AND. It is used as follows:

```
140 IF NOT (hp > = 30000 OR cp > = 5000) THEN PRINT "Do not
    sell" ELSE PRINT "Sell."
```

Notice that we have had to change the order of the messages so as to make sure that the conditions still work correctly. Notice the use of brackets round the complete conditional clause.

The last Boolean operator is EOR which is short for 'exclusive or'. This is used in the situation where if either of the two conditions are met then do one thing. But if neither condition is met or indeed both conditions are met, then do something else. It is possible to use combinations of these conditionals in the same sentence. Here is an example, based on the house and car example above.

```
140 IF hp > = 30000 OR cp > = 5000 OR hp + cp > = 35000
    THEN PRINT "Sell" ELSE PRINT "Do not sell."
```

In this case any one of the three conditions will result in the response Sell. Or, to put it the other way, all three conditions would have to fail to get the response 'Do not sell'.

The final example uses a combination of OR and AND as follows:

```
140 IF (hp > = 30000 OR cp > = 5000) AND hp + cp > = 35000
    THEN PRINT "Sell." ELSE PRINT "Do not sell."
```

Try lots of examples with this and try to understand it. It means that the sum of the two prices must be greater than 35000, no matter what else. The use of AND here gives the condition that follows a sort of veto. As well, if both of the other two fall below the required price then this too fails.

In this sort of situation the AND operator has logical precedence over the OR. This means that the computer will go to the AND first, then to the OR. In general the order of precedence among Boolean operators is NOT, AND, OR(EOR), the last two having equal precedence. (For more about precedence see page 144 in the handbook).

Graphics with IF and THEN

We will now write a short program which demonstrates the use of conditional or IF statements in drawing pictures on the screen. To begin with we are going to choose a starting point on the screen and then draw a line diagonally across the screen. When the line reaches the edge of the screen we want it to turn at right angles to its previous direction and move back across the screen again. This process continues with the line bumping off the screen edges like a billiard ball. Begin as follows:

```
100 CLS
120 INPUT"Choose an X starting point  " X
140 INPUT"Choose a Y starting point  " Y
180 MODE 5
200 MOVE X,Y
```

Lines 120 and 140 allow us to choose the point on the screen where we will begin to draw the line. Remember that X can run from 0 to 1279 and Y can run from 0 to 1023. Line 180 chooses MODE 5 because of its graphics facility and its four colors. If you have a Model B machine try MODE 1. Line 200 moves the cursor to the starting point, without actually making any mark on the screen.

We now need to increase the two co-ordinates by a fixed amount each time and then DRAW a short line joining this new point to the last point. And we want to go on doing this.

```
220 incX = 5 : incY = 5
240 X = X + incX : Y = Y + incY
260 DRAW X,Y
320 GOTO 240
```

Type these lines in and RUN the program. It will produce one long line across the screen, but then nothing else. You will have to press the Escape key to stop it. Then type in MODE 7 and press RETURN so that it is easy to read. Remember that in MODE 5 the letters are twice as broad.

We now use IF THEN to check for the left and right edges of the screen, as follows

```
280 IF X <0 OR X >1275 THEN incX = -incX
```

And a similar line is needed to check the top and bottom of the screen.

```
300 IF Y <0 OR Y >1018 THEN incY = -incY
```

Try this and the line should now bounce off the walls of the screen and make a continuous crisscrossing line. Press the ESCAPE key when you wish to stop it.

We now wish to change the color of the line each time it bounces off a wall. To do this we must change lines 280 and 300 by adding a short identical statement to the end of each as shown. This can be done very quickly using the COPY key.

```
280 IF X < 0 OR X > 1275 THEN incX = -incX : GCOL 0, RND(3)
300 IF Y < 0 OR Y > 1018 THEN incY = -incY : GCOL 0, RND(3)
```

This statement, GCOL 0, RND(3), changes the color of the line each time. The expression RND(3) becomes one of the three numbers 1, 2 or 3 each time, but the choice is made randomly, so that the color changes will be random. The complete program now looks like this:

```
100 CLS
120 INPUT "Choose an X starting point "X
140 INPUT "Choose a Y starting point "Y
180 MODE 5
200 MOVE X,Y
220 incX = 5 : incY = 5
240 X = X + incX : Y = Y + incY
260 DRAW X,Y
280 IF X < 0 OR X > 1275 THEN incX = -incX : GCOL 0, RND(3)
300 IF Y < 0 OR Y > 1018 THEN incY = -incY : GCOL 0, RND(3)
320 GOTO 240
```

There are two other points to be made about this program. The use of the statement GOTO in line 240 can be avoided by using the words REPEAT, UNTIL and FALSE. These are described in detail later in this book. For the moment we will use them as follows where their meaning is fairly obvious so long as we know that UNTIL FALSE really means forever in this case. Put in line 230 and change line 320 as follows:

```
230 REPEAT
320 UNTIL FALSE
```

The second point is that, we can change the values of the increases to X and Y as declared in line 220. This can produce very interesting results. For example, change line 220 to this and RUN the program again.

```
220 incX = 20 : incY = 1
```

Problems

1. Write a program which allows you to input a set of 10 numbers. The program should first test each number to check as to whether or not it is a whole number. If it is not it should reject it with a message. It should then test as to whether the number is between 0 and 9, between 10 and 19, or greater than 19. When all ten numbers have been entered it should print them out in three separate lists.

2. Write a program which invites you to input two numbers, and then asks you to choose which of the four arithmetical operations (add, subtract, multiply, divide) you wish to perform with the two numbers. Use the words ON, GOSUB and RETURN.

CHAPTER 5
LOOPS AND REPETITIONS

Introduction to loops

One of the many powers of computers is their ability to be repetitive; that is, to do the same thing over and over again without becoming bored or tired. Such repetitions are done by making LOOPS round and round the same process. A simple diagram will illustrate the idea.

START PRINT "HELLO" RETURN TO START

A program to make the computer loop like this will print the word "HELLO" over and over again without stopping. There are a number of ways of doing this sort of thing, that is making loops, and we will consider three of them in turn. They are:

1. Using GOTO
2. Using FOR NEXT
3. Using REPEAT UNTIL

Using GOTO

We will begin by using the word GOTO to produce a program which will repeatedly print HELLO. We start with this way of doing it because it is the easiest to understand. Later on we will encourage you to use the other methods rather than using GOTO. This is because using GOTO can cause difficulties especially if used often in a program.

First type in NEW to remove any program in the memory and then type in this short two-line program, remembering to press the RETURN key at the end of each line.

```
120  PRINT "Hello"
180  GOTO 120
```

Now type in RUN and press RETURN. The computer will now print an unending column of the word Hello on the screen. The program does not tell the machine when to stop, and for this reason it is a bad program. The only way it can be stopped is for you to intervene and press the ESCAPE key. Do this now. There are two essentially different ways of knowing when a loop has been repeated enough times.

(a) When you know exactly how many loops you want to make. An example of this would be if you wished this program to print the word Hello exactly 7 times. We will call a loop of this kind a COUNT-LOOP.

(b) When some condition has been fulfilled. This condition might be that a set of numbers should be written by the computer on the screen, one after another, until the number 99 is reached. Then the looping should stop. We will call this a CONDITION-LOOP.

Using GOTO the two kinds of loops are dealt with in a similar way. Suppose we wished to change the two-line program already in the machine so that it prints the word Hello exactly 10 times. This is a COUNT-LOOP and the following new lines need to be added to the program. Be careful not to put the variable name count in upper case.

```
100 count = 0
140 count = count + 1
160 IF count = 10 THEN GOTO 200
200 END
```

Now RUN this program and check if it does in fact print Hello 10 times. LIST the program now and look at it. The word 'count' is used to stand for the number of times the computer circuits the loop. In other words it counts the number of circuits. In line 100 count is put equal to zero, and in line 140 it is increased by one during each circuit. That is, the number in the unit of memory labelled count has one added to it. This is an unusual use of the equality sign. We could read line 140 as : the value of count is to be put equal to the value of count plus one. Line 160 checks to see if 10 circuits have been completed and, if so, the program ends at line 200.

Now for another example, this time of a CONDITION-LOOP. Suppose we wished to input some numbers, square them, and print the results on the screen. In this case we do not know how many of these numbers there are. We will first produce a program to handle the input and calculation process, and we will then consider the need for a stopping routine which will have to take the form of a CONDITION-LOOP. First type in NEW to remove the program in memory, then type in this program and then RUN it.

```
100 INPUT number
140 PRINT number, number*number
160 GOTO 100
```

A question mark will appear on the screen in response to line 100. That is, the machine is expecting the input of a number from you. Type in 7 and press RETURN. The computer will make the variable called number equal to 7 as a result of line 100. In line 140, this number i.e.7 and its square 49, are printed on the screen. Then line 160 sends the program back to line 100 to wait for another input.

Now press the ESCAPE key to return to COMMAND MODE, so that some new lines can be added to the program. These will allow you to escape from the program at any time. To do this we use a dummy number, and we must choose one that we are unlikely to wish to find the square of. In this case we have used 999 as the dummy number. Type in the lines:

```
120 IF number = 999 THEN 180
180 END
```

Line 120 is the CONDITIONAL line which is used to end the program's run whenever we wish. To test this type in RUN and press RETURN. As before a question mark will appear on the screen. This time type in 999 and the program will end.

Using FOR NEXT

This type of loop is best used when we have what is called a COUNT-LOOP, that is a loop where we know in advance how many times we wish to repeat some statement or process. The words used are FOR, NEXT and TO. Later on we also use STEP. We will begin with a short example. First type in NEW and then this program. Remember to press RETURN after each line.

```
100 FOR count = 1 TO 6
120 PRINT "Loops are about repeating"
140 NEXT count
```

Now RUN this program, and the result is as follows:

```
Loops are about repeating
Loops are about repeating
Loops are about repeating
Loops are about repeating
Loops are about repeating
Loops are about repeating
>-
```

RUN the program a few times and each time, count how often the line "Loops are about repeating" is printed. Now look at the program. Lines 100 and 140 go together and all statements occuring between these lines are repeated six times. Line 140 can be replaced by:

```
140 NEXT
```

In other words the variable name, in this case count, can be left out but this can lead to confusion so in this book the variable will always be included along with the word NEXT.

Using the counter

Sometimes the statement that is repeated, that is the statement within the loop, is simple and obvious as in this example. But it can be more complicated and can be related to the variable doing the counting. Here is another example to type in and try. (Remember to use NEW first).

```
100 FOR loopnumber = 1 TO 8
120 PRINT loopnumber
140 NEXT loopnumber
```

The output will look like this:

```
                 1
                 2
                 3
                 4
                 5
                 6
                 7
                 8
>-
```

That is to say, the actual value of the variable loopnumber itself is printed for each circuit of the loop. Now change line 120 as follows:

```
120 PRINT 3*loopnumber
```

This time the output will be

```
                   3
                   6
                   9
                   12
                   15
                   18
                   21
                   24
>-
```

So, this time each value of the variable 'loopnumber' is multiplied by 3, and these results are printed. We can use this technique to print multiplication tables. First type in the word NEW and then type in this program.

```
100 FOR count = 1 TO 9
120 PRINT "3 times "; count; "  is  "; 3* count
140 NEXT count
```

Now RUN this and see what happens. You will notice that we changed the variable name first to 'loopcounter' and then back to 'count'. This is just to demonstrate that you can choose the word you wish to use for the variable name.

Now another example illustrating how the statement to be executed within the loop may be closely related to the count number. Suppose you wished to add the numbers 3, 4, 5, 6, 7, and 8. The answer is of course 33, as you can check. First use NEW to remove the old program and then type in this program.

```
100 sum = 0
120 FOR count = 3 TO 8
140 sum = sum + count
160 NEXT count
180 PRINT "The total is  "; sum
```

When this is RUN the response is:

```
The total is 33

>_
```

On line 100 the variable 'sum' was declared as zero. Then in line 140 the total is cumulated by adding to sum successively the values of the variable 'count' as the program loops round. The procedure can be pictured as follows:

```
                    sum = 0
count = 3           sum = 3
count = 4           sum = 7
count = 5           sum = 12
count = 6           sum = 18
count = 7           sum = 25
count = 8           sum = 33
```

The word STEP

The process that allows us to use the value of the variable counting the loops is even more useful when we allow the value to change in different ways. For example suppose we were interested in odd numbers only. To get access to these we use the new word STEP. First use NEW to remove the old program and then type in this example and RUN it. The result is shown after the program.

```
100 FOR count = 1 TO 11 STEP 2
120 PRINT count
140 NEXT count
```

```
                     1
                     3
                     5
                     7
                     9
                     11
 >-
```

That is to say the value of the variable called count changes by 2 (the STEP value) each time. We can also use this procedure to count backwards. Change line 100 to this, and then RUN it

```
100 FOR count = 9 TO 1 STEP -1
```

DIM lists and arrays

Normally we use variable names like number and count to stand for individual pieces of information. But there are occasions when we wish to deal with sets or lists of information and it would be a very tedious business to have to give each one of these a separate name. So, in these situations we can use what is called an Array variable. Suppose for example we had a list of names to deal with. We will use four only but the number could be much larger than this. The four names are : John, Paul, George and Ringo. The array variable we will use is called, appropriately, beatle$ and is used like this:

```
John   is stored in beatle$(1)
Paul   is stored in beatle$(2)
George is stored in beatle$(3)
Ringo  is stored in beatle$(4)
```

In other words the same variable name, in this case beatle, is used for each case, but a different number inside brackets after the variable name is used to distinguish one name from another.

We must always declare in advance that we are going to use an array variable, and to do this we use the word DIM which is short for dimension. An example would look like this:

```
100 DIM beatle$(4)
```

The word DIM would inform the computer that we were booking some memory space; the word beatle is the variable name; the dollar sign means that we are dealing with strings, and the 4 in brackets means that we want four units of memory to be reserved. This might be visualized like this:

	beatle$(1)
	beatle$(2)
	beatle$(3)
	beatle$(4)

That is we have booked a set of four units of memory and given these units names as shown. So if we then say, beatle$(1) = "John", the word John will be stored in the first of the memory units.

Notice that we used the first line number that is, 100, for this. All dimension declarations should come as early in a program as possible and should not occur within a loop as the computer will give an error message if it meets the declaration more than once.

We can of course declare more than one array. Here is an example where we need both a string array and one for numbers. A grocer wishes to store the names of items on his stock list along with the quantity of each that he has. To do this he needs to declare two arrays, both quite large. A line like this would be needed:

```
100 DIM item$(200), quantity(200)
```

This means that he is booking space for 200 different grocery items like tea, sugar, potatoes, and so on. He is using the variable 'item$' for these. He is also booking space for the number of each in store and is using the variable 'quantity' for this. So, if the 23rd item on his list was tins of coffee, and he had 73 of these in store, then this information would be stored as:

```
item$(23) = "tins of coffee"
quantity(23) = 73
```

It is also possible to have arrays with two (or more) dimensions. Suppose for example the grocer separated his items of food into two categories, with fruit and vegetables in one category and everything else in the other category. He would then declare his intentions as follows:

```
100 DIM item$(2,100), quantity(2,100)
```

He would then have two lists of items, side by side, labelled as item$(1,100) and item$(2,100). We can show this in a diagram as follows:

item$(1,1)	Apples	Tins of coffee	item$(2,1)
item$(1,2)	Oranges	Sugar	item$(2,2)
item$(1,3)	Potatoes	Tea	item$(2,3)
item$(1,4)	Plums	Butter	item$(2,4)

The quantity array would reflect this picture exactly, except that the variable would be quantity instead of item and the contents of the units of memory would be numbers. Arrays of these kinds are used a great deal in loops and examples of these now follow.

Loops with strings

We can also use loops with strings. First type in NEW and then this program:

```
100 FOR count = 1 TO 6
120 A$ = A$ + "DO"
140 PRINT A$
180 NEXT count
```

Now RUN this and the response should look like this:

```
DO
DODO
DODODO
DODODODO
DODODODODO
DODODODODODO
>-
```

Now suppose we wished to use a set of stores in which to keep the names and examination marks of a class of students. First we need to declare two arrays, one for the names and one for marks. (It would be possible to combine these in one two-dimensional array, but we will try to keep it simple for the moment).

```
100 DIM name$(14),mark(14)
```

We have chosen the variable-array name$(14) to hold the names of the students and the variable-array mark(14) to hold the marks. We will now put the names into two data lines as follows: (We could have put them all on one data line, but it would have looked rather long).

```
120 DATA Cranston, Darby, Everton, Farren, Greer, Griffith,
    Hart
140 DATA Jenkins, Marriott, Murray, Nesbitt, O'Hara, Short,
    Sullivan
```

We then put the marks one for each name into a further DATA line.

```
160 DATA 12,31,73,26,34,18,93,63,70,8,23,30,41,60
```

We now need a FOR NEXT loop to READ each of these sets of DATA into the appropriate arrays.

```
180 FOR count = 1 TO 14 : READ name$(count) : NEXT count
200 FOR count = 1 TO 14 : READ mark(count) : NEXT count
```

We now wish to print the two columns side by side on the screen. But first we will put in a screen-hold routine, so that we can decide when to begin this printing.

```
220 PRINT'' "Press the space-bar"
240 Z = GET
```

Then the print routine to print the two columns:

```
260 FOR count = 1 TO 14
280 PRINT name$(count), mark(count)
300 NEXT count
```

Now RUN this program to see if it works. The complete program looks like this.

```
100 DIM name$(14),mark(14)
120 DATA Cranston, Darby, Everton, Farren, Greer, Griffith,
    Hart
140 DATA Jenkins, Marriott, Murray, Nesbitt, O'Hara, Short,
    Sullivan
160 DATA 12,31,73,26,34,18,93,63,70,8,23,30,41,60
180 FOR count = 1 TO 14 : READ name$(count) : NEXT count
200 FOR count = 1 TO 14 : READ mark(count) : NEXT count
220 PRINT '' "Press the space-bar."
240 Z = GET
260 FOR count = 1 TO 14
280 PRINT name$(count), mark(count)
300 NEXT count
```

When it is run the screen result should look like this:

```
Cranston     12
Darby        31
Everton      73
Farren       26
Greer        34
Griffith     18
Hart         93
Jenkins      63
Marriott     70
Murray        8
Nesbitt      23
O'Hara       30
Short        41
Sullivan     60
>-
```

Problems with loops

Sometimes it is necessary to jump out of a loop because some condition has been satisfied. This procedure should be avoided wherever possible and it usually is possible with a little thought to avoid it. If it is absolutely necessary, then you should try to use a REPEAT UNTIL loop as described later in this chapter, where it can be accomplished with less difficulty. To illustrate the problem and to indicate a possible solution, type in this example:

```
100 DATA 3,5,11,4,9
120 FOR count = 1 TO 5
140 READ number
180 PRINT number
200 NEXT count
220 END
```

Now RUN this and see how it works. The list of 5 pieces of data in line 100 are read, one at a time, by line 140 and printed by line 180. Now suppose that you wanted to leave the loop and go on to the next part of the program as soon as a number is read that is greater than 10. To achieve this you could add the following lines to the program:

```
160 IF number > 10 THEN 240
240 PRINT "This number is too large."
260 PRINT "The count is still at  ";count
```

Now RUN the program again. This time, when line 140 reads the third number, that is the number 11, it jumps out of the loop. But as line 260 indicates the count variable is still at 3. This means that somewhere inside, the computer is waiting for it to go on to 4 and then to 5. This can on occasions lead to problems. One way of avoiding it is to change line 160 as follows:

```
160 IF number > 10 THEN count = 5 : NEXT count : GOTO 240
```

There is another unusual feature of loops on this machine that you must be careful about. A loop is always executed at least once, no matter what the numbers involved are. Here is an example. First type in NEW and then type this in and RUN it.

```
100 FOR count = 7 TO 6
120 PRINT count
140 NEXT count
```

Even though the suggested loop is impossible, the computer does not give an error message. It just goes round the loop once.

Nested loops

It is possible to place one loop inside another as shown in this example. Remember to use NEW to remove the previous program from the memory.

```
┌──100 FOR tens = 1 TO 5
│ ┌120 FOR units = 0 TO 9
│ │140 PRINT;10*tens + units;" ";
│ └160 NEXT units
│  180 PRINT
└──200 NEXT tens
```

Now RUN this program. It will print all the whole numbers from 10 to 59 in succession. There are two points to notice about it.

1. The units loop is counted in the lines 120 to 160. The tens loop is placed round and outside this in the lines 100 to 200. This pattern must always be used, that is with one loop completely contained inside another. The square brackets at the side of the program above are put in to show this nesting pattern.

2. The space in inverted commas followed by a semi colon on line 140 is there to ensure that the numbers are printed on the same line across the screen with a space between them. The PRINT statement on line 180 is there to make sure that the printing begins on a new line when the value of the variable 'tens' changes.

Now for another example of nested loops using a two-dimensional array. Suppose we had two columns of matching words as shown below which we are going to use as a test within a program.

	Column 1	Column 2
Row 1	Red	Coat
Row 2	Blue	Moon
Row 3	Yellow	Lines
Row 4	Black	Spot
Row 5	White	Collar
Row 6	Green	Grocer

This is a two-dimensional array of words, or strings, and we need a variable to store them in. First we need to declare the array variable using DIM. Type in this line and press RETURN.

```
100 DIM colour$(6,2)
```

The effect of this is to prepare the computer to receive a set of 12 strings in an array of six by two. The array can be set out as follows:

	Column 1	Column 2
Row 1	colour$(1,1)	colour$(1,2)
Row 2	colour$(2,1)	colour$(2,2)
Row 3	colour$(3,1)	colour$(3,2)
Row 4	colour$(4,1)	colour$(4,2)
Row 5	colour$(5,1)	colour$(5,2)
Row 6	colour$(6,1)	colour$(6,2)

This means that a unit of memory within the computer will be labelled colour$(1,1) and that the string 'Red' will be stored in that unit. Similarly another unit of memory will be labelled colour$(1,2) and the string 'Coat' will be stored in that unit, and so on. You can get the idea quite quickly if you look at the two tables and compare them.

Now we need a routine to enter the list of words. We will use READ and DATA statements and begin by placing the strings in DATA statements like this:

```
120 DATA Red,Coat,Blue,Moon,Yellow,Lines
140 DATA Black,Spot,White,Collar,Green,Grocer
```

A nested loop can be used to READ these words into the array labelled colour. This is done as follows:

```
160 FOR row = 1 TO 6
180 FOR column = 1 TO 2
200 READ colour$(row,column)
220 NEXT column
240 NEXT row
```

You might now wish to check that the procedure has worked properly. To do this, type in the following PRINT routine. (In a real program this routine may not be needed, but it can be typed in quickly as a check and then deleted again).

```
260 FOR row = 1 TO 6
280 FOR column = 1 TO 2
300 PRINT colour$(row,column),;
320 NEXT column
340 PRINT
360 NEXT row
```

The combination of a comma and a semicolon at the end of line 300 ensures that the words are printed on the screen in two columns side by side.

Color and graphics

We will now show you how to make use of loops using FOR in some simple graphics routines. The following short program shows all the possible colours that are available, first in MODE 5. First type in NEW and then this program.

```
100 MODE 5
120 FOR shade = 0 TO 3
140 COLOUR shade
160 PRINT'' "The color now is  ";shade
180 Z = GET
200 NEXT shade
```

Now RUN it. To begin with you will not see anything because the color variable will be at zero so the writing is in black, which is the same color as the screen. The screen is held by line 180, so press the space-bar to get the next color, and continue in this way.

If you have a Model B machine change two lines as follows to display all 16 colors.

```
100 MODE 2
120 FOR shade = 0 TO 15
```

The next program illustrates an interesting way of producing colored printing on different coloured backgrounds in MODE 7. The result is the same as the print style used in Viewdata facilities on T.V. The technique makes use of the string function CHR$ (short for character-string) which will be discussed in more detail in Chapter 9. In this case it must be accepted for the moment. In MODE 7 this CHR$ function is used with certain numbers to produce colors, as follows:

CHR$ 128	White
CHR$ 129	Red
CHR$ 130	Green
CHR$ 131	Yellow
CHR$ 132	Blue
CHR$ 133	Magenta
CHR$ 134	Cyan

So the program begins like this:

```
100 MODE 7
120 FOR shade = 128 TO 134
140 PRINT CHR$ shade; "BBC micro"
180 NEXT shade
```

Type this in and RUN it. The phrase BBC micro should appear 7 times each time in a different color. We can now make the background color different each time by putting in CHR$ 157 after CHR$ shade each time in line 140 like this:

```
140 PRINT CHR$ shade; CHR$ 157; "BBC micro"
```

Type in this new version of line 140 and RUN the program again. This time a set of 7 bands of colour appear across the screen, but the phrase 'B.B.C. Micro' can no longer be seen, since it has not changed color. So to make it change color and appear again add another CHR$ to line 140, like this: (Notice that shade+1 must be put in brackets).

```
140 PRINT CHR$ shade; CHR$ 157; CHR$(shade+1); "BBC
    micro".
```

Now RUN it again. There is, finally one last possible embellishment. Add yet another CHR$ to the end of this row, that is CHR$ 141 like this:

```
140 PRINT CHR$ shade; CHR$ 157; CHR$(shade+1); CHR$ 141;
    "BBC micro"
```

Now use the COPY key to make an exact copy of this line, except change the line number to 160. That is to say, have two identical lines numbered 140 and 160. Now RUN the program again. This time the letters and the bands of color should be of double height. This doubling effect is caused by CHR$ 141, and when it is used the line containing it must be used twice. The complete program looks like this:

```
100 MODE 7
120 FOR shade = 128 TO 134
140 PRINT CHR$ shade; CHR$ 157; CHR$(shade+1); CHR$ 141;
    "BBC micro"
160 PRINT CHR$ shade; CHR$ 157; CHR$(shade+1); CHR$ 141;
    "BBC micro"
180 NEXT shade
```

The last program in this section on graphics loops uses a FOR loop to draw a mathematical curve. The equation of the curve is Y = X * X + 50. This is a quadratic equation, and the curve representing it is called a parabola. But do not worry if your mathematics is not too strong. It is possible to type in the program and watch it work without completely understanding the mathematics. As well as this, the process itself should help you to understand the mathematics a bit better. Begin as follows:

```
100 MODE 1
140 FOR count = 0 TO 70 STEP .25
180 Y = count * count + 50
260 NEXT count
```

Line 100 sets the MODE. If you have a MODEL A machine use MODE 5, and if you are using a black and white monitor as well use MODE 4. The loop in lines 140 and 180 uses the variable count to represent X and, in line 180, Y is made equal to the square of this variable added to 50. We must now scale these numbers so that they fit easily into the screen. The values of count range from 0 to 70, which is too small, so we will scale this up by multiplying by 10. The values of Y on the other hand are too large (think about the value of 70 * 70 + 50, for example) so we must scale them down by a factor of 5. These changes are made in the new line 200.

```
200 X = 10 * count : Y = Y/5
```

We will generate the curve by drawing a series of lines from the bottom of the screen. These will be equal in length to the values of Y. This means that at each circuit of the loop we must move across the bottom of the screen a distance equal to X. This is done in line 220.

```
220 MOVE X,0
```

Then, draw the lines from each of these points.

```
240 DRAW X,Y
```

Type in these extra lines and RUN the program. If you have a color monitor or T.V. add this line and then RUN the program again.

```
120 GCOL 0,1
```

This version of the curve shows that part of it for which X is positive. If we wanted to look at a wider range, we can change lines 140 and 200 as follows:

```
140 FOR count = -70 TO 70 STEP  .25
200 X = 10 * count + 640 : Y = Y /5
```

RUN this and the result should be a beautiful colored parabola. Finally if we wish to show the negative side a different color from the positive type in this line and then RUN the program.

```
160 IF count = 0 THEN GCOL 0,2
```

The complete program now looks like this

```
100 MODE 1
120 GCOL 0,1
140 FOR count = -70 TO 70 STEP  .25
160 IF count = 0 THEN GCOL 0,2
180 Y = count * count + 50
200 X = 10 * count + 640 : Y = Y/5
220 MOVE X,0
240 DRAW X,Y
260 NEXT count
```

Using REPEAT UNTIL

This type of loop is best used for what we have called a CONDITION-LOOP, that is a loop where we do not know in advance how many times we wish to repeat a statement or process. The words used are REPEAT and UNTIL.

We will begin with a short example. First type in NEW and then this program. Remember to press RETURN after each line.

```
100 REPEAT
120 INPUT number
140 PRINT number, number*number
160 UNTIL number = 999
```

This is almost identical in its effect to the program on page 76 which uses GOTO, and this one is clearly shorter and simpler. Type in RUN and press RETURN. A question-mark will appear on the screen and you respond to this with any number, for example 7. This is stored in the variable called number by line 120. Line 140 prints 7, and its square, 49, on the screen and then another question mark will appear on the screen. This process will continue or REPEAT until you put in 999. Then line 160 will bring the program to an end. However it will print 999 itself, and its square, and in this it is different from the original program. The two words REPEAT and UNTIL always work together in this way.

Here is an example which uses strings. These words are placed in data statements on line 100, and the last of these is used to test for the end of the loop.

```
100 DATA JAN,FEB,MAR,APR,MAY,JUN
120 REPEAT
140 READ month$
160 PRINT month$
180 UNTIL month$ = "JUN"
```

The data in line 100 are read, one at a time, by line 140 and each is then printed on the screen by line 160. Line 180 uses the last word, i.e. JUN, to bring the process to an end.

This next example makes use of the BASIC word COUNT. (Notice that this is in upper case and has a special meaning in BASIC. It must not be confused with variable-word 'count' in lower case that we sometimes use in a loop). This is used to establish when a loop has been repeated enough times. First type in NEW and then this short two-line program:

```
100 REPEAT PRINT " " ;
120 UNTIL COUNT = 30 : PRINT
```

Now type in RUN and press RETURN. The result should be a single horizontal line across the screen made up of 30 hash signs, i.e. like . There are four small points to notice about this short program.

1. The PRINT statement appears on the same line as the word REPEAT. This is an example of a case where it is possible to put a command on the same line as REPEAT.

2. The semi-colon at the end of line 100 ensures that all the signs are printed on the same line.

3. The extra PRINT on line 120 then moves the cursor to the next line on the screen after the row of hashes has been printed.

4. The 30 on line 120 can be changed to any other whole number up to 255. If you go above 255 the computer will then go on printing forever.

It is often the case that at the end of a program, the user must be asked whether the program is to be repeated or ended.

Here is an example where the procedure to be repeated is very simple and is used as an example. It should be recognized that normally this part would be much longer. In this case, the user is asked to put in a number and the computer prints out its square root.

First type in NEW and then this program:

```
100 REPEAT
120 PRINT "This program takes any number"
140 PRINT "and finds its square root"
160 INPUT "Put in your number now  ",A
180 PRINT "The square root of "; A; " is "; SQR(A)
200 PRINT "If you wish to find the square root of"
220 INPUT "another number, put in YES now  ", answer$
240 UNTIL answer$ <> "YES"
```

To begin with notice that the first line is the REPEAT line, and that the last line is the UNTIL line. This means that everything in between these two lines will be repeated as often as is wished. The condition for repetition shown in line 240 is that the variable answer$ should be the word YES. In lines 200 and 220 the user is requested to type in YES if the program is to be repeated. The response is stored in the variable answer$. So therefore if anything other than YES is typed in, the condition in line 240 is met and the program comes to an end.

REPEAT with TIME

The word TIME (notice the capital letters) represents a built-in timer or clock which measures the time from the moment that the machine is switched on. Unfortunately, in some ways, it uses a unit of one hundredth of a second and so does not give the time in hours, minutes and seconds. There is a good deal more about this function in chapter 7 page 121. Here we simply want to use it with REPEAT to make a delay inside a program. There are a number of ways of doing this. The first in line 140 puts the value of TIME back to zero and then uses the loop to test for the passage of four seconds. Type it in and try it.

```
100 CLS
120 PRINT "When this appears, count to four."
140 TIME = 0 : REPEAT UNTIL TIME > 400
160 PRINT "Time is up."
```

Sometimes however it is not wise to put the time to zero as its actual value may be useful in another part of the program. In this case, change line 140 as follows:

```
140 time = TIME : REPEAT UNTIL TIME - time > 400
```

TRUE and FALSE

The computer has two built-in functions called TRUE and FALSE. These are known as Boolean functions. Again notice that they are in capital letters. You can check that the computer knows these by typing in directly. PRINT TRUE and then press RETURN. The response should be -1. So, TRUE = -1. Now type in PRINT FALSE and press RETURN. This time the result should be 0 or zero. So, FALSE = 0.

They can be used in REPEAT loops and the best way to begin to understand how they work is to try them. So, first of all type in NEW and then this:

```
100 REPEAT
120 PRINT "Hello there."
140 UNTIL FALSE
```

Then RUN this program. It will go on printing the phrase 'Hello there.' for ever, and will only stop when you press the ESCAPE key. Now change line 140 to this, and RUN the program again.

```
140 UNTIL TRUE
```

This time it prints 'Hello there.' once and when it reaches line 140 it stops. So, UNTIL FALSE means go on repeating the loop indefinitely, while UNTIL TRUE means stop after one loop. The computer translates the phrase UNTIL FALSE as meaning something like, 'It is false that the end of this loop has been reached'.

There are occasions, especially in games when an indefinite or infinitely repeating loop is necessary. In these cases the procedure REPEAT.....UNTIL FALSE is very useful.

However the more usual way of using these words is to establish conditions for staying with or leaving the loop; and the usual way to do this is with a variable. Here is an example.

```
100 cond = FALSE
120 REPEAT
140 INPUT score
160 PRINT score
180 IF score > 20 THEN cond = TRUE
200 UNTIL cond
220 PRINT'' "End of loop."
```

First of all, in line 100 we set a variable cond equal to FALSE. Then we use a REPEAT (line 120) UNTIL cond (line 200) loop. Since cond is FALSE this loop will repeat indefinitely, unless we change the value of cond So, in line 180 we set up the condition that if the number in the variable score is greater than 20, then the variable cond is changed to TRUE. Type this in and RUN it. If you put in any number less than 20 the loop continues; but as soon as you put in something like 32, it stops and the message in line 220 is printed out.

This program could be shortened even more as follows. Remove line 100 and change line 180 to this:

```
180 IF score > 20 THEN cond = TRUE ELSE cond = FALSE
```

(More information about the use of words like IF, THEN and ELSE can be found in Chapter 4.)

Another way to handle situations like this is to leave the loop at two separate points: that is, to use the word UNTIL twice, once with FALSE and once with TRUE. Here is an example, a bit like the last one, but handled in this double-exit way.

```
100 REPEAT
120 INPUT score
140 IF score < 20 THEN PRINT score : UNTIL FALSE
160 UNTIL TRUE
180 PRINT'' "End of loop."
```

On line 140 the condition that the loop should continue, i.e. if the score is less than 20, leads to the UNTIL FALSE statement which, as we know from above, allows the loop to repeat. However, if this condition does not maintain, then the program goes to line 160 where UNTIL TRUE brings it to an end. Type this one in and try it. It is worth pointing out that this kind of double-exit routine can lead to difficulties and should be avoided if possible.

Problems

1. Write two programs, to do the same task, but in one of them use FOR, TO, STEP, NEXT and in the other use REPEAT UNTIL. The task is to print out the square roots of all the numbers 10, 20, 30 .... up to 100.

2. Use the words DIM, DATA, READ and FOR loops to read the names of the months of the year and the number of days in each into two arrays. Then print this information on the screen.

3. Use the techniques with CHR$ and MODE 7 described on pages 87 to 89 to produce a colourful screen message for Christmas. Make use of all the colours and the double height facility.

CHAPTER 6
FILE MANAGEMENT

Introduction

When you type a program into the computer it is stored in the computer's memory. However when you turn the computer off, this program is lost, so that when you turn it on again, the program must be completely retyped. This can be very frustrating so the problem has been solved by making it possible to save programs (and lists of data) on cassette tapes using an ordinary tape-recorder. These can then be recovered quite quickly when the computer is switched on again. Another even quicker form of external (or off-line) storage is floppy-disk storage and this is described in Appendix A, page 266.

To begin with the tape-recorder must be connected to the computer, and the way to do this is described in some detail in the User Guide, starting at Page 11. When this has been done, the optimum tone and volume settings must be established. This can be done using the Welcome tape provided with the machine. The procedure for doing this is also described in the User Guide on page 12. Most tape-recorders work very well, however, if the tone setting is put at maximum and the volume setting is put just below the middle point of the range. A little bit of experiment with a short program and the techniques now described will help you to decide the best volume setting for your machine. (Ordinary tape cassettes can be used with the tape recorder but you are well advised to use the shorter heavy-duty low-noise cassettes).

Program saving

The sequence of actions now described needs to be gone through each time you wish to keep or store or save a program so that it can be used again at a later date. If you are using this process for the first time or have very little experience of using it, then you should begin by practising with an unimportant short program. Here is an example:

```
100 CLS
120 PRINT "This is a test program"
140 END
```

This practice period is necessary because it is possible for things to go wrong, and if you have spent a long time typing in a program, you do not want to lose it at this stage. The sequence of actions is as follows:

(a) If you have not already done so, type in the program that you wish to keep.

(b) Put a blank cassette into the tape-recorder.

(c) Decide on a name for the program file. As soon as you save it on a cassette it is called a file. The name of the file must have at most ten symbols, must begin with a letter and must contain no spaces and no punctuation marks. We will call this one EXAMPLE. So type in :

```
SAVE "EXAMPLE"
```

and press the RETURN key. The computer will respond by printing a short message so that the screen now looks like this:

```
>SAVE "EXAMPLE"
RECORD then RETURN
```

(d) However, do not try to respond to this to begin with. Instead make sure that the tape is completely rewound by pressing the REWIND key. Now press the counter reading to make it zero. Then press the PLAY key, or the FAST FORWARD key and move the tape forward to a suitable point. If you are using the tape for the first time then you need to move it forward far enough to get beyond the tape-leader. If you have used the tape before then you should have a record of how far forward you need to go on the counter to get to the next bit of blank tape. In either case make a note of the counter reading now.

(e) The message on the screen is a little confusing. It means press the RECORD and the PLAY keys on the tape recorder, so that both are down. Then press the RETURN key on the computer. As soon as you do this the computer begins to record the program on the tape. After a few seconds it will indicate that it is doing this by printing a message on the screen like this:

```
EXAMPLE        00
```

As the program is saved this 00 may change to 01 and then 02 and so on. This is a measure of the amount of space needed to hold the program, and the unit of measure used is called a block. At the end of the process the screen looks something like this:

```
EXAMPLE    04  04BB
>_
```

Just as it completes the saving process the computer signals this by making a little buzzing sound.

(f) When the program has been saved on tape, the tape recorder may stop of its own accord or you may have to stop it. This depends on the form of the connection between the recorder and the computer. In either case you will know that the process of saving the program has been completed because the computer will make the sound described above and the prompt sign (>) will appear. Then press the STOP key on the recorder and make a note of the counter reading. You should now have two counter readings showing where the beginning and ending of the program is on the tape.

(g) You should now check as to whether or not the program has been saved properly. To do this, type in the following and press RETURN.

```
*CAT
```

First press the REWIND key on the recorder and by using the counter move the tape back to before the point on the tape where your program starts. Then press the PLAY key on the recorder. This word CAT is short for CATALOGUE and it means that the computer will, if you start at the beginning, produce a list of all the programs that have been properly saved on this cassette.

(h) If all is well the computer will print on the screen the same sort of message as that described when the program was saved. When it has completed this, press the ESCAPE key on the computer and, if necessary, press the STOP key on the recorder. However, if there is an error it will print something different, such as:

```
DATA?
REWIND TAPE
```

In this case, the program must be saved again. So go back to (a) on page 96 and follow the instructions again, but remember that you do not have to type the program in again. If the error messages persist, however, there may be something else wrong.

For example, the volume may not be high enough on the recorder, or its heads may need cleaning.

(i) If there has been no error, remember to label the cassette carefully with the name of the program file and the counter numbers.

Usually there are no problems with saving programs, and the process is much simpler in practice than it looks on paper. However, difficulties do occasionally occur, and it is as well to take precautions.

If the program in question is a long one and you need to spend some hours working with it, it is a good idea to stop at regular intervals and save the current version on the tape. That is, save unfinished programs which you intend to go on working with. This means that, if something does go wrong (for example a power failure or a machine fault) then at least something has been saved. You can always save newer versions on top of the previously less complete one, so there is no waste of tape. It is also a good practice to save each program twice so that, if there is a difficulty with one of them, the other can then be used.

Program loading from tape

We use the word LOAD to recover a program that has been saved on tape. The technique is very simple and is similar to that used when saving a program.

(a) Insert the cassette into the tape-recorder.

(b) Type in LOAD "EXAMPLE" and press the RETURN key. Of course you must change the word EXAMPLE to whatever name you have given to your program. The computer responds with this screen message:

```
>LOAD "EXAMPLE"
SEARCHING
```

(c) Now press the REWIND key on the tape to move it back to the beginning. Then press the tape-counter to make it zero. If your program is the first one on the tape then press the PLAY key. If it is not the first one, use the FAST FORWARD key to move the tape forward to the appropriate place, and then press the PLAY key. The computer will then search for the program and when it finds it the message on the screen will look something like this:

```
Loading
EXAMPLE   04  04BB
>_
```

The tape recorder will then make some rather unpleasant noises (unless you have done something to stop this). These noises mean that you can actually hear each block of the program being loaded.

If you have any difficulties or if the screen message does not look like this, or if there is no screen message at all, then press the ESCAPE key on the computer and the STOP key on the recorder. Then rewind the tape and try again.

(d) When the cursor returns and the computer makes a buzzing sound this means that you have successfully loaded the program. If necessary, press the STOP key on the recorder.

(e) Now type in RUN and press RETURN.

The word CHAIN

We can use the word CHAIN as a replacement for the word LOAD. So instead of typing in LOAD "EXAMPLE", we could type in CHAIN "EXAMPLE" and proceed as before. The only difference is that the word CHAIN combines the words LOAD and RUN, so that when the program has been transferred to the computer it begins to run immediately. The word can also be used in two other ways:

(a) If you have forgotten the name of the program that you wish to load then you can type in CHAIN "" (that is CHAIN followed by two sets of quotation marks, with no space between them), and press RETURN. In this case the computer will load the first program that it finds on the tape. (You can of course always use *CAT to find out what programs are on the tape). It is also possible to use LOAD "" in the same way.

(b) You can use the word CHAIN to load a program from within a program. The word is used with a line number in the usual way and the name of the program to be loaded is put in inverted commas as normal. For example to load and run a program called "SECOND" you would need a line like this:

```
300  CHAIN "SECOND"
```

Data saving

One of the most important uses of computers is the storage and retrieval of data. The techniques used to do this are usually written as part of programs, or routines within programs. These data files can take many forms such as lists of names, or addresses, or book titles or examination marks or prices.

In order to illustrate this process we will write a complete program which will allow us to save and retrieve some example data. We will again use this opportunity to illustrate some of the structuring techniques that can be used in designing programs so that they are more readable and easier to change and correct. We will build up the program in a number of small separate units or subprograms, and then, near the end, we will link them together into a properly organized coherent unit.

We will begin with a short routine to input a set of four names and test marks to the computer's memory. Later we will extend this so that you can choose how many names and scores to enter, but to make this introduction simpler we will use four names and scores only. It will also be very easy to amend the final program so that you can use it to save any other kind of data rather than names and scores. It is called Subprogram 2, because it is one of a set of subprograms that we will write. The line numbers may seem a bit odd, but they will make sense when the complete program is written.

Subprogram 2

```
100 DIM name$(4),score(4)
380 REM INPUT ROUTINE
400 CLS
420 FOR count = 1 TO 4
440 INPUT' "Input name of pupil   "name$(count)
460 INPUT' "Input score of pupil  "score(count)
480 NEXT count
```

First type this in and we will consider it line by line.

(a) Line 100 declares the two necessary data arrays. This idea has been described on page 79 . The first is a string array called 'name$' and it will be used to store the four names. The second is an array for numbers called 'score' and is used to store the four scores.

(b) Line 400 clears the screen.

(c) Lines 420 and 480 make a loop using the variable 'count' to count from 1 to 4.

(d) Lines 440 and 460 allow you to input the four names and scores.

Now type in RUN and press RETURN. Then follow instructions as they appear on the screen. This is of course a practice exercise since we have not yet written the rest of the program.

We now wish to write a new subsection of the program, that is the part that will allow us to save this data onto a cassette tape. This section is shown below, as Subprogram 3. Type it in first and we will then explain it line by line.

Subprogram 3

```
560 REM SAVE ON TAPE ROUTINE
580 CLS
600 X = OPENOUT"names"
620 PRINT'' "DATA now being stored on tape."
640 FOR count = 1 TO 4
660 PRINT # X,name$(count)
680 NEXT count
700 CLOSE # X
720 PRINT' "Names now stored on tape"
```

(a) Line 600. The word OPENOUT warns the computer that it is about to print data of some sort 'OUT' to a file. The word with quotation marks round it is the name given to this file. We choose this and in this case we have called it 'names'. Later on, when we wish to retrieve this data from this file we can do so by referring to the file by this name. The letter X is allocated a number by the computer, and this is the number of the channel through which the data is going to be read out. Each file of data is connected to the computer by a file channel number and this ensures that the correct set of data is recalled, later on, through the same channel. We could of course have used any other variable name in place of X. For example, we could have used file number. We could also have used a string variable for the name of the file like this: A$ = "names". We would then write

```
X = OPENOUT A$
```

(b) Lines 640 and 680 make a loop as usual, which allows us to deal in turn with each of the four names.

(c) Line 620 is PRINT # X,name$(count). This means, print to the tape using channel number X the strings represented by name$(count). Remember that this is the same X referred to in line 600, so if you used another letter there, you must also change it here. The symbol # is used by computers as a shorthand for the word number.

(d) Line 700 closes down the channel numbered X, and it is always essential to remember to close down an open channel in this way.

The next section of the program (subprogram 4), prints the four scores on tape in almost exactly the same way. First type it in:

Subprogram 4

```
740 X = OPENOUT"scores"
760 FOR count = 1 TO 4
780 PRINT#X,score(count)
800 NEXT count
820 CLOSE#X
840 PRINT' "Scores now stored on tape"
```

The only important difference is that the name of the file on line 70 is changed to scores, and the variable name on line 780 is changed to score(count).

Now put a blank cassette into the tape-recorder, type in RUN and press RETURN. Then follow the instructions as they appear on the screen. This will mean that you will type in four names and four scores, and when you have completed this the computer will, with your help, store these on the tape. It is probably a good idea at this stage to save this incomplete version of the program on tape.

It is worth pointing out that we could very easily have combined these two data-saving routines into one. In other words we need only have opened one file, and we could have put the line 780 beside the line 660 inside the first loop. This has some advantages, but on this occasion we want to have two separate files.

Data recovery

We must now have some routines for recovering this data from the tape. Since they were saved in the order 'names' and then 'scores' we will put in recovery routines in the same order. The first one, subprogram 5, recovers the names. Type it in and we will then discuss it.

Subprogram 5

```
 920 REM DATA RECOVERY ROUTINE
 940 CLS
 960 PRINT' "Press play on the recorder"
 980 PRINT'' "DATA now being recovered from tape."
1000 X = OPENIN"names"
1020 FOR count = 1 TO 4
1040 INPUT#X,name$(count)
1060 PRINT name$(count)
1080 NEXT count
1090 CLOSE#X
1100 PRINT' "names now recovered from tape."
```

(a) On line 1000 we open a channel to the tape recorder and its number is called X. The word which informs the computer that we are recovering data is OPENIN; that is, data is coming in from the tape. The name of the file is, as usual, put in quotation marks as shown.

(b) Lines 1020 and 1080 combine to make a loop to read in the four names one at a time.

(c) Line 1040 actually recovers the data, one name at a time. INPUT#X can be contrasted with PRINT#X on line 660. When data is being put out to a tape it is 'printed' on the tape as in 660. When it is being brought back it is 'input' from the tape as in this line.

(d) Line 1060 simply prints the data on the screen as it is recovered so that you can see the data coming in off the tape.

Now the scores can be recovered using an almost identical routine, as follows. It is subprogram 6. Type it in now.

Subprogram 6

```
1120 X = OPENIN"scores"
1140 FOR count = 1 TO 4
1160 INPUT#X,score(count)
1180 PRINT score(count)
1200 NEXT count
1210 CLOSE#X
1220 PRINT' "Scores now recovered from tape."
```

The only important differences are on lines 1120 where the file name is now scores and on lines 1160 and 1180 where, again, the word score appears.

Structuring the program

The complete program as we have constructed it so far allows you to do three things:

(a) to enter data into the machine (lines 100 to 480).
(b) to save this data on tape (lines 560 to 840).
(c) to recover this data from tape (lines 920 to 1220).

However as it is currently written, these three activities must be done in exactly this order. For example, we have already used the first two parts to enter and save data. If we now wish to recover that data we cannot choose to go directly to the third routine. So the program has very limited value in this state. We need some kind of organisation or structure that allows us to choose which one of these routines to use at any time, or indeed to choose which order to use them in.

There are a number of ways to do this and in this case we will use what is often called a MENU structure. This was first described in chapter 4. Using this method the list of possible options is presented and the user chooses which to use. The first part of this is called Subprogram 1. Type it in and we will discuss it.

Subprogram 1

```
120 CLS
140 PRINT' "Which routine do you wish to use?"
160 PRINT' "         Data entry......1"
180 PRINT' "        Data saving......2"
200 PRINT' "      Data recovery......3"
260 PRINT' "Choose one of the NUMBERS."
280 INPUT N
```

(a) Lines 140 to 260 present a MENU of options on the screen and the user is invited to choose one of these by inputting an appropriate number.

(b) Line 280 accepts the number chosen and stores it in the variable N.

We must now use this value of N to decide which of the three routines to send the computer to. We could use a series of IF-THEN statements as described on page 64 , but we can also use the word ON which is also described on that page, but this time we will use it with GOSUB instead of GOTO. Type in line 340 as follows:

```
340 ON N GOSUB 380,560,920
```

The computer interprets this to mean:

When N = 1, then go to the subroutine at line 380;

When N = 2, then go to the subroutine at line 560;

When N = 3, then go to the subroutine at line 920.

Obviously using the word ON like this is more efficient and less cumbersome than using a series of IF-THEN statements. However, it does produce a sequence of line numbers (in this case 380,560 and 920) which do not in themselves suggest very much about what they are doing to the reader. It is possible to change this to a combination of two lines like this. (Do not type them in).

```
330 enter = 380 : save = 560 : recover = 920
340 ON N GOSUB enter,save, recover
```

This is obviously much easier to read and understand since it clearly implies that when N = 1, the subroutine to be used is to 'enter' data; when N = 2 the subroutine is to 'save' data, and so on. However the disadvantage is that, if you use RENUMBER to change the program line numbers, then the variables on line 330 are not changed by this, and line 340 will become incorrect. For this reason it is a dangerous technique and cannot be recommended. However we can make line 340 slightly more clear with a line in front of it like this. Type it in now

```
320 REM ON N GOSUB ENTER, SAVE, RECOVER
```

A glance at this helps to make sense of line 340. (Ideally we would use Procedures rather than GOSUB, but with this version of BASIC it would be rather complicated). Add two more lines to the program as follows.

```
300 IF N < 1 OR N > 3 THEN 120
```

This line is simply an error-checking device, or failsafe line. It checks that the number chosen from the menu is not less than 1 or greater than 3. If a wrong number outside this range is chosen, the program returns to the start of the menu.

```
360 GOTO 120
```

This line ensures that, when the subroutine has been completed, the program returns to the menu. The completed first part of the program (Subprogram 1) now looks like this:

Subprogram 1

```
100 DIM name$(4),score(4)
120 CLS
140 PRINT' "Which routine do you wish to use?"
160 PRINT' "            Data entry......1"
180 PRINT' "           Data saving......2"
200 PRINT' "         Data recovery......3"
260 PRINT' "Choose one of the NUMBERS."
280 INPUT N
300 IF N < 1 OR N > 3 THEN 120
320 REM ** ON N GOSUB ENTRY,SAVE,RECOVER,
340 ON N GOSUB 380,560,920
```

We must now remember that, on line 340, we used GOSUB and this means that each of the three routines must be turned into genuine 'subroutines'. This is done simply by putting a line at the end of each with the word RETURN on it. We will now do this, but we will also add a simple two-line routine to hold the screen at the end of each subroutine. (This simple technique was described on page 52). First, type in these three lines at the end of the data entry routine.

```
500 PRINT'' "That was the last one. Press space-bar"
520 Z = GET
540 RETURN
```

Then a similar three lines at the end of the data saving routine.

```
860 PRINT' "Press the space-bar."
880 Z = GET
900 RETURN
```

And finally, at the end of the data recovery routine.

```
1240 PRINT' "Press the space-bar."
1260 Z = GET
1280 RETURN
```

The complete program up to this point should now look like this. List your version on the screen and check that this is the same. You will find that the listing is too long and that you have to list it in chunks. You can make it stop listing by holding both the CTRL key and the SHIFT key at the same time. You can then make it begin to list again by releasing one of these. When you are sure that your version is the same as this one you can then use it to type in some names and scores, save them on tape and recover them from tape. You should also remember to save this version of the program on tape.

```
100 DIM name$(4),score(4)
120 CLS
140 PRINT' "Which routine do you wish to use?"
160 PRINT' "          Data entry......1"
180 PRINT' "         Data saving......2"
200 PRINT' "       Data recovery......3"
260 PRINT' "Choose one of the NUMBERS."
280 INPUT N
300 IF N < 1 OR N > 3 THEN 120
320 REM ** ON N GOSUB ENTER,SAVE,RECOVER
340 ON N GOSUB 380,560,920
360 GOTO 120
380 REM INPUT ROUTINE
400 CLS
420 FOR count =1 TO 4
440 INPUT' "Input name of pupil  "name$(count)
460 INPUT' "Input score of pupil  "score(count)
480 NEXT count
500 PRINT'' "That was the last one. Press space-bar"
520 Z = GET
540 RETURN
560 REM SAVE ON TAPE ROUTINE
580 CLS
600 X = OPENOUT"names"
620 PRINT'' "DATA now being stored on tape."
640 FOR count = 1 TO 4
660 PRINT#X,name$(count)
680 NEXT count
700 CLOSE#X
720 PRINT' "Names now stored on tape."
740 X = OPENOUT"scores"
760 FOR count = 1 TO 4
780 PRINT#X,score(count)
800 NEXT count
820 CLOSE#X
840 PRINT' "Scores now stored on tape"
860 PRINT' "Press the space-bar"
880 Z = GET
900 RETURN
920 REM DATA RECOVERY ROUTINE
940 CLS
960 PRINT' "Press play on the recorder"
980 PRINT'' "DATA now being recovered from tape."
1000 X = OPENIN"names"
1020 FOR count = 1 TO 4
1040 INPUT#X,name$(count)
1060 PRINT name$(count)
1080 NEXT count
1090 CLOSE#X
1100 PRINT' "Names now recovered from tape."
1120 X = OPENIN"scores"
1140 FOR count = 1 TO 4
```

```
1160 INPUT#X,score(count)
1180 PRINT score(count)
1200 NEXT count
1210 CLOSE#X
1220 PRINT' "Scores now recovered from tape."
1240 PRINT' "Press the space-bar."
1260 Z = GET
1280 RETURN
```

Further routines

This program should now work very well. However, it does have two further limitations.

(1) There is no routine which allows you to look at the data once you have entered it (or after you have recovered it from a tape).

(2) There is no routine which allows you to Finish or Stop using the program.

We will now add these two routines. In doing this we can demonstrate how, now that we have established a properly organized structure, it is a relatively simple matter to extend a program by adding new routines to it.

First a routine for displaying the data on the screen.

Subprogram 7

```
1300 REM DATA DISPLAY ROUTINE
1320 CLS
1340 PRINT'' "NAMES","SCORES"
1360 FOR count = 1 TO 4
1380 PRINT' name$(count),score(count)
1400 NEXT count
1420 PRINT' "   Press the space-bar"
1440 Z = GET
1460 RETURN
```

There is nothing new in this routine needing explanation, so we now add on a routine for ending the program.

Subprogram 8

```
1480 REM FINISH ROUTINE
1500 PRINT' "Thank you for now.  If you wish to start"
1520 PRINT' "again, type in RUN and press RETURN."
1540 END
```

This is therefore an exit from the program and line 1540 is the only line in the whole program with END. As a consequence of these two new routines we must add two new lines to the menu, and change three other lines (that is lines 300,320 and 340). The new menu lines are:

```
220 PRINT' "       Display data......4"
240 PRINT' "    Finish for now......5"
```

The changed lines are:

```
300 IF N < 1 OR N > 5 THEN 120
320 REM ON N GOSUB ENTER,SAVE,RECOVER,DISPLAY,FINISH
340 ON N GOSUB 380,560,920,1300,1480
```

Type these in and RUN the program and try each of the five menu options.

Making it more general

This program is now complete. Remember however that it is meant as an example only. If you wished to make it a more generally useful program it would have to be changed so that it dealt with more than 4 names and scores. To do this, it is necessary to change a very small number of lines. These are now described.

(a) Change line 100 so that the declared arrays can hold more data. For example, we might change it to:

```
100 DIM name$(200),score(200)
```

(b) Add a line to the INPUT routine as follows:

```
410 INPUT' "How many names do you wish to enter  ",total
```

This means that, at the beginning of the program we must know how many names we are going to use and, in this case, it will be stored in the variable 'total'.

(c) Change the lines where we have used the number 4 to represent the number of names or scores to be entered. For example, line 420 becomes

```
420 FOR count = 1 TO total
```

As well as this, lines numbered 640,760,1020,1140 and 1360 must be similarly changed. The completed program is shown below. (Remember to save it on tape). List it on the screen and make sure that your version is identical to this one.

```
 100 DIM name$(200),score(200)
 120 CLS
 140 PRINT' "Which routine do you wish to use?"
 160 PRINT' "            Data entry......1"
 180 PRINT' "           Data saving......2"
 200 PRINT' "         Data recovery......3"
 220 PRINT' "          Display data......4"
 240 PRINT' "        Finish for now......5"
 260 PRINT' "Choose one of the NUMBERS."
 280 INPUT N
 300 IF N < 1 OR N > 5 THEN 120
 320 REM ON N GOSUB ENTER, SAVE, RECOVER, DISPLAY, FINISH
 340 ON N GOSUB 380,560,920,1300,1480
 360 GOTO 120
 380 REM INPUT ROUTINE
 400 CLS
 410 INPUT' "How many names do you wish to enter "total
 420 FOR count = 1 TO total
 440 INPUT' "Input name of pupil  "name$(count)
 460 INPUT' "Input score of pupil  "score(count)
 480 NEXT count
 500 PRINT'' "That was the last one.  Press  space-bar"
 520 Z = GET
 540 RETURN
 560 REM SAVE ON TAPE ROUTINE
 580 CLS
 600 X = OPENOUT"names"
 620 PRINT'' "DATA now being stored on tape."
 640 FOR count = 1 TO total
 660 PRINT#X,name$(count)
 680 NEXT count
 700 CLOSE#X
 720 PRINT' "Names now stored on tape"
 740 X = OPENOUT"scores"
 760 FOR count = 1 TO total
 780 PRINT#X,score(count)
 800 NEXT count
 820 CLOSE#X
 840 PRINT' "Scores now stored on tape"
 860 PRINT' "Press the space-bar"
 880 Z = GET
 900 RETURN
 920 REM DATA RECOVERY ROUTINE
 940 CLS
 960 PRINT' "Press play on the recorder"
 980 PRINT'' "DATA now being recovered from tape."
1000 X = OPENIN"names"
1020 FOR count = 1 TO total
1040 INPUT#X,name$(count)
1060 PRINT name$(count)
1080 NEXT count
1090 CLOSE#X
```

```
1100 PRINT' "Names now recovered from tape."
1120 X = OPENIN"scores"
1140 FOR count = 1 TO total
1160 INPUT #X,score(count)
1180 PRINT score(count)
1200 NEXT count
1210 CLOSE #X
1220 PRINT' "Scores now recovered from tape."
1240 PRINT' "Press the space-bar."
1260 Z = GET
1280 RETURN
1300 REM DATA DISPLAY ROUTINE
1320 CLS
1340 PRINT'' "NAMES","SCORES"
1360 FOR count = 1 TO total
1380 PRINT' name$(count),score(count)
1400 NEXT count
1420 PRINT' "    Press the space-bar"
1440 Z = GET
1460 RETURN
1480 REM FINISH ROUTINE
1500 PRINT' "Thank you for now.  If you wish to start"
1520 PRINT' "again, type in RUN and press RETURN."
1540 END
```

Using REPEAT-UNTIL

One of the difficulties with the program that we have just written is that it assumes that we know at the beginning of an exercise exactly how many pieces of data we are intending to store. Very often this is not the case, and this is even more true when we wish to recover data.

We will now write two short programs. The first will input and then save data on tape when the exact number of pieces of data is not known: the other will recover this data again without needing to know how many pieces of data were stored. No attempt will be made to link these two programs or to produce a complete program as in the last section. However, it would be very easy to use these two routines within the overall structure of the long complete program.

We begin more or less as before by declaring two arrays, this time they are both string arrays and refer to a record collection. The line is as follows:

```
100 DIM artiste$(100),album$(100)
```

We could, of course, extend this and enter much more information about the collection, and we could also have used a two-dimensional array. Next we clear the screen, and, since we do not know how many records we are going to enter, we will use a dummy-word to indicate when we have finished. The word we have chosen is LAST, and so we need a couple of lines of explanation, like this:

```
120CLS
140PRINT' "When you have entered all the records"
160PRINT' "enter the word LAST (in capitals)."
180PRINT' "Then press RETURN twice."''
```

We have to press RETURN twice (line 180) because the REPEAT UNTIL loop will not check until the end of the loop, and we will be entering two pieces of data (the name of the artiste, and the name of the record) each time. We will use the variable 'Listno' to count the entries, so, to begin with we make it equal to zero.

```
200 listno = 0
```

Then we have the complete REPEAT UNTIL loop, as follows. First type it in.

```
220 REM ENTER DATA
240 REPEAT
260 listno = listno+1
280 PRINT'' "This is number "listno
300 INPUT' "What is the name of the artiste"
artiste$ (listno)
320 INPUT' "What is the name of the record "album$(listno)
340 UNTIL artiste$(listno) = "LAST"
360 listno = listno-1
```

Line 340 checks each time to see if the word LAST has been entered. If it has, the looping ceases at line 340. The program then goes on to line 360, which reduces the value of the counting variable, listno, by 1, so that the words LAST are not retained as part of the data.

The next routine stores the two sets of data, side by side, on tape. Since, at this stage, the computer knows how many records have been entered we can now use a FOR NEXT loop. The routine is more or less identical to the one used in the long example program just completed. Type it in and try it. That is to say, save some example data on tape. This means that not only do you check if the program works, but you can make a check on the next program which recovers the data.

```
380 REM STORE DATA ON TAPE
400 PRINT'' "The data will now be stored on tape."
420 PRINT "Move the tape to the correct position."
```

```
440 PRINT "Press PLAY and RECORD and then RETURN"''
460 X = OPENOUT"records"
480 FOR count = 1 TO listno
500 PRINT #X,artiste$(count),album$(count)
520 NEXT count
540 CLOSE #X
560 PRINT' "Data now stored on tape."
```

Data recovery with REPEAT

A completely separate program is now described which can be used to recover from tape the data about records stored in this first exercise. However the line numberings are such that it can be attached on to the first one. As well as this the first two lines are simply repeated from the first program. Type it in and we will discuss it. (You must decide for yourself whether or not to use NEW to remove the first program).

```
100 DIM artiste$(100),album$(100)
120 CLS

600 REM RECOVER DATA FILE
620 PRINT "Move the tape to the correct position"
640 PRINT "and then press the PLAY key."
660 listno = 0
680 X = OPENIN"records"
700 PRINT' "Data file now being recovered."
720 REPEAT
740 listno = listno+1
760 INPUT #X,artiste$(listno),album$(listno)
780 PRINT artiste$(listno),album$(listno)
800 UNTIL EOF #X
820 CLOSE #X
```

The only really new statement is on line 800. The letters EOF stand for End Of File, so that line can be read:

"Until End Of File Number X"

This means that the computer continues to input data from the file until it reaches the end of the file and then stops. This of course means that it is not necessary to remember how many pieces of data were saved. Line 760 actually retrieves the data. Note that is a faithful copy in its format of line 500 in the previous program. Line 780 prints the data on the screen as it is recovered.

Final comments

There are a number of other words used in association with data file handling that we have not dealt with in detail. Of those the two most important are BPUT and BGET. These correspond to PRINT and INPUT except that they work with single bytes of information rather than with full strings or numbers. The programming procedures involved are almost identical to those just described but the data to be saved (using BPUT instead of PRINT) or to be recovered (using BGET instead of INPUT) must be carefully organized into a sequence of single identifiable bytes.

The saving and recovering of data files is much more quickly handled with disk drives, so the procedures necessary for disk drives are shown in Appendix A.

Problems

1. Write a program that will store the numbers 1 to 100 on a cassette tape file, and will then recover them. Make sure you have a menu (as described on page 104) which allows you to choose whether to store data or recover data.

2. Write a mailing list program which allows you to input, save and recover a list of names and addresses.

CHAPTER 7
FURTHER PROGRAMMING

Introduction

In this chapter we intend to bring together some of the very considerable number of techniques and facilities which are available to the user of the B.B.C. microcomputer. Some of these arise out of the design of the actual machine itself, and some from the version of BASIC used by the machine. None of these separate pieces is long enough to justify a full chapter but each is of considerable importance and interest.

The red keys

We have already used these red user defined keys on page 8. There are ten of them along the top of the keyboard with the symbols f0, f1 and so on up to f9 written on them. Each one can be programmed to produce a command or a statement or even a full programming phrase. We can begin to demonstrate this as follows. Type in the following and then press the RETURN key.

```
*KEY 0 FOR count = 1 TO number
```

This phrase 'FOR count = 1 TO number' is one that is used a great deal, so let us suppose that we needed it in line 240 of a program. Type in 240 and then press the red key f0. The phrase will immediately appear on the screen beside 240. Then press the RETURN key. So, as a result of programming the key f0 the whole line after the line number can be entered with two key presses.

In fact it is possible to include the return key in the programming of the red key. Type in the line exactly as before, but do not press the RETURN key yet. Now hold the SHIFT key and press the key with the symbols \ and ¦ on it. It is the key on the left of the arrow-left key (←). In MODE 7 this produces the symbol || . Then press the letter M immediately (with no space) and press the RETURN key. The line now looks like this (in MODE 7).

```
*KEY 0 FOR count = 1 TO number || M
```

Now type in a line number as before and then press the f0 key. Once again the correct phrase will appear after the line number but this time, since pressing the RETURN key has also been programmed, the cursor will have gone on to the next line. In other words this whole line after the line number can be entered simply by pressing the key f0.

However it is normal to use these red keys for a variety of simpler statements and commands. We will demonstrate this as follows. Type in *KEYO AUTO 100,20 || M and then press RETURN. This time we have programed the key f0 so that it will automatically number the first line of a program as 100, the next line as 120 and so on. We will use this now to put in a simple program which we will then use for further demonstrations. Press the key f0. Then type in this program. When you press RETURN at the end of each line the next line number appears automatically.

```
100 PRINT' "This is a demonstration program"
120 PRINT' "which we will use for the"
140 PRINT' "user defined function keys."
160 -
```

Now press the ESCAPE key to get out of the automatic numbering routine. Then type this in and press the RETURN key

```
*KEY1 LIST || M
```

The spacing in these lines is not important except that there must not be a space between the sign and the letter M (representing the RETURN key). Now press the key f1. The program will list immediately and without the need to press any other key.

We can program the key f2 by typing in the following and pressing RETURN.

```
*KEY2 RUN || M
```

To test this press the key f2 and the program will run automatically. We can go on in this way, using each of the ten keys to hold a different word or command. This is a most useful facility but it can be a bit tedious having to type in these key-programming lines each time that we turn on the computer. One way to avoid this is to write a short program to do it, save this, and then load and run it each time we want to begin. First we must decide on the set of words that we want to use.

The ten that we have chosen are, LIST, RUN, AUTO, PRINT, INPUT, MODE, PROC, RENUMBER, MOVE and DRAW, but you can change any or all of these if you wish. The program then looks like this. Type in NEW to remove the old program and then type this in.

```
100 *KEY0 LIST ||M
120 *KEY1 RUN ||M
140 *KEY2 AUTO 100,20 ||M
160 *KEY3 PRINT
180 *KEY4 INPUT
200 *KEY5 MODE
220 *KEY6 PROC
240 *KEY7 RENUMBER
260 *KEY8 MOVE
280 *KEY9 DRAW
```

Type in RUN and press RETURN. The ten keys are now programmed. Notice that for LIST, RUN and AUTO we have included the RETURN key, but not for the others. This is because we would normally wish to write something after a word like INPUT before pressing the RETURN key. If you now save this program it will be available to be loaded and used when needed. (You can deprogram a key by typing in *KEY and then the number and then pressing RETURN. That is, program it to do nothing).

Now look at the keyboard. Just above the red keys there is a length of plastic which can be lifted so that a strip of paper or card can be placed beneath this. This makes it possible for us to write the words that we have programmed for each key on this paper and then we can see at a glance what each key stands for.

Other user defined keys

Although there are only ten of these red keys, it is in fact possible to program six other keys if wished. This will work only with later versions of the machine operating systems. These are shown below with their corresponding numbers.

BREAK	KEY 10
COPY	KEY 11
→	KEY 12
←	KEY 13
↓	KEY 14
↑	KEY 15

The BREAK key is a particularly useful example. Normally when this key is pressed any program in the machine is lost and can only be recovered by typing in OLD followed by pressing RETURN. However this difficulty can be got round by programming this key so that it contains this OLD instruction. Type it in like this and press RETURN

```
*KEY10 OLD ||M
```

Now press the BREAK key and then try to list the current program (using the key f0).

Numbers on the computer

We are here concerned with real numbers, that is numbers that include decimals as well as whole numbers. To begin with we are interested in how the machine handles large numbers and the maximum size of number it can cope with. To test this, try the program shown. Type it in and run it.

```
100 MODE 7
120 FOR count = 1 TO 10
140 PRINT 10↑count
160 NEXT count
```

This prints out all the powers of 10 up to 10 to the power of 10. The screen looks like this

```
         10
        100
       1000
      10000
     100000
    1000000
   10000000
  100000000
        1E9
       1E10
>-
```

The last number printed out in full is 1 followed by eight zeros. 1 followed by 9 zeros is printed as:

```
1E9
```

This conventionally means 1 multiplied by 10, nine times. This is called scientific notation. Now subtract one from each of the numbers and print this out by retyping line 140 like this:

```
140 PRINT 10↑count, 10↑count -1
```

This produces the same set of numbers as before, and, more or less beside them, the result of subtracting one from each of them. But the important thing, from our point of view, is that the machine prints 999,999,999 (i.e. nine times) in this form, but when one is added to this it prints it as 1E9, i.e. in scientific notation. In other words nine nines is the largest whole number that the computer can cope with. After this it gives you an estimate only. Now change line 140 so that the program looks like this:

```
100 MODE 7
120 FOR count = 1 TO 10
140 PRINT 999999995 + count
160 NEXT count
```

This asks the computer to print all the whole numbers, starting with 999,999,996 and going up to 1,000,000,005. Run the program and see what happens.

We will now try to see how the computer handles decimals. First type in this program:

```
100 MODE 7
120 INPUT num
140 PRINT 1/num
160 GOTO 120
```

Notice that line 160 sends the program back to the INPUT line, line 120. This means that you can go on inputting numbers for the variable num and then examining the decimal caused by dividing num into 1. That is, you can look at 1/3 or 1/7 or 1/103 as decimals. (When you wish to leave the program press ESCAPE). Run the program.

Line 120 will make the computer put a question mark on the screen. Type in 3 and press RETURN. Then type 7; then 53; then 179. Try as many numbers as you like. Remember that our problem is to try to understand how the computer writes decimals.

Obviously some fractions, like 1/9, produce straightforward decimals, with nine significant figures. But other decimals like 1/23 produce less accurate answers in scientific notation form. At what stage does the changeover take place? That is, when are decimals too small to be written normally?

Run this program again, and put in 10. The response is, not surprisingly, 0.1. Now put in 11. This number will be smaller than 0.1 and the response is in scientific notation. In fact the computer will translate any number smaller than 0.1 into scientific notation, and at the other extreme any number greater than 999 999 999 into scientific notation.

The conclusions then are as follows:

(a) Any number numerically less than 0.1 is changed into scientific notation.

(b) Any number numerically greater than 999 999 999 is changed into scientific notation.

(c) Any number between these two limits is written as an ordinary number or decimal.

(d) If this number or decimal has more than nine digits, only the first nine are recorded. If the 10th digit is 6, 7, 8 or 9, then the ninth digit has a 1 added to it.

Integers

The BBC micro has available a number of words and techniques for handling integers. Normally it is assumed that we are dealing with real numbers, that is numbers which can have both integers and decimal (or fractional) parts. When we deal with integers we are dealing with whole numbers. Unlike real numbers this means that we have complete accuracy.

We can indicate to the computer that we are dealing with integers by putting the % (percent) sign after the variable name. Here is an example. First type it in.

```
100 MODE 7
120 INPUT number%
140 PRINT number%
```

Run this and respond with a whole number like 34. Then run it again and respond with a real number like 34.84. In both cases line 140 will produce the number 34. In other words the variable number% will always be treated as an integer.

As well as this there is a set of what are called resident integer variables. These are labelled A%, B%, C% and so on up to Z%. That is, each of the 26 upper case letters followed by the percent sign. These are special in that they retain their value until the computer is switched off. This means that they can be transferred from program to program. They are unaffected by any of the BASIC words like RUN or CLEAR. You can test this as follows. Type this in directly and then press RETURN.

```
A% = 99 : A = 5
```

Then type in PRINT A% , A and press RETURN. The computer will print 99 and 5 on the screen. Now press the BREAK key. Then immediately type in, PRINT A%,A and press RETURN. The response will be 99 followed by an error message 'No such variable'. In other words the computer retains the value for A% but not for A. This is why it is called a resident integer variable. The only way to remove the value 99 from A% is to reallocate it by, for example, typing in A% = 47, or by switching the machine off and on again. After switching on again all the resident integer variables will be treated as equal to -1 or 0, depending on which version of the machine you own.

There are two words specially associated with integers and these are DIV and MOD. These assume that the numbers being dealt with are integers. For example, type the following in directly:

```
PRINT 13 DIV 5
```

The answer will be 2, because if you divide 13 by 5 the answer is 2 wholes with a remainder of 3. In this case the remainder is ignored. However if you wanted to know the remainder you would use the word MOD as follows:

```
PRINT 13 MOD 5
```

The answer this time is 3, that is the remainder on division by 5. Here is a short program which illustrates this idea.

```
100 MODE 7
120 FOR count = 10 TO 16
140 PRINT'''' count ; "  divided by 3 gives  " ; count DIV
     3
160 PRINT' "Remainder when  " ; count ; " is divided by 3
    is  " ; count
    MOD 3
180 PRINT'' "Press space bar" : Z = GET
200 NEXT count
```

Type in RUN and look very carefully at the results. This should make it clear what the effects of DIV and MOD really are. These words are used at various points in this book, and a good example is shown on page 123.

TIME

The computer has an internal clock which keeps time very well and which begins to count as soon as the machine is switched on. It measures time in units of one hundredth of a second and this number is stored in the reserved variable or function denoted by the word TIME. Here is a short program to illustrate how it works. Type it in and run it and we will then discuss how it works. The odd spacing of the line numbers is deliberate.

```
120 CLS
140 REPEAT
220 PRINT TAB(1,3); "Since your computer was switched on"
240 PRINT TAB(15,5); TIME
320 PRINT TAB(1,9); "hundredths of a second have passed."
340 UNTIL FALSE
```

Most of the words have been used before and so do not need a lot of explanation. The REPEAT UNTIL FALSE loop ensures that the program goes on running for ever. The TAB statements are described in detail on page 192. Here they place the messages on exactly the same points of the screen on each loop. The new word is TIME on line 240. When the program is run the screen looks something like this:

```
Since your computer was switched on
              516912

hundredths of a second have passed.
```

The last two digits on the right, in this case 12, are changing very rapidly as they represent hundredths and tenths of a second. The next digit, in this case 9, represents seconds. The 6 represents 60 seconds, and so on. Although it is interesting to watch time fly in this way, it doesn't really help us to get a worthwhile or usable measure of time. So we can change the number represented by TIME in various ways as follows. First put in two new lines as follows, and then run the program again.

```
160 seconds = TIME DIV 100
300 PRINT TAB(10,8); seconds"  Seconds"
```

This time there are two changing times on the screen. The first is the same as before created by line 240. The next is reached by using the variable seconds along with the integer function DIV as shown on line 160. This means that the current value of TIME is divided by 100 and the remainder is ignored. So the lower changing number is a measure of the time in seconds, and is written by line 300. The word Seconds in quotes is preceded by two spaces.

If you watch this for a while you will find that, unlike a clock or digital watch, it does not return to zero after sixty seconds have passed but just goes on counting. To solve this we need to change line 160 again as follows.

```
160 seconds = TIME DIV 100 MOD 60
```

The effect of the addition of MOD 60 is to bring the number of seconds back to 0 when it reaches 60. Type in RUN and try this. You will notice also that the word seconds becomes secondss. This is because the change from a two-digit number (like 60) to a one-digit number (like 0) moves the word seconds one place to the left . The last extra s is the remaining part of the word seconds before this shift to the left.

We now know the number of seconds but for a proper watch we need to know the minutes and the hours as well. So now put in the new lines that follow, and run the program again.

```
180 minutes = TIME DIV 6000 MOD 60
280 PRINT TAB(10,7); minutes"  Minutes"
```

Line 180 uses the same technique as line 160 except that there are 6000 hundredths of a second in a minute and so that is what we must divide by. The MOD 60 remains as before because there are sixty minutes in an hour. Line 280 prints this on the line above the seconds line.

To sort out the hours we need these three lines, the last of which is a change.

```
200 hours = TIME DIV 360000 MOD 24
260 PRINT TAB(10,6); hours"  Hours"
320 PRINT TAB(1,9); "have passed"
```

Line 200 results from the fact that there are 60x60x100 or 360000 hundredths of a second in any hour. The new version of line 320 makes sure that the screen message make sense. Then remove line 240 by typing in 240 and pressing RETURN. Now run the program and the screen should look something like this:

```
 Since your computer was switched on

          2 Hours
          37 Minutes
          0 Seconds

have passed.
```

One last point. You may wish to put the time to a specific number at the start. For example, suppose you wished the time to begin at zero. In that case the first line should be:

```
100 TIME = 0
```

The complete program looks like this:

```
100 TIME = 0
120 CLS
140 REPEAT
160 seconds = TIME DIV  100 MOD 60
180 minutes = TIME DIV 6000 MOD 60
200 hours = TIME DIV 360000 MOD 24
220 PRINT TAB(1,3); "Since you started running this
    program"
260 PRINT TAB(10,6); hours"  Hours"
280 PRINT TAB(10,7); minutes"  Minutes"
300 PRINT TAB(10,8); seconds"  Seconds"
320 PRINT TAB(1,9); "have passed."
340 UNTIL FALSE
```

TIME and delays

There are a number of ways to make the computer wait for a while before going on to the next line of the program. We have already met Z=GET on page 52. This waits until some key is pressed and then continues. In a moment we will use some variations on this and we will also use INKEY. Here we will show how to use TIME to make a delay. There are really two very similar techniques. The first involves putting TIME equal to zero as follows. Type in this example:

```
100 CLS : PRINT "From now until...."
120 TIME = 0 : REPEAT UNTIL TIME = 500
140 PRINT'' "   Now "TIME/100"   Seconds have passed."
160 PRINT'' "......"
```

Run this and see what happens. Line 120 creates a delay of 5 seconds. We could avoid having to set TIME equal to zero by changing lines 120 and 140 as follows:

```
120 time = TIME : REPEAT UNTIL TIME - time = 500
140 PRINT''"...Now "(TIME - time)/100 "  seconds have
    passed."
```

GET

We now look at the word GET. This is a function which waits for a key to be pressed and then has the ASCII code of that number stored in the variable associated with GET. Type this program in and run it.

```
100 Z = GET
120 PRINT CHR$ Z, Z
140 GOTO 100
```

Now press the letter A. Immediately the letter A and its corresponding ASCII number 65 appear on the screen. (The word CHR$ turns an ASCII number into a letter or symbol. See page 178). So in line 100 the variable Z is put equal to GET, and in line 120 this variable is printed as a number. The number associated with the spacebar is 32, and this can be checked using the above program. Now change line 120 as follows, and run the program.

```
120 IF Z = 32 THEN PRINT "Space bar"
```

This indicates a way of using GET to make decisions about what the program will do next. The string word corresponding to GET is GET$ and this returns the actual letter or symbol rather than the number associated with it. Rewrite the program as :

```
100 Z$ = GET$
120 PRINT Z$
140 IF Z$ = " " THEN PRINT "Space bar"
160 GOTO 100
```

In line 140 there is a single space between the two quotation marks. Now RUN this and check that it works. Both of these words GET and GET$ hold the screen indefinitely so there are two other comparable words which hold the screen for fixed and specified lengths of time. First type in NEW to remove the last program and then type in the following.

```
100 Z = INKEY(200)
120 PRINT Z
140 GOTO 100
```

Run the program and watch it for a while. The number -1 will appear repeatedly on the screen with a delay of two seconds. The number 200 causes this delay as it is measured in hundredths of a second. If we change it to 400 then the delay will be one of four seconds. Now press the letter A and the number 65 will appear on the screen exactly as with the word GET. So the only real difference between GET and INKEY is that GET waits indefinitely and INKEY waits a specified time. If we wished the program not to wait at all we would use INKEY(0). This is very useful when for example we wish to make a program cycle round a loop but remain susceptible to an interruption from the screen. A good example of this appears on page 253 where a program to play a game is being discussed. We want the program to go on moving a ball about the screen with a loop, but we also want to be able to interrupt this to move a paddle about.

Finally the word corresponding to GET$ and the companion of INKEY is INKEY$ and this is used in exactly the same way as INKEY except that, like GET$, the letter or symbol is returned rather than the ASCII number.

Random numbers

Random numbers are frequently needed when writing games programs or producing simulations on the computer. This is done using the built-in random number function which is activated by the statement RND (short for random). First type in this program and then run it.

```
100 CLS
120 INPUT seed
140 FOR count = 1 TO 5
160 PRINT RND(seed)
200 NEXT count
```

The machine responds by first clearing the screen in line 100, and then printing a question mark in response to line 120. This means that it is waiting for you to put in a number to be stored in the variable 'seed'. Then a loop is generated by lines 140 and 200 and this is cycled round five times. During each cycle the function RND(seed) is printed. This is a random number connected in a specific way to the value chosen for the variable seed. There are a number of possible responses to this, and we will deal with each in turn. First put in a fairly small positive whole number like 4 and press the RETURN key. When we did this the result is shown below. Your result may well be different.

```
1
4
3
1
2
```

Run it again a few times, and respond with 4 each time. After a while you will notice that the only numbers produced by this are the numbers 1, 2, 3, and 4. You will also notice that they do not appear in any pattern or with any obvious regularity. RND(4) is always equal to one of the numbers 1, 2, 3 or 4, but we can never predict which one it is going to be. We can even get a run of two or three identical numbers. This, in simple terms, is what we mean when we call them random numbers.

Now run it again a few times and respond to the question mark each time with a 5. The only difference will be that the number 5 is now likely to appear occasionally among the five numbers that appear on the screen each time. Now change the program as follows:

```
140 FOR count = 1 TO 100
160 PRINT ; RND(seed)" ";
```

This means that we can print out 100 random numbers each time. The two semi-colons and the single space within quotation marks in line 160 ensures that we can see them all on the screen. Now run the program and put in a 2. The screen should now contain a lot of ones and twos. There ought to be roughly the same number of each. This is rather like tossing a coin and calling one side of the coin 1, and the other 2. We can change the program so that it counts how many ones and how many twos actually occur. The new program looks like this:

```
100 CLS
140 FOR count = 1 TO 100
160 coin = RND(2) : PRINT coin;
180 IF coin = 1 THEN heads = heads + 1 ELSE tails =
    tails + 1
200 NEXT count
220 PRINT'' "Number of heads is ";heads
240 PRINT'' "Number of tails is ";tails
```

We have not changed lines 100, 140 or 200. Line 120 is removed since we know that the seed in this case is 2. For this reason line 160 is changed as shown. Then line 180 uses IF THEN ELSE to count the number of heads or tails. Finally the results are given as lines 220 and 240. Type all this in and run it a few times. Make a note of how close to 50-50 the results come out each time.

If we wanted a number within a specified range, it is easy to convert this sort of procedure to do this. Suppose for example that we were writing a game and wished to choose a spot randomly on the screen between two vertical walls. Remember that the screen ranges from 0 to 1279 across the bottom. Suppose the walls were at the points 300 and 900, and so we want a number somewhere between these. This is a range of 600, so we will use RND(600) to give us a random number in this range. We then add 300 to this to make it a random number in the required range, i.e. 300 to 900. This technique is actually used in Chpater 13.

We will now return to the original program and try some different numbers. First type in NEW and press RETURN. Then type in this program again.

```
100 CLS
120 INPUT seed
140 FOR count = 1 TO 5
160 PRINT RND(seed)
200 NEXT count
```

We have already shown how, if the number chosen for the variable 'seed' in line 120 is a positive whole number like 9, then the result of line 160 is to print out five numbers from the range of numbers 1,2,3,4,5,6,7,8,9.

Try it again a few times by typing in RUN and then responding with numbers like 5 or 7 or 2. You might now wonder what would happen if you used the number 1 as the seed. This would seem to mean that the computer will choose number between 1 and 1. Type in RUN and try it. That is, respond to the question mark with a one. The result when we did it was:

```
0.51067642
0.654073761
0.567598962
0.15318275
0.692124873
```

That is to say, the response to 1 is a set of numbers all lying between 0 and 1. This will always be the case. Now type in RUN and respond with zero or 0. This time the set of five numbers will be identical decimals between 0 and 1. These five numbers, all the same, are dependent on what was going on before they were produced. That is to say, although they are all equal to each other, the next time you use 0 may (depending on the circumstances) produce a different set of 5 identical numbers.

The only whole numbers left to try are negative numbers. Type in RUN and respond to the question mark with the number -3. The result is that the computer prints -3 five times. This would appear to have no value but in fact it has one advantage in that it makes the random number generater go to a new starting point. When the computer is first switched on, it begins to generate random numbers at exactly the same point (or number) each time. The result is that if you are playing a game, for example, the game begins with the same random number and proceeds through the same sequence of random numbers each time you switch on and load the program. The way to avoid this is to force the random number generator to begin at a different point in its sequence, and this is done using a negative number. The problem is that the negative number itself should be fairly random. One solution is to use the built in clock function called TIME. (See page 121). This begins to count in hundredths of a second as soon as the computer is switched on and so when the program is run it is likely to have a different numerical value each time. So, we can help to ensure that we begin with a genuinely random sequence by using a line like this early in the program.

```
firstseed = RND ( - TIME)
```

It is also possible to use the word RND by itself without a number in brackets after it. So if you write PRINT RND and press RETURN the computer produces a whole number from the range:- -2147483648 to +2147483647.

The word PLOT

This word PLOT is very versatile. It can be used to draw lines, place points on the screen, draw complete triangles, make all of these disappear again, decide on color, and other things. It is always followed by three numbers. Here is an example:

```
PLOT 85,600,250
```

The first number gives the computer information about what to draw (a point or a line or a triangle) what color it is to be, and so on. The other two numbers give the computer information about where on the screen to draw these things. In order to understand how it works we must begin by learning to understand the difference between the two words 'absolute' and 'relative' as used, for example, in the phrases:

1. Draw the line absolute.
2. Draw the line relative.

We will use a diagram to represent part of the screen and we have put some co-ordinates on as shown along the bottom and along the side. (Ignore the point A for the moment).

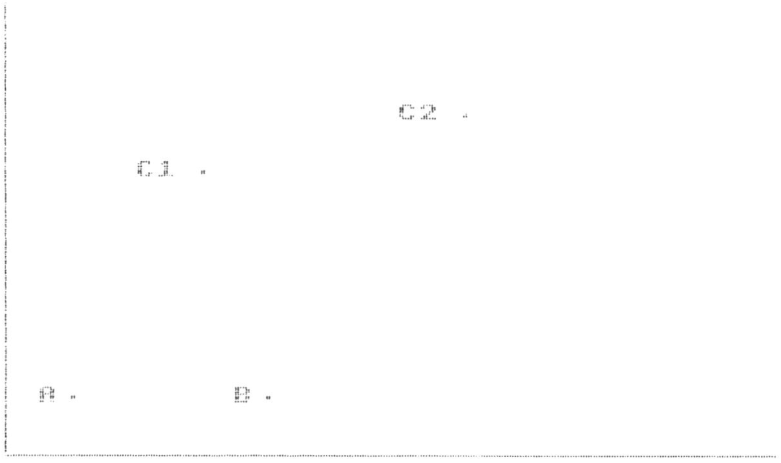

Now imagine that the cursor is at the point B(400,100) that is across 400 and up 100. We now wish to draw a line joining B to the point C(300,500) that is across 300 and up 500. There are two possible positions for C, and they are marked as C1 and C2.

When C is taken to be at position C1, then we have found C by beginning at the origin (the point O) and moving over 300 and up 500 from there. In this case we have drawn the line BC (or BC1) ABSOLUTE. When we draw a line absolute we always begin at the origin.

When C is taken to be a position C2, then we have found C by beginning at the point B and moving over a further 300 - to make it 700 altogether - and moving up a further 500 - to make it 600 altogether. In this case we have drawn the line BC (or BC2) RELATIVE. When we draw a line relative we always take the last point plotted as the origin and move to the new point from there.

We will now write a program to illustrate how all of this works in practice. First type it in and we will then discuss it.

```
100 CLS
120 REPEAT
140 INPUT' "Choose value for N " N
160 MODE 5
180 GCOL 0,1
200 MOVE 100,100 : REM A
220 MOVE 400,100 : REM B
240 PLOT N, 300,500 : REM C
260 UNTIL FALSE
```

Line 100 clears the screen. Lines 120 and 260 combine to make a repeating loop so that we can use the program repeatedly. Line 140 allows the user to choose the value of N to use in line 240. Line 240 is the crucial line and we will use a series of different values for N in this to see if we can sort out the effects of each. Line 160 uses MODE 5 because it has four colors and we want to demonstrate how PLOT affects colour. Line 180 uses GCOL 0,1 to make the chosen color red. Lines 200 and 220 use MOVE to move the cursor successively to the points A(100,100) and then B(400,100). These points are shown on the diagram on page 129. Remember that the word MOVE tells the computer to move to the points detailed but makes no mark on the screen to indicate that this move has happened. The computer however retains a memory of the location of these points.

Now run the program and respond with 0, then with 1, then with 2 and then with 3. The numbers to be used are shown below along with a description of what result to expect for each number. These descriptions refer to the diagram on page 129 and in particular to the effect of line 240.

N = 0 Nothing appears to happen but the cursor has been moved to the point C2, that is to the relative point.

N = 1 The line BC2 is drawn relative, that is as though B were the origin. It is colored red as a result of our choice of colour on line 180.

N = 2 The line BC2 is drawn again relative, but the color this time is white. White and Red are inverse colors. In line 180 we choose color red, so N = 2 changes this to its inverse color, that is white.

N = 3 The line BC2 is drawn again relative, but you cannot see it as it is drawn in the same color as the screen, that is in black.

These four results are characteristic with respect to color of much of what follows. All the numbers that can be used for N in line 280 can be put together in groups of four, where the first moves the cursor to the next point, the second uses the color chosen by the user, the third uses the color which is the inverse of the chosen color, and the fourth uses the background color.

To demonstrate this we will now use the next set of four numbers, that is 4, 5, 6 and 7. RUN the program again if you have stopped it, and respond with these four numbers in succession.

N = 4 Nothing appears to happen but this time the cursor has moved to the point C1, that is to the absolute point.

N = 5 The line BC is drawn absolute, that is with respect to the true origin at O. It is colored red as a result of our choice of color in line 180.

N = 6 The line BC is drawn again absolute, in the color inverse to red, that is in white.

N = 7 The line BC is drawn again absolute but cannot be seen as it is drawn in the screen background color that is black.

All of this means that the numbers 0 to 3 refer to relative movement and the numbers 4 to 7 refer to absolute movement. We can summarize these results so far, as follows with reference to the statement PLOT N, X, Y.

Relative plotting numbers for N	Absolute plotting numbers for N	Effect of PLOT N, X, Y.
0	4	Move to the point X, Y
1	5	Draw a line to X, Y in the chosen color
2	6	Draw a line to X, Y in inverse of chosen color
3	7	Draw a line to X, Y in screen background color

The next eight numbers for N, that is 8 to 15, produce results that are identical to these to look at, but in fact leave off the last point in each line. Use the program and test this by comparing 0 with 8, 1 with 9, 2 with 10 and so on. The next eight numbers for N, that is 16 to 23 produce dotted lines each time, but apart from this the results are identical to those produce by 0 to 7 and the next eight, 24 to 31, again produce dotted lines with the last point missing. We then skip to 64 for the next set of eight points which runs from 64 to 71. In this case only the points C1 and C2 are drawn and the lines are left out. Run the program and check that this works.

The final set of eight numbers runs from 80 to 87 and these produce triangles filled with the appropriate colors. These are the triangles ABC1, or ABC2 depending on whether we wish to use absolute or relative numbers. Note that when drawing triangles we use the last two points plotted on the screen and this is why we put A into the diagram at the start.

Two of these versions of PLOT are used so much that they have been given special words to themselves. The first is N = 4 and so PLOT 4, X, Y is the same as MOVE X,Y. The second is N = 5 and so PLOT 5, X, Y is the same as DRAW X,Y. The complete range is summarized in this table.

Plotting Relative
That is the origin is at the last point plotted

Line	Line without last point	Dotted line	Dotted line without last point	Point only	Triangle	Color	Effect
0	8	16	24	64	80	no mark made	move to (X, Y)
1	9	17	25	65	81	chosen color	draw to or at (X, Y)
2	10	18	26	66	82	inverse of chosen color	draw to or at (X, Y)
3	11	19	27	67	83	screen back-ground	draw to or at (X, Y)

Plotting Absolute
that is origin is at 0,0

Line	Line without last point	Dotted line	Dotted line without last point	Point only	Triangle	Color	Effect
4	12	20	28	68	84	no mark made	move to (X,Y)
5	13	21	29	69	85	chosen color	draw to or at (X,Y)
6	14	22	30	70	86	inverse of chosen color	draw to or at (X,Y)
7	15	23	31	71	87	screen back-ground	draw to or at (X,Y)

We will now use this informatiom to write a program to produce random squares on the screen using absolute plotting. Then by changing one number we will turn this into relative plotting and produce a quite different sort of pattern. The program is as follows. An explanation of what it does follows.

```
100 MODE 5
120 REPEAT
140 GCOL 0,RND(4)
160 X = RND(800) : Y = RND(800)
180 MOVE X,Y : MOVE X + 100,Y
200 PLOT 85,X,Y + 100
220 PLOT 85,X + 100,Y + 100
240 UNTIL FALSE
```

In line 100 we chose MODE 5 because it has four colors; then lines 120 and 240 together make a continuous loop. Line 140 uses GCOL and RND(4) to choose, randomly, one of the four available colours. (There is more detail about GCOL on page 201). In line 160 the coordinates of the bottom left corner of the square X and Y are chosen randomly as some numbers between 1 and 800. The squares will have a side equal to 100, so in line 180 the word MOVE is used to plot the two bottom corners of the square at (X,Y) and (X + 100,Y). Then line 200 used PLOT with 85 to produce the triangle which is the left half of the square; and line 220, in a similar way, produces the triangle which is the right half of the square.

Type in RUN and watch the screen for a while. It should quite quickly be covered with randomly displayed squares. Now change lines 200 and 220 as follows:

```
200 PLOT 81,X,Y + 100
220 PLOT 81,X + 100,Y + 100
```

The number 81 indicates that, this time the plotting is relative, rather than absolute, and so the pattern this time will not be of squares. Try it and see.

MODES

The computer Model A can have four MODES numbered 4, 5, 6 and 7. The Model B machine can have eight MODES numbered 0, 1, 2, 3, 4, 5, 6 and 7. These are screen display modes and we will now try to understand how they differ from each other. We can describe each mode with respect to four different characteristics, that is Graphics, Colors, Text and Memory used. These are shown in the table below:

MODE	Graphics	Colors	Text	Memory needed	Memory available to user MODEL A	MODEL B
0	640 x 256	2	80 x 32	20	--	12
1	320 x 256	4	40 x 32	20	--	12
2	160 x 256	16	20 x 32	20	--	12
3		2	80 x 25	16	--	16
4	320 x 256	2	40 x 32	10	6	22
5	160 x 256	4	20 x 32	10	6	22
6		2	40 x 25	8	8	24
7		1	40 x 25	1	15	31

It is of course unlikely that you will be able to remember all of this detail but there are certain characteristics of the various modes that are easily remembered when they have been used for a while. But first we should consider for a moment why we might need so many different modes. The reason is that there will be occasions when we will want to use the screen primarily to draw pictures or graphics of some kind. In this case we want to be able to break the screen down into as many small units or dots as possible. Look for example under graphics in the table. Obviously MODE 0 is better for graphics than MODE 1 or MODE 4. These in turn are better than MODES 2 and 5. And MODES 3, 6 and 7 do not allow this kind of graphics at all. However, the better the graphics resolution the more memory is needed.

There will be occasions when we will want to use the screen for text and numerical work and will not wish to use graphics at all. In this case it will be best to use MODE 3 or 6 or 7. But then the problem of color becomes important, and you will now notice that because MODE 6 allows two colors (black or white text) that it uses a great deal more memory than MODE 7. So the choice of mode depends on your needs with respect to graphics, text, color and memory. You can now see why MODES 0 to 3 are not available in Model A machines, there is not enough memory.

It is worth pointing out that, in some ways, the table gives a false picture. This is because it refers mainly to graphics colors. For example we have already demonstrated in chapter 5 that it is possible to have text and background colors by using CHR$ in MODE 7.

We will now develop a short program to demonstrate both graphics and text in all the modes, the available colors and the amount of free memory available in each. The program begins like this. Type in NEW to clear the memory and then these lines, which demonstrate how text appears in the different modes.

```
100 CLS
120 INPUT'' "What MODE  ", mode
160 MODE mode
280 PRINT' "Mode " ;mode
320 GOTO 120
```

Run this, and respond to the question 'What MODE' each time with one of the numbers starting at 7, and then 6 and so on down to 0. Each time line 160 will put the screen into the requested mode and line 280 will print a message on the screen about the mode. But this printed message will also give an indication of what text looks like in this mode. For example when Mode 5 appears the text is of double width because, as the table shows, there are only 20 columns across the screen in this mode. If you are using a Model A machine then when you reach 3 in your inputs there will be an error message, 'Bad MODE at line 160'. (You will also get this message on both types of machine if you use MODE inside a procedure or a function). We now add some lines which will allow us to demonstrate the graphics facilities in each mode. Type these in now, and run the program.

```
200 MOVE 100,100
220 DRAW 1000,250
240 DRAW 600,700
260 DRAW 100,100
```

Respond as before with 7, then 6 and so on. In these first two cases no picture appears because these two modes have no graphics facility. But when the response is 5, a triangle will appear on the screen; and then when the response is 4 the same triangle appears, only drawn with finer resolution.

We now wish to show the colors that are available in each mode. So once again we add some lines, as follows.

```
140 INPUT'' "What color  ",colour
180 GCOL 0,colour
```

We also change lines 220 and 240 as follows:

```
220 MOVE 1000,250
240 PLOT 85,600,700
```

Line 180 produces the graphics color and line 240 uses PLOT with 85 to make a triangle. Run this program and see what colors the triangle can be made. For example if we choose MODE 5 and then one for the color we produce a red triangle. Two for the color produces a yellow triangle, and so on. Finally add this line:

```
300 DIM P% - 1 : PRINT "Memory  "; HIMEM - P%
```

(The word HIMEM and this use of P% are not explained in detail here. They refer to specific memory locations within the machine). This gives a measure of the amount of free memory still available, in bytes, and gives a very clear indication of the consequence, in terms of memory, of each mode chosen. This program is now complete and you should play with it a great deal while looking at the table on page 135. In this way you can become familiar with what the various modes can do.

MODE 7 is in some ways different from all the others. It uses a slightly different set of characters for example, and this means that pressing some keys while in MODE 7 produces symbols different from those written on the key. It also uses a set of chunky graphics. All of these differences are discussed on page 181. The reason for the differences between MODE 7 and the others is that there are two international standards for character sets. One is Teletext which is used by British television and this set is the one available in MODE 7. The other is called ASCII and this set is used by the other modes.

LISTO

The word LISTO is used to change the format of the listing of a program. (Note that the last character in LISTO is the letter O and not the numeral zero). This is particularly useful when we wish to see the way in which the loops occur within a program. To demonstrate this, type in a simple example as follows:

```
100 MODE 7
120 PRINT "Start"
140 FOR count = 1 TO 4
160 PRINT count
180 NEXT count
200 PRINT '''
240 REPEAT
260 PRINT "Hello"
300 UNTIL TRUE
```

Now list this program on the screen and proceed as follows, carefully noting the results on the screen each time.

1. Type in LISTO 1 and press RETURN. Then LIST the program. This time there will be a space each time between the line numbers and the words of the line. That is each line is indented by one space.

2. Type in LISTO 2 and press RETURN. Then LIST the program. This time there will be no space between the line numbers and the words. But there will be two spaces between the line numbers 160 and 180 - that is the contents of the FOR loop - and the beginning of the line. The FOR loop could then be described as indented by two spaces.

3. Now type in LISTO 3 and press RETURN. Then list the program. This time it will do both of the things caused by LISTO 1 and LISTO 2.

4. Now type in LISTO 4 and press RETURN. Then list the program. This time the REPEAT loop is indented by two spaces.

5. Now type in LISTO 5 and press RETURN. Then list the program. This time the combination of 4 and 1, that is 5, means that each line will be indented by one and each REPEAT loop will be indented by 2 spaces.

6. LISTO 6 represents a combination of LISTO 4 and LISTO 2.

7. LISTO 7 is a combination of all three, that is LISTO 1, LISTO 2 and LISTO 4.

Try all of these and check that they work.

COUNT

The word COUNT is used to count all the characters printed using PRINT. To demonstrate this, type in NEW and then this two line program. The run it.

```
100 PRINT "AAAAA";
120 PRINT COUNT
```

The result is that the computer prints the five As on the line 100 and then prints 5 as a result of line 120. That is to say the word COUNT is a measure of the number of characters inside the quotation marks in line 100. The semi colon after the quotation mark is essential otherwise the cursor returns to the left margin of the screen and then COUNT is equal to zero. A better known example of using this is as follows:

```
100 REPEAT PRINT "+";
120 UNTIL COUNT = 10
```

Run this and try to understand what is happening.

Errors and bugs

When the computer is asked to do something that it finds impossible it usually prints an error message on the screen. The favorite such message is the single word Mistake, and you will probably have got used to seeing this one. When the computer prints an error message on the screen it remembers a number associated with the message. To test this, press a few keys at random on the keyboard and then press RETURN. The computer will respond, as usual, with Mistake. Now type in PRINT ERR and press RETURN. This time the computer will print 4. This means that the error number associated with the error message Mistake is 4. All the error messages have numbers and a list of these is given on page 482 of the User Guide. There you will find the number 4 beside the message Mistake. The computer always stores the errror number of the last error message in the reserved variable name ERR.

Most error messages are more useful than Mistake. Try another example. Type in PRINT "Hello and leave out the last quotation mark. Now press RETURN. The response will be Misssing ". Now find the number of this message by typing in PRINT ERR. This time the response is 9.

However if mistakes occur whenever a program is running then, usually, the program stops running and prints an error message. This can cause great difficulties. For example if a program has been running for a considerable time and has done a great deal of work, it can be very disappointing if a mistake occurs and the program aborts. So there are ways of avoiding this. For example, type in this program:

```
100 MODE 7
140 REPEAT
160 INPUT den : REM denominator
180 PRINT 100/den
200 UNTIL den=99
240 END
```

Now run this and respond to the question mark with some numbers. Then respond with the number zero. The response will be an error message as follows and the program will stop.

```
Division by zero at line 180
```

We will now add these lines to the program which will produce a message and will ensure that the program does not abort on an error.

```
120 ON ERROR GOTO 260
260 IF ERR = 18 PRINT "Division by zero.  Try again."
280 GOTO 140
```

Line 120 ensures that, if and when an error occurs, the program does not stop. It goes to line 260. There it checks if the error is number 18 (which is the number for the division by zero error) and if it is, a message appears on the screen and the program returns to line 140 and goes on. But no matter what the error is the program will not stop until the input is 99 as specified by line 200. So this is a way of ensuring that a mistake or error will not make a program stop but will return it to an appropriate line in the program. If you can predict what the error is likely to be then the error number can be used to print a message on the screen.

We can also turn this error-reporting facility off when we wish to by using ON ERROR OFF. For example we can add this line to the above program.

```
220 ON ERROR OFF
```

Any errors that occur in the program after line 220 will not make use of the routine described above and so as soon as another error is detected the computer will stop running again. This is because the ON ERROR command is now off. In this case, this is not a very real example since the program then ends. You can also ask for a report on the last error that occurred using the reserved word REPORT. Just type the word in and press RETURN. The word can also be included as a line in a program. Finally we can get the computer to report the line number on which the error occured. This is always stored in the reserved variable name ERL. We can test this as follows. Type in this program and run it:

```
100 MODE 7
140 PRINT 2 ↑ 130
```

This produces the error message 'Exp range at line 140'. Now add these lines and run the program.

```
120 ON ERROR GOTO 160
160 PRINT "Error number ";ERR
180 PRINT "at line number ";ERL
```

We can also try to check where an error has occurred by using the words TRACE ON. This makes the computer print on the screen all the line numbers that it uses when running through a program. Here is an example:

```
100 MODE 7
120 add = 5 : total = 30
140 count = 0
160 REPEAT
180 count = count + 1
200 total = total + add
220 UNTIL total = 70
240 PRINT count
```

This program begins with 'total = 30' and repeatedly adds 5 to it using the variable add for 5. It uses the variable count to count the number of times this addition must be done until total is equal to 70. Then in line 240 it prints the value of count. Run it and the answer will be 8. That is, add 5 to 30 eight times and the result will be 70. Now let us make a deliberate mistake. Suppose we put the variable add equal to zero in line 120. Change it to this now as shown below and run it again.

```
120 add = 0 : total = 30
```

This time the condition in line 220 will never be satisfied and so the loop will continue for ever. In order to stop it you will have to press the ESCAPE key. Now let us suppose that we cannot spot this mistake and so do not know how to correct the program. Type in these lines:

```
110 TRACE ON
210 Z = GET
```

The first new line turns the trace facility on and line 210 simply holds the screen occasionally. Now run the program and press the space bar a few times. The screen will look like this:

```
120   140   160   180   200   210   220
  180   200   210   220   180   200   2
10   220   180   200   210
```

These are line numbers and will in fact have arrows on each side, but these are not reproduced here. (In other modes these arrows become square brackets). A little study of these will quickly identify a repeating loop made up of the lines (180,200,210,220). Now keep pressing the space bar and the screen will fill up with repeated sets of these numbers. If we then turn to the program, we will quickly realize that the loop is being repeated endlessly and this will make clear what the difficulty is.

It is also possible to turn the trace off with the words TRACE OFF. Finally, if it is needed, it is possible to specify the last line of the program beyond which trace will not work.

The CTRL key and control-operations

Some very interesting and useful things can be achieved by holding the key marked CTRL (meaning CONTROL) and then pressing various other keys. It is easiest to demonstrate this if you have a program in the computer. If you have not, load one from tape or type in a few dummy lines, like this:

```
100 REM
120 PRINT "This is a dummy program"
140 END
```

First LIST the program. Then hold the CTRL key and press the key marked L. This should clear the screen. List the program again and try to clear the screen again in the same way. So, when combined with the CTRL key, the key marked L clears the screen.

This concept of what are called 'control-operations' is an important aspect of the BBC microcomputer, and the functions which such control-operations perform can often be achieved in a variety of ways. The first of these ways has just been demonstrated, and, as we will discover, the combination of holding the CTRL key and pressing another key produces some sort of result for a great many of the other keys. But before we look at some of the other keys we will examine other ways of achieving the same result as the combination of CTRL and L, that is clearing the screen.

Imagine that each letter of the alphabet was numbered starting with A being 1. Then B is 2, C is 3 and so on. So you will find that L is 12. We now come to a new word, that is VDU. List the program so that there is something on the screen and then type in VDU12 and press RETURN. Again the screen will clear. So we have the equivalent combination shown below:

```
          L .... 12
 CTRL and L .... VDU 12
```

This sort of equivalence between CTRL and some letter on the one hand, and VDU followed by the letter's numerical partner on the other, holds all the time. Sometimes one is more easy to use than the other and as you go along you will find that the VDU statement can have a very great variety of uses.

In chapter 9 we will be discussing at length string functions of various kinds. Included in this will be the word CHR$ which is short for character string. This often has the same effect as VDU, except that we must put the word PRINT in front of it. So LIST the program again and then type in, PRINT

CHR$12, and press RETURN. Once again the screen will clear. But, as well as this, we already know that the word CLS followed by RETURN will clear the screen. So now we have these four equivalents.

1. CTRL and L
2. VDU12 followed by RETURN
3. CLS followed by RETURN
4. PRINT CHR$12 followed by RETURN

The close equivalence of VDU12 and CLS illustrates another point about control operations. Obviously this particular operation of clearing the screen is one that will be used a great deal, so it is useful to have a special word for it, one that is easy to remember. This is why the word CLS was made part of the machine's language. There are a number of other VDU operations which have been given special easily remembered names like this, such as COLOUR, MODE, GCOL.

We will now return and look at some other of the more immediately or directly useful control-operations. We will move through these in alphabetical order.

1. CTRL B. If you have a printer attached to the computer this has the effect of turning it on so that everything after this is printed on the printer as well as on the screen. It is of course the equivalent of VDU2, since B is the second letter of the alphabet. VDU2 is most useful when you wish to output to the printer in the middle of a program-run. For example, if you have a program which is doing a series of long calculations and you want to print the final answer each time on the printer you can use a line like this:

```
400 VDU 2 : PRINT"The answer is  "total : VDU 3
```

VDU 2 turns the printer on. The message about the answer is then printed on the paper as well as on the screen, and VDU 3 turns the printer off again.

We can also program one of the red keys to activate the printer, and to turn it off, or even to do something like line 400 above. For example if we wished to be able to use a red key to LIST a program we could use the following:

```
* KEY 2 ¦ B LIST ¦ M ¦ C
```

We have already used the symbol (or || in MODE 7). It stands for CTRL in this context, so this line means that KEY 2 is programmed to turn the printer on (¦ B), LIST the current program on paper (LIST¦ M), and then turn the printer off (¦ C).

2. CTRL C. We have already used this in the last section. It turns the printer off and has as an equivalent VDU 3.

3. CTRL D and CTRL E. We will deal with those two together, since CTRL D has the effect of cancelling the effect of CTRL E. Very often when drawing graphs or pictures we wish to place messages or numbers on specific points of the screen. We can do this reasonably well using the TAB facility but without much accuracy. The reason for this is that the screen is numbered differently for text and for graphics. So we can talk about the 'text cursor'. This moves on a screen which is numbered from the top left and which ranges from 80x32 to 20x32 and 40x25 depending on the mode. But we can also talk about the 'graphics cursor' which moves on a screen which is numbered from the bottom left and which is 1280 by 1024. The effect of CTRL E or VDU 5 is to join the two cursors together and make this joint cursor behave like the graphics cursor.

First of all we will do it directly. Type in MODE 4 and press RETURN. Then hold the CTRL key and press E. The result of this is that the combined cursor becomes invisible, but it is still there. Then type in the following invisible line and press RETURN:

```
MOVE 500,500 : PRINT "Center"
```

The result will be that the word Center appears at approximately the screen center. Now hold the CTRL key and press D. This turns the facility off.

There are a number of side-effects of this operation. If you repeat the above sequence and, before turning the facility off, repeat the line as follows, with the word CENTER in capitals this time.

```
MOVE 500,500 : PRINT "CENTER"
```

The effect is that the new word overwrites the other, that is it is superimposed on it. Other side-effects include the effect that the screen does not scroll, and the colors used for both text and graphics are graphics colors.

A final demonstration uses the VDU version of this operation within a short program to put an X at the start and a list of numbers on the rest of the X axis. Type it in and try it.

```
100 MODE 4
120 VDU 5
140 MOVE 0,500 : PRINT "X"
160 FOR X = 100 TO 900 STEP 100
180 MOVE X, 500 : PRINT ; X/100
200 NEXT X
220 VDU 4
```

4. CTRL G. Hold the CTRL key and press G. A sound is caused by this. This is often called the Bell for historical reasons. Since G is the seventh letter of the alphabet, we can achieve the same result with VDU 7 and RETURN. This can be used as a quick way of getting sound into a program.

5. CTRL with H,I,J and K. These four move the cursor around the screen. The equivalent VDU numbers are 8,9,10,11. They can be shown on a diagram as follows

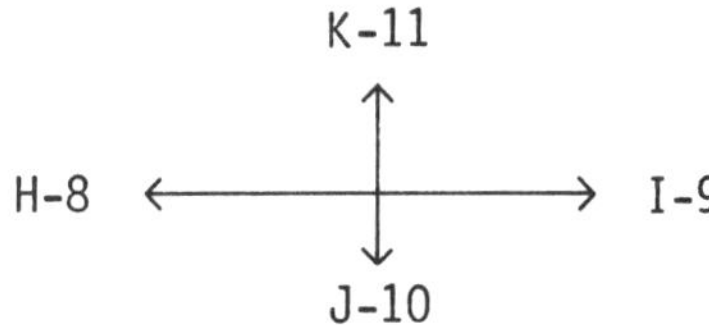

These four cursor movements can be used in place of TAB to put the text cursor on a specific point on the screen. The example that follows allows us to demonstrate another of the VDU facilities; that is you can put a string of numbers after it separated by commas and it will act on each in turn. Suppose we wished to move the cursor down five lines and across three spaces, and then print "Hello". This program will do it.

```
100 CLS
120 VDU 10,10,10,10,10,9,9,9
140 PRINT "Hello"
```

6. CTRL L and CTRL P. These clear the screen. We have already discussed CTRL L at length at the beginning of this section. CTRL P (or VDU 16) can be used to clear the graphics screen. It is equivalent to CLG.

7. CTRL M. Holding CTRL and pressing M has the same effect as pressing the RETURN key. It is used most often with the programmable red keys.

8. CTRL N and CTRL O. To demonstrate these two properly we need a long program. Either wait until you have typed one in or load one from the WELCOME tape. Then type in LIST and press

RETURN. Now hold CTRL and press N. Then LIST it again. This time only a bit of the listing will appear and then it will stop. Then press either of the two SHIFT keys and another section will be listed. This is called paging and CTRL N turns on paging. Similarly CTRL O turns it off.

Turn paging off now and then LIST the program again. Then hold CTRL and press the SHIFT key. This allows you to stop the listing at any point and is a very useful facility.

9. CTRL P. See number 6.

10. CTRL Q. This is the equivalent of COLOUR. Type in MODE 5 and press RETURN. Then hold CTRL and press Q. This must be done carefully. Put one finger on CTRL and hold it. Then press Q. Then let both keys go. Then press the number 1. Then type in some letters. They will print in RED. Use CTRL and Q again, and then press 2. Again type in some letters. This time they will be in yellow. We can of course use VDU 17 since Q is the 17th letter of the alphabet. Try this short program.

```
100 MODE 5
120 FOR color = 0 TO 3
140 VDU 17, color
160 PRINT "COLOR"
180 NEXT colour
```

Now run this program. Line 140 will change the color each time a loop is made. That is:

```
VDU 17,0  makes the letters black
VDU 17,1  makes the letters red
VDU 17,2  makes the letters yellow
VDU 17,3  makes the letters white
```

11. CTRL R. This is the equivalent of GCOL and can be used, usually as VDU 18, to change the color of graphics. There is more about this in chapter 11.

12. CTRL^. This is the symbol on the key below the BREAK key. Used with CTRL it has the effect of putting the cursor in the top left hand corner of the screen, that is in the HOME position. It is the equivalent of VDU 30. Sometimes it is useful to be able repeatedly to write a changing message on the top line of the screen. We could use TAB to do this, but here is an alternative. Try this program:

```
100 CLS
120 PRINT "This is the top line."
140 Z=GET
160 VDU 30
180 PRINT "This is again the top line."
```

When this is run the first message appears at the top of the screen. Then press any key to release line 140 and the second message will completely replace the first message on the top line of the screen.

In this section we have only skimmed the surface of the possibilities with VDU and control-operations generally. There is a good tightly-written description of the whole range in the User Guide, and we will refer to them again in chapter 11 on graphics. Here is a summary of what we have just covered:

CTRL B	VDU 2	Turns on printer
CTRL C	VDU 3	Turns off printer
CTRL D	VDU 4	Separates two cursors
CTRL E	VDU 5	Joins two cursors
CTRL G	VDU 7	Bell
CTRL H	VDU 8	Cursor left
CTRL I	VDU 9	Cursor right
CTRL J	VDU 10	Cursor down
CTRL K	VDU 11	Cursor up
CTRL L	VDU 12	Clears text screen. CLS.
CTRL M	VDU 13	RETURN
CTRL N	VDU 14	Turns on paging
CTRL O	VDU 15	Turns off paging
CTRL P	VDU 16	Clears graphics screen. CLG.
CTRL Q	VDU 17	COLOUR
CTRL R	VDU 18	GCOL
CTRL ^	VDU 30	Homes cursor.

Problems

1. Using the random number function, write a program to simulate the tossing of a single dice.

2. Copy the digital clock program on page 124 and then change it so that a message can be flashed on the screen at a specified time.

3. Continue this process of adaptation so that the digital clock becomes a stopwatch with laptimes.

4. Write a program which repeatedly draws random sized rectangles of random color on the screen. Use PLOT 85, and the random number function.

CHAPTER 8
PROCEDURES AND FUNCTIONS

Introduction

In most programs there are routines, often fairly standardized, that are self-contained or self-dependent in some way. These routines are quite often used more than once within a program. We have met and used this notion at various places in this book and we have so far used two forms of definition of these.

The first most useful and versatile form which we have met is called a procedure. We first met this idea on page 46, and we have used it fairly freely at a number of other places in the book so far. A second form is called a subroutine and we first met this on page 65. A subroutine is an inferior form of procedure and should be used only when when the use of a procedure would be awkward or difficult. Our main use of it has been when faced with a situation demanding the use of a multiple choice as, for example, when dealing with a menu. There is one other form of this sort of routine. It is called a function and we will deal with this later in this chapter. At the end we also deal with the word EVAL which is also used with functions.

There is a sense in which all such separated routines represent our definition of a new word for the computer to use. For example, on page 49, we developed a procedure for making line spaces on the screen. It took the form and title, PROCspace(number) where the number is a variable and so was called on with examples like PROCspace(3) or PROCspace(6). So, in a sense we have defined a new word in the computer's vocabulary. Once defined we can use this word over and over again.

The first consequence of using procedures in a program is that it becomes much easier to read, follow, and understand. This is especially so if some care is taken with the choice of names given to procedures. The second consequence is that the program is more carefully structured and organised with all the lines of a particular routine placed close together, and markers put at the beginning and end; as well as this, all the routines can be put in careful and logical succession in separate recognizable units. The third consequence is the absence of complex knock-on effects when bugs (or errors) occur. This can mean, in less carefully structured programs, that an error in line 300, if corrected, produces three more errors in lines 400, 1000, and 5000. With structured programs, using procedures, such difficulties are less likely to occur.

We will now try to bring together in one place all the information and techniques associated with procedures and similar routines. This means that, to begin with, there will be a little repetition of material already covered in a rather sketchy form earlier in the book. We repeat it here so that proper full explanations can be given.

Simple procedures

In order to demonstrate the ideas involved we will begin with a very simple example. Suppose we wished to be able to make a four-line space on the screen. To begin with type in NEW to remove any program in memory. Here is the first line of the procedure:

```
300 DEF PROCspace
```

All procedures begin in this way. The name, which we always choose, is in this case 'space'. Although it is permitted to use both upper and lower case when choosing names for procedures, we will always put such names in lower case. The other two words are DEF and PROC. These are not chosen by us and are always used in this order, at the beginning of a procedure. There should never be any spaces within the variable name, and there can be no space left between the word PROC and the word space.

The last line of any procedure is always ENDPROC. Like this:

```
340 ENDPROC
```

Between these two lines we put the actual routine which we wish the procedure to perform.

```
320 FOR count = 1 TO 4 : PRINT : NEXT count
```

This makes a four-line space. There are of course easier ways to effect this line, such as PRINT''', but this way is more versatile as we will see in a moment. Now we need to write that part of the program which calls or makes use of this procedure.

Type this in, and then run the program to make sure that it works.

```
100 MODE 7 : PRINT "There are 4 line-spaces between this line"
120 PROCspace
140 PRINT "and this line."
160 END
```

In line 120 the procedure is called using the title space that we gave to it on line 300. We have placed the complete procedure at the end of the program by itself away from the main logical flow of the program in lines 100 to 160. It is not required that this be done, but it seems wise to develop a consistent and organized system and this is the way we will do it.

Procedures with parameters

This particular routine is not very versatile since the number of line-spaces is completely determined by the 4 in line 320. But it is a very simple matter to change this so that you can have whatever number of line-spaces you wish. Retype the procedure as follows beginning with line 300:

```
300 DEF PROCspace(number)
```

The word number in brackets is a variable to which we can give a number when we call the procedure. This is shown below in line 120. Now retype line 320 as follows:

```
320 FOR count = 1 TO number : PRINT : NEXT count
```

This line ensures that the number of spaces is determined by the variable number, and we can decide what this is to be in line 120 by putting an appropriate number in brackets. Now type in this:

```
100 PRINT "This is line one"
120 PROCspace(10)
140 PRINT "There are 10 line-spaces above this line."
```

Now run this program and see what happens. Clearly we can put whatever number we wish inside the brackets in line 120 when we call the procedure. This sort of technique allows procedures to be very versatile. When used in this way a variable is called a parameter.

Here is another example. On page 78 we had a three-line program which allowed us to print the three-times table on the screen. We can put this into a procedure and use a parameter (i.e. a variable) so that we can put any multiplication table that we wish on the screen. First we will look at the procedure which we call, appropriately enough, tables. Remember to type in NEW before beginning to type this in.

```
260 DEF PROCtables(number)
280 FOR count = 1 to 9
300 PRINT' number; "  times "; count; "  are  ";
    number * count
320 NEXT count
340 ENDPROC
```

Now we need a short program to call this procedure, as follows:

```
140 INPUT'' "Which table do you want ",number
160 PROCtables(number)
240 END
```

Run the program a few times and then add these lines to allow you to repeat the process as often as you wish.

```
100 MODE 7
120 REPEAT
180 INPUT'' "Another table(YES/NO) ",ans$
200 UNTIL ans$ = "NO"
220 PRINT'' "Thank you for now."
```

Now run it again and try some other numbers. It is of course possible to have more than one parameter associated with the procedure. Here is a simple one which allows you to multiply any two numbers together. It is very like the last program in its structure. Type in NEW and then the procedure, as follows:

```
280 DEF PROCmultiply(first,second)
300 PRINT'' "The answer is  "first * second
320 ENDPROC
```

Now a program to call this using REPEAT and UNTIL in exactly the same way as before.

```
100 MODE 7
120 REPEAT
140 INPUT'' "What is the first number ",one
160 INPUT'' "What is the second number ",two
180 PROCmultiply(one,two)
200 INPUT'' "Another. (YES/NO) ",ans$
220 UNTIL ans$ = "NO"
240 PRINT' "Thank-you"
260 END
```

This program could also have been written using a function and these are described later in this chapter.

Using procedures

We will now develop a slightly longer though incomplete program which uses a number of procedures in order to illustrate one way of structuring such a program. We will first of all describe the purpose of the program, then we will describe the procedures that it will use, and finally the main body of the program.

The program will allow us to input the names of items on a stock list, then the number of each item actually in stock, and finally it will print the stock-list in two columns on the screen. It would normally be necessary to have many more procedures than this, but we will leave most of them out to stop the example becoming too long.

A short example of the two lists would look like this:

Items	Quantity
Hammers	20
Spanners	300
Saws	80
Planes	10
Chisels	10

First the procedure to input the list of items on the stock-list, that is the list like the one on the left above. Type it in and then we will discuss it.

```
340 DEF PROCstocklist
360 INPUT' "How many items are on the list ",list
380 FOR count = 1 TO list
400 INPUT' "Put in the next item's name "item$(count)
420 NEXT count
440 PRINT' "That was the last one."
460 PROCholdscreen
480 ENDPROC
```

Line 340 declares the procedure and calls it stocklist. The rest of the procedure finds out how many items there are on the list, using the variable list, and then invites the user to put the names of the items in one at a time. These items are stored in the array variable item$ and so we must remember to declare this variable. In line 460 another procedure called holdscreen is called. This is a procedure for holding the screen until the user is ready to move on to the next part of the program. The technique has already been described on page 52. Its presence here illustrates that it is possible to call a procedure from within a procedure.

```
780 DEF PROCholdscreen
800 PRINT'' "Press the space bar now"
820 Z = GET
840 ENDPROC
```

Next we need a procedure to input how many of each item are actually in stock. First type it in and we will discuss it.

```
500 DEF PROCquantity
520 FOR count = 1 TO list
540 PRINT'' "The item is  ";item$(count)
560 INPUT "How many are there ",number(count)
580 NEXT count
600 PRINT'' "That was the last one."
620 PROCholdscreen
640 ENDPROC
```

This is quite like the earlier procedure PROCstocklist. It is defined and named in line 500. Lines 520 and 580 produce the necessary loop. Line 540 tells the user the name of the item being considered and line 560 invites the user to input the quantity or number of this item in stock. This quantity is stored in the array variable number so this must also be declared in the program.

Now we need a procedure to print the data on the screen so that we can read the list of items and the number of each in stock. Type it in now:

```
660 DEF PROCshowlist
680 FOR count = 1 TO list
700 PRINT item$(count),number(count)
720 NEXT count
740 PROCholdscreen
760 ENDPROC
```

We will also put the title into a procedure, although this could be just as easily done outside a procedure at the start. We do it here so that the whole program can be described with a very few words, each representing a procedure.

```
240 DEF PROCtitle
260 PRINT TAB(15,1);"STOCK LIST"
280 PRINT TAB(15,2);"**********"
300 PRINT''
320 ENDPROC
```

The beginning of the program then looks like this

```
100 MODE 7
120 DIM item$(30), number(30)
140 PROCtitle
160 PROCstocklist
180 PROCquantity
200 PROCshowlist
220 END
```

This use of procedures means that it is possible to read this program and make sense of it just by looking at these first few lines. Clearly it begins by establishing a title, then a stocklist, then the quantities associated with this, and then it shows the list. The complete program is now shown and in this listing extra lines full of stars have been put in to highlight the various procedures.

```
100 MODE 7
120 DIM item$(30), number(30)
140 PROCtitle
160 PROCstocklist
180 PROCquantity
200 PROCshowlist
220 END
239 REM ****************************************
240 DEF PROCtitle
260 PRINT TAB(15,1);"STOCK LIST"
280 PRINT TAB(15,2);"**********"
300 PRINT''
320 ENDPROC
339 REM ****************************************
340 DEF PROCstocklist
360 INPUT' "How many items are on the list ",list
380 FOR count = 1 TO list
400 INPUT' "Put in the next item's name "item$(count)
420 NEXT count
440 PRINT' "That was the last one."
460 PROCholdscreen
480 ENDPROC
499 REM ****************************************
500 DEF PROCquantity
520 FOR count = 1 TO list
540 PRINT'' "The item is  ";item$(count)
560 INPUT "How many are there ",number(count)
580 NEXT count
600 PRINT'' "That was the last one."
620 PROCholdscreen
640 ENDPROC
659 REM ****************************************
660 DEF PROCshowlist
```

```
680 FOR count = 1 TO list
700 PRINT item$(count),number(count)
720 NEXT count
740 PROCholdscreen
760 ENDPROC
779 REM *************************************
780 DEF PROCholdscreen
800 PRINT'' "Press the space bar now"
820 Z = GET
840 ENDPROC
```

A procedure with graphics

Now for a fairly short example of how we might use procedures to call up a particular graphics routine when we wanted it. This program will draw randomly colored squares of random size at randomly chosen place on the screen. The procedure to be used will be called PROCsquare. The main part of the program which call this procedure is as follows:

```
100 MODE 5
120 start = RND(-TIME)
140 REPEAT
160 PROCsquare
180 Z= INKEY(100)
200 UNTIL FALSE
220 END
```

Assuming that we know what PROCsquare does, this first part of the program is self-explanatory. Line 120 makes sure that the random number sequence begins at a random point and line 180 makes a short delay between each loop. The procedure which draws the squares looks like this:

```
240 DEF PROCsquare
260 X = RND(1000) : Y = RND(900) : REM bottom corner of
    square
280 side = RND(400) : REM length of square's side
300 col = RND(3) : REM color of square
320 GCOL 0, col
340 MOVE X, Y : MOVE X + side, Y
360 PLOT 85, X, Y + side : PLOT 85, X + side, Y + side
380 ENDPROC
```

Now run the whole program and try it.

LOCAL variables

Sometimes we may wish to use, or we may even inadvertently use, the same variable name twice within a program. This can lead to errors and logical difficulties and is best avoided. Fortunately it is very easy to ensure that no problems arise in procedures (or functions) by declaring the variable to be a LOCAL one. We will now show, using an example, what this means.

We will write a procedure which takes a number that is given to it (a parameter passed from the main program) and raise this number to the power of 2, then to the power of 3, and finally to the power of 4. For example it would take the number 3 and produce the set of numbers 9, 27, and 81.

The procedure looks like this. Type it in now:

```
240 DEF PROCpowers(number)
280 FOR count = 1 TO 4
320 PRINT "The answer is " ; number↑count
340 NEXT count
360 ENDPROC
```

The little upward pointing arrow on line 320 is the symbol for 'to the power of' in MODE 7. In the other modes it looks like this^. We will now use this procedure to calculate this set of powers for all the integers from 2 to 6 ,as follows:

```
100 MODE 7
120 FOR count = 2 TO 6
140 PRINT''
160 PROCpowers(count)
180 PRINT'' "Press the space bar." : Z = GET
200 NEXT count
220 END
```

Note that the loop, set up in lines 120 to 200, runs from 2 to 6 and contains a call on the procedure in line 160. Now run the program. The first set of results will be correct and the screen will look like this:

```
The answer is 2
The answer is 4
The answer is 8
The answer is 16

Press the space bar.
>-
```

But when the space bar is pressed the next set of answers will be as follows:

```
The answer is 6
The answer is 36
The answer is 216
The answer is 1296

Press the space bar.
>-
```

The logic of the program would seem to suggest that this should have calculated the powers of 3, not these of 6. Press the spacebar again, and, exactly the same set of results, that is the powers of 6 will appear. In fact this set of answers will now continue to appear forever. We will have to get out of this loop by pressing ESCAPE.

What has gone wrong? List the program on the screen and look closely at it. In line 120 the variable count becomes 2. Then in line 280, within the procedure, the same variable name is used, so count runs from 1 to 4.

However, when this loop has been completed, that is when count gets to 4, it goes on and becomes 5, although this 5 is not used. But when we now return to line 120, it moves the value of count on one more, so it becomes 6. And this process happens every time thereafter. Hence the closed loop.

The way to avoid this difficulty is to declare the variable count inside the procedure to be a LOCAL variable. This means that, in a sense, the computer now holds two different versions of count, in different parts of the memory, that is the local count in the procedure and the main variable count. To do this add this line:

```
260 LOCAL count
```

Now RUN the program again and all will be well. We can of course declare more than one variable to be local, and we can also declare local variables within functions as well as procedures. There will be examples of these among the programs that now follow.

Functions

Functions are rather like procedures in a number of ways. They have to be declared using the word DEF; they are normally placed at the end of the program well out of the way; and they are used to perform routines which may be needed more than once within a program. We begin with a very simple example. This is so simple that there are other better ways of doing it, and so it is used here only to illustrate how functions work.

Suppose you were working on a fruit farm for the summer and that you were being paid 127 cents for every basket that you filled. You want a program which allows you to put in the number of baskets and tells you how many cents you have earned. We begin by defining the function as follows:

```
180 DEF FNwages(baskets) = 127 * baskets
```

The word DEF must always be used, followed by a word which always begins with FN, which is short for function. The last part of this second word is chosen by you and is the name of the function. Notice also that the function is put equal to a number, can be thought of as a number, and will therefore be used in a PRINT statement.

We now need a short program to call or to make use of this function. Type this in.

```
100 MODE 7
120 INPUT "How many baskets  ",baskets
140 PRINT "You earned  " FNwages(baskets)
160 END
```

Notice that the function name, that is FNwages, appears as we suggested in a PRINT statement. This is always the case with functions, unlike procedures where there is no PRINT and the title of the procedure is simply declared. Run this program a few times and each time put in a diferent number in response to the question.

A function always produces a single number or string. (We will deal with strings later). This number is the result of a set of computations or arithmetical operations and the numbers on which this set of operations is performed are declared as variables in the definition of the function.

The next example allows the user to put in two numbers. The function then squares each of these and adds the two squares together and finds the square root of the sum. It is of course the length of the hypotenuse of a right-angled triangle. It looks like this.

```
100 MODE 7
120 INPUT' "Put in the two numbers " one, two
140 PRINT FNhyp(one,two)
160 END
180 DEF FNhyp(opp,adj)
200 = SQR(opp ↑2 + adj ↑2)
```

The two numbers are put in as one and two. The function on line 180 becomes equal to the square root of the sum of the squares of the two parameters which are called opp and adj. This means that the values which the user puts in, and which are contained in the variables one and two, are passed to the variables opp and adj so that opp becomes equal to one and adj becomes equal to two. Notice that the last line of the function begins with an equality sign. This is usually the case, and is a sign that the function has been completed. Sometimes there is a choice of ending and so the function might end with an IF THEN ELSE. Here is an example of such an ending. (Remember to type in NEW first).

```
100 INPUT num
120 PRINT FNexample(num)
140 END
160 DEF FNexample(variable)
180 IF variable = 1 THEN = 1 ELSE = 10 * variable
```

This means that the function, FNvariable, equals 1 if variable = 1; and that it equals 10 * variable in any other case.

Here is another slightly more complicated example of a function. In this case a single number is passed from the main body of the program to the function which then operates on it according to the definition. The problem can be described as follows. Begin with any whole number greater than 0, say 5. If the number is even, divide it by two. If it is odd multiply by three and add one. So, beginning with 5 leads to a sequence of numbers as follows. We will call this a chain.

5, 16, 8, 4, 2, 1, 4, 2, 1, ...

Notice that, after 1 is reached the sequence recurs. The program to produce this sequence or chain begins as follows and uses the function FNchain.

```
100 MODE 7
120 INPUT "Which number  "num
140 PRINT''' num;
160 REPEAT
180 num = FNchain(num)
200 PRINT num;
220 UNTIL num = 1
240 END
```

In line 120 we are invited to put in the number which will begin the chain. It is called num and is printed in line 140. This first number, num, is replaced in line 180 by a new value of num which has been generated by the function which we will define below. The outcome of this is printed by line 200. The process then recurs and this repetition, caused by lines 160 and 220, continues until the number 1 is reached. The sequence then stops. Now for the function.

```
260 DEF FNchain(num)
280 IF num MOD 2 = 0 THEN = num DIV 2 ELSE = 3 * num +1
```

It may be necessary to remember that num MOD 2 is equal to the remainder on division by 2 and obviously this will equal zero only if num is even. In this case num is divided by 2; otherwise it is multiplied by 3 and 1 is added. Run this program a few times and make sure that it works.

Functions with strings

We have now considered the use of functions with numbers. When a function acts on another number, or set of numbers, it produces a resulting number. That is to say a single number or set of numbers goes into the function, get operated on in some way, and a single resultant number comes out. It is possible to do this with words or strings as well. In the example which follows, a word is put in. The function, called FNspaces, puts a couple of spaces between each two letters of the word; that is to say, it spaces the word out. The result is printed by line 140.

```
100 MODE 7
120 INPUT"What is the word ",word$
140 PRINT'' FNspaces(word$)
160 END
```

The definition of the function now follows. First of all the function is given a name in line 180 using the variable spaces. Then, in line 200 the string variable newword$ is made equal to a null string.

```
180 DEF FNspaces(var$)
200 newword$ = ""
```

Then a loop is set up using the two lines 220 and 260. Then in line 240, the MID$ function and the variable are used to put two spaces after each letter of the word. (The MID$ function is described in detail in Chapter 9). This means that you must be careful when typing it in to put two spaces between the quotation marks at the end of line 240.

```
220 FOR count = 1 To LEN(var$)
240 newword$ = newword$ + MID$(var$,count,1) + "  "
260 NEXT count
```

Finally, in line 280, the function is made equal to the new word including the spaces.

```
280 FNspaces = newword$
```

Recursion

A function may be asked to call itself. This process is called recursion. This is for many people a difficult concept so we will show how it works in a number of simple examples. The first example uses a recursive function to add up all the integers, that is the whole numbers, from 1 to wherever you choose. The body of the program therefore looks like this

```
100 MODE 7
120 PRINT "This program adds up all the integers"
140 PRINT' "from 1 to wherever you choose."
160 INPUT' "Where do you choose ",integer
180 PRINT'' "The sum is  " FNsum(integer)
200 END
```

The effect of this program is to add up all the integers from 1 to whatever number is contained in the variable 'integer'. The function is called in line 180 and is called sum. The parameter is integer. The function now follows. Type it in first, then run it a few times using small numbers like 3 (answer 6) or 4 (answer 10) to check that it works. We will then explain it.

```
220 DEF FNsum(number)
240 IF number = 1 THEN = 1 ELSE = number +FNsum(number - 1)
```

In order to explain this we must choose a value for number and work through it step by step. Suppose we choose the number three. Then line 220 would define the function as FNsum(3). When this statement FNsum, followed by a number in brackets appears, then line 240 goes into action. This can be read as follows.

(a) IF number = 1 then the function also equals 1. That is to say
FNsum(1) = 1

(b) However if number does not equal 1, then the function equals number + FNsum(number -1). That is to say, the function is defined in terms of itself. That is what is meant by recursion. So we proceed as follows.

number = 3

Line 1. FNsum(3) = 3 + FNsum(2) (using (b) above).
But then

Line 2. FNsum(2) = 2 + FNsum(1) (again using (b) above).
And then

Line 3. FNsum(1) = 1 (using (a) above).

This process stops here. But originally we asked, what is the value of FNsum(3) and we do not know yet. To use the above three lines to work this out we must begin at line 3, then to line 2 and then finally up to line 1.

Line 3. FNsum(1) = 1

Line 2. FNsum(2) = 2 + FNsum(1) = 2 + 1 = 3

Line 1. FNsum(3) = 3 + FNsum(2) = 3 + 2 + 1 = 6

And so we have reached the answer.

The next example involves the well-known sequence of numbers called the Fibonacci sequence. This begins with the two numbers 1, 1. The third number is got by adding these two, so it is 2. The fourth number is got by adding the second and third; and so on. So the sequence looks like this:

1, 1, 2, 3, 5, 8, 13, ...

The function which calculates the terms of this sequence looks like this:

```
240 DEF FNfib(num)
260 IF num = 1 OR num = 2 THEN = 1
280 IF num ½ 2 THEN = FNfib(num -1) + FNfib(num - 2)
```

Notice that in line 280, the function calls itself twice so that each term in the sequence is equal to the sum of its two predecessors. The program which uses this function looks this:

```
100 MODE 7
120 INPUT'' "How many terms  ",terms
140 FOR count = 1 TO terms
160 PRINT count, FNfib(count)
180 NEXT count
200 PRINT
220 END
```

Now run this and put in 20 in response to line 120. You will find that, as the number becomes bigger, the process of recursion takes a long time. In fact it is not usually the most economical way of solving a problem. To demonstrate this here is another program which also calculates Fibonacci numbers using a simple procedure. This one works a great deal faster than the recursion method. In this case we ask only for the first twenty numbers in the sequence.

```
100 MODE 7
120 first = 1 : second = 1
140 PRINT first'second
160 FOR count = 1 TO 18
180 PROCfib
200 NEXT count
220 END
240 DEF PROCfib
260 third = second + first
280 PRINT third
300 first = second : second = third
320 ENDPROC
```

There is one other important point about recursion. Since the computer must keep a record of all the proceedings involved in a recursion, the number of times that a function can go on calling itself is limited by the amount of memory available. If it is asked to do so too often the error message 'No room' will be printed on the screen.

The last example of the use of recursion involves the situation where a set of data is stored in an array and we wish to find the sum of this data. The body of the program looks like this:

```
100 MODE 7
120 DIM num(30)
140 DATA 10, 20, 30, 40, 50
160 FOR count = 1 TO 5 : READ num(count) : NEXT count
180 PRINT "The sum of the data is  " ; FNarray(5)
200 END
```

Now the function, with the recursion on line 240.

```
220 DEF FNarray(list)
240 IF list = 1 THEN = num(1) ELSE = num(list) +
    FNarray(list - 1)
```

The effect of this is to add together all the data on line 140. The example data given here are chosen so as to make it easy to check whether or not the program works properly.

EVAL

This word allows us to input a mathematical function during the run of a program in exactly the same way as we can input a number or a string. This is most easily demonstrated by using an example. First type in this example.

```
100 MODE 4
120 INPUT "What is the function  ",function$
140 FOR x = 1 TO 5
160 y = EVAL(function$)
180 PRINT x, y
200 NEXT x
```

RUN this program and respond to the question with a function in x, such as x 2 or x 3 - 10. (Remember that this ↑ or ^ sign means 'to the power of'). The result will be two sets of numbers representing x and y. We can then use these to draw a curve. However there is no very simple way of ensuring that this curve fits easily into the screen. To solve this we will now write a more extended program. First type in NEW to remove this program. The curve-drawing program that we now present is written as a series of procedures which have been given names that are intended to be self-expanatory. So the main body of the program looks like this. Type it in and then we will discuss what the sequence of procedures is intended to do.

```
100 MODE 7
120 PROCinputs
140 PROCfindmaxmin
160 PROCscaling
180 MODE 1 : REM MODE 5 for model A
200 PROCdrawcurve
220 END
```

The first procedure called 'inputs' will invite the user to put into the machine all the information that it needs in order to draw the curve. The next procedure called 'findmaxmin' will calculate the range of values that both x and y will cover so that we can make best use of the whole screen. To do this it is necessary to use a loop which runs through the whole range of x values, calculates each corresponding y value, and keeps a note of the smallest value of y and of the largest value of y. The third procedure called 'scaling' will calculate a scale-factor for each of x and y so that later the actual calculated values can be scaled up or down to fit on the screen. The final procedure is called 'drawcurve' and this one actually draws the curve. Notice that the word MODE cannot be used within a procedure, and so is used twice in the main body of the program. Line 180 will be MODE 1 on Model B machines, and MODE 5 on Model A machines.

The first procedure is shown below. It begins by inviting the user to type in the actual function to be used. This must be done quite carefully using the computer's own symbols. For example if the curve was e (the exponential) to the power of x-squared, then it will be typed in as EXP(1 - x ↑2).

```
240 DEF PROCinputs
260 maxy = 0 : miny = 0
280 INPUT'' "What is the function ",function$
300 INPUT'' "What is the lower limit ",lower
320 INPUT'' "What is the upper limit ",upper
340 INPUT'' "What is the step ",step
360 ENDPROC
```

The only other information needed to draw the curve is the lower limit for x, the upper limit for x and the size of the step. These are needed for the loop that will be written as shown below later on in the program. (Do not type this in now).

```
FOR x = lower TO upper STEP step
```

Line 260 establishes early on in the program the existence of a greatest value for y and a least value for y. These are called maxy and miny and have been put equal to zero.

The next procedure runs through the complete range of x and calculates each y using this new word EVAL on line 440.

```
380 DEF PROCfindmaxmin
400 FOR count = lower TO upper STEP step
420 x = count
440 y = EVAL(function$)
460 PROCmaxmin
480 NEXT count
500 ENDPROC
```

During each circuit of this loop the procedure called maxmin is called and this is a very simple procedure for checking and upgrading the values of maxy and miny each time. It appears at the very end of the program but is shown here for convenience.

```
 980 DEF PROCmaxmin
1000 IF y > maxy THEN maxy = y
1020 IF y < miny THEN miny = y
1040 ENDPROC
```

So at the end of the findmaxmin procedure the computer has established the largest and smallest values of y, and these are stored in maxy and miny.

The next procedure, shown below, uses all the information available to establish the values of a series of parameters associated with x and y, and necessary for the screen scaling procedure. They are as follows:

1. The range of x and y. That is the difference between the lowest value and the highest value of each. These are called rangex and rangey. Assume that the upper values of both x and y are positive : then if the lower values of x and y are negative the origin is included for each and so the range in each case is just the upper value minus the lower value. For x this will be (upper - lower) and for y this will be (maxy - miny). However if, in either case, the lower value is positive, then the range will not include the origin and so the range will simply be from the origin to the upper value - which is the upper value. So, in this case, x will be upper and y will be maxy. This is done in lines 540 and 560.

```
520 DEF PROCscaling
540 IF lower < 0 THEN rangex = upper - lower ELSE rangex =
    upper
560 IF miny < 0 THEN rangey = maxy - miny ELSE rangey =
    maxy
580 scalex = 1280 / rangex
600 scaley = 1024 / rangey
620 IF lower > 0 THEN xcenter = 0 ELSE xcenter = scalex *
    (-lower)
640 IF miny > 0 THEN ycenter = 0 ELSE ycenter = scaley *
    (-miny)
660 ENDPROC
```

2. Then when the ranges of x and y are established as rangex and rangey we need a scale factor for each. This is done by dividing the actual range of each into the total available range. This is done in lines 580 and 600. Remember that, across the screen there are 1280 points and up the screen there are 1024 points.

3. The origin or centre of the curve must then be established and this is done in lines 620 and 640 where the coordinates are called xcentre and ycentre. Again there are two

possibilities in each case. If the lower values of each of x and y are positive then the origin is at (0,0). Otherwise it must be moved either over or up or both.

The last procedure draws the curves, making use of all the information generated by the preceding procedures. Once again it uses the EVAL function in line 880. Most of it is self explanatory but we will write some notes about the less obvious points.

```
680 DEF PROCdrawcurve
700 GCOL 0,1
720 REM next 2 lines draw y axis
740 MOVE xcentre,0
760 DRAW xcentre,1023
780 REM moves origin
800 VDU 29, xcentre ; ycentre;
820 REM draw curve
840 FOR count = lower TO upper STEP step
860 x = count
880 y = EVAL(function$)
900 MOVE scalex * x,0
920 DRAW scalex * x, scaley * y
940 NEXT count
960 ENDPROC
```

Line 700 sets the colour to red. Line 740 and 760 draw the y axis. The x axis is normally created just by the curve drawing procedure. In line 800 we use VDU 29 to establish the new origin. The coordinates of this were calculated earlier in lines 620 and 640. Notice the two semi-colons. Do not leave either of these out.

This is the complete program. Type it in and try it. To get some spectacular looking curves try these examples using -5, 5, and .05 for lower, upper and step.

(a). x - x↑3 / 12 + x↑5 /120

(b). SIN(x) * COS(2 * x)

(c). EXP(1 - x↑2)

Problems

1. Write a program which uses the word EVAL to produce a set of number-pairs for any function between two limits which the computer invites the user to input. The program should be made up of three procedures, PROCbegin, PROCvalues, PROCdisplay and should begin as follows:

```
100 MODE 7 : DIM x(100), y(100)
120 PROCbegin
140 PROCvalues
160 PROCdisplay
180 END
200 DEF PROCbegin
220 ..........
```

2. Write a program, using FN and PROC which allows you to input a three digit number and then produces a new number from this which is equal to the sum of the squares of the digits of the original number. For example, 123 would become (1 * 1) + (2 * 2) + (3 * 3) or 14. The program should give the option of continuing this process with the new number, in this case 14.

CHAPTER 9
STRINGS

Introduction

We have met strings at various times in this book (see page 16), and this chapter is about ways of manipulating and displaying them. In order to do this effectively, the computer has a set of quite powerful string functions. Each function separates out a part of the string or changes numbers into strings or strings into numbers. We will consider each of these functions in turn.

Definition of strings

More often than not strings are made up entirely of letters of the alphabet and are simply English words. However, it is not necessary for this to be so. A string can be made up of any collection of symbols or graphics or numerals, and the important point is that quotation marks must be put around strings when they are used in programs.

A string can be made up entirely of numerals so that it looks exactly like a number, except for the quotation marks.

```
A = 47          A is a number
A$ = "47"       A$ is a string
```

This may not seem to be a very important distinction, but it is vital and the importance rests in the different sort of manipulations that can be performed with numbers as opposed to strings. For example, numbers can be added together in the conventional sense. Type this in and run it:

```
100 first = 20
120 second = 30
140 sum = first + second
160 PRINT sum
```

The result of this addition of 20 and 30 is, not unexpectedly, 50. But suppose these were in the form of strings. Type in the program below and run it. (Remember to type in NEW first):

```
100 first$ = "20"
120 second$ = "30"
140 ans$ = first$ + second$
160 PRINT ans$
```

The result is 2030. That is, addition of strings results in what is called concatenation rather than normal arithmetic addition. To think of this in another way, if these two strings had contained alphabet letters or other non-numeric characters, then placing them side by side would seem less strange.

The VAL function

The first string function that we consider is the VAL function. It can be used to "translate" strings into numbers, according to the following rules. Firstly, if the string in question is made up of, or begins with, letters, graphics, or any non-numeric characters, then use of the VAL function produces 0. Some examples:

```
A$ = "Joe"      VAL(A$) = 0
B$ = "SD007"    VAL(B$) = 0
C$ = "A99"      VAL(C$) = 0
```

This process can be tested within a program.

```
100 PRINT VAL ("Joe")
120 A$ = "PC49"
140 PRINT VAL(A$)
```

Type this in and run it. The result should be two zeros.

Secondly, if the string is made up entirely of numerals the VAL function translates this string into the corresponding number.

```
A$ = "99"       VAL(A$) = 99
B$ = "1234"     VAL(B$) = 1234
C$ = "4.7"      VAL(C$) = 4.7
```

Again, you can test this within a program as follows. Type this in and run it:

```
100 PRINT VAL("99")
120 A$ = "4312"
140 PRINT VAL(A$)
```

Thirdly, if the string begins with numerals, but also contains letters or symbols, the VAL function translates this string into the initial number value, disregards the letters etc., and disregards any numbers which follow them.

```
G$ = "12AB"     VAL(G$) = 12
H$ = "4X5Y"     VAL(H$) = 4
I$ = "987Q"     VAL(I$) = 987
J$ = "9PQ2"     VAL(J$) = 9
```

This function can be useful in programs when checking whether or not an input is appropriate. Here is an input program, where the second line simply prints the input.

```
100 INPUT "Write your name "name$
140 PRINT name$
```

Run this program and respond to the question mark with Joe - or something similar. The computer accepts this quite happily and then prints it on the screen. Now run the program again, but this time respond to the question mark with a number; say 87. Again, the computer accepts this quite happily because name$ in line 100 is a string, and both Joe and 87 are acceptable strings. Therefore, when the input variable name$ is a string variable then the computer cannot distinguish numbers from words. In order to change this add line 120 to the program so that it now looks like this:

```
100 INPUT "Write your name "name$
120 IF VAL (name$) <> 0 THEN 100
140 PRINT name$
```

Then run it again and try responding with a number, say 43. This time the computer will not accept it and returns to line 100. This is because in line 120 if VAL (name$) is not equal to zero then the program returns to line 100. Obviously VAL (name$) is only equal to zero when name$ is not a number, that is, when name$ is a letter or symbol combination. (Or of course when name$ is in fact zero).

Many programmers would argue that all input statements should use string variables and that number variables should not be used at all. The argument is that if a number input is needed, it is possible to use the VAL function to turn it into a number, once it has been input as a string. But, more importantly, when input as a string it is possible to use all the string functions to manipulate it, format it and validate it in a way that is difficult, if not impossible, with numbers.

This kind of manipulation and formatting can be demonstrated as follows. (First type in NEW). Suppose, at the start of a program, the user is invited to input the date and suppose further that this is done according to a fixed format. That is June 14th 1902 would be entered as 061402. Similarly February 5th 1912 would be 020512. The first two digits represent the month, and if it is one digit, a zero is written in front of it. The third and fourth digits represent the day, and the fifth and sixth digits represent the year.

```
100 MODE 7
120 INPUT "What is the date ",date$
```

We now wish to break this six-character string into three parts in order to make the date easier to read. We must first remember that, since we used date$ in line 120, this six-figure digit is a string and not a number; so we first use the VAL function as follows:

```
140 date = VAL(date$)
```

'date' is now a six-digit number which can be subjected to normal arithmetic manipulation, and so the rest of the program, shown below, applies simple arithmetic to this to separate the month, the day and the year. 'aux' is a temporary variable brought in to hold a number until the arithmetic has been completed.

```
160 year = 1900 + date MOD 100
180 aux = date DIV 100
200 month = aux DIV 100
220 day = aux MOD 100
240 PRINT'' "Month","Day","Year"
260 PRINT'' TAB(1); month; TAB(11); day; TAB(20); year
```

The words DIV and MOD are described on page 121.

There are also three functions which allow us to isolate particular bits of individual strings. They are LEFT$, RIGHT$ and MID$. We will consider each in turn, as well as the LEN function.

The LEFT$ function

This is best explained using examples. Type in the program below and run it. The resulting printouts are shown on the right. Make sure that, in each case, there is no space between the word LEFT$ and the opening bracket.

Program	Printout
100 PRINT LEFT$("Basic",1)	B
120 PRINT LEFT$("Basic",2)	Ba
140 A$ = "Educational"	
160 PRINT LEFT$(A$,9)	Education

So the LEFT$ function prints the specified number of characters starting on the left of the string. This function is often very useful in programs because it allows us to test input by examining its first letter only.

```
100 PRINT "Do you wish to:-"
120 PRINT' " Begin again."
140 PRINT' " Read list."
160 PRINT' " Save on tape."
180 INPUT ans$
200 IF LEFT$(ans$,1) = "B" THEN 1000
220 IF LEFT$(ans$,1) = "R" THEN 2000
240 IF LEFT$(ans$,1) = "S" THEN 3000
```

In this incomplete program the first letter of the response is examined and compared with the first letter of each possible response. This technique is used frequently and is demonstrated in the next short routine, which is also incomplete. The two lines 1000 and 2000, referred to in lines 120 and 140, have not been included.

```
100 INPUT "Do you wish to play again "ans$
120 IF LEFT$(ans$,1) = "Y" THEN 1000
140 IF LEFT$(ans$,1) = "N" THEN 2000
160 PRINT "Try again" : GOTO 100
```

This routine shows how to isolate the first letter of strings. We now look at a routine which prints the first letter; then the first two letters; then the first three letters, and so on. First type in NEW and press RETURN. Then type in this program:

```
100 MODE 7
120 INPUT word$
140 FOR count = 1 TO 7
160 PRINT LEFT$(word$,count)
180 NEXT count
```

Now type in RUN and, when the question mark appears, type in a word like STRETCH. The figure 7 in line 140 can be changed to whatever number you wish. Do not remove this program for a moment as it will be used again with the next string function.

The LEN function

This function simply counts the number of characters in a string. The word LEN is short for length. One immediate use of this can be found in the last program. Type in the new line 130 below and also change line 140 as shown.

```
130 len = LEN(word$)
140 FOR count = 1 TO len
```

Now type in RUN and press RETURN. Respond to the question mark by typing in any word. Line 130 finds the number of characters in this word, and calls it len. Line 140 sets up the loop to run len times.

We can now use this LEN function to demonstrate how long a string the computer can handle. First remove the old program by type in NEW. Then type in the following, noting that in line 120 word$ is to contain exactly 63 As. Line 130 actually prints out the number so you can first run the program and check that it is exactly 63.

```
100 MODE 7
120 word$ = "AAAA..."
130 PRINT LEN(word$)
```

When you are sure that the word$ in line 120 is a string made up of 63 As then remove line 130 by typing in 130 and pressing RETURN. Now add this line:

```
140 newword$ = word$ + word$ + word$ + word$
```

newword$ is, therefore, a string made up of four times 63 or 252 As. Again use a temporary line to see how this looks. Type in this line and then run the program.

```
150 PRINT newword$
```

The result of this should be that over six full rows of As appear on the screen. Now remove line 150 and type in these three lines.

```
160 INPUT extra$
180 newword$ = newword$ + extra$
200 PRINT newword$,LEN(newword$)
```

Line 160 invites you to input another string. Line 180 joins this new string to the end of the 252 As already in newword$. Line 200 prints this extended string newword$, and its length. When the question mark appears on the screen as a result of line 160, input a string of five As. Then press RETURN. The computer responds like this:

```
String too long at line 180
>-
```

Therefore, the existing 252 As joined to this new input of five As (making a total of 257 As) produces a string that the computer considers to be too long. Run the program again and put in four As. Again, an error message appears. Run it again with three As and the new enlarged string is printed out by line 200. At the end it also prints 255, which is the length of the string, or the number of characters it contains. So the longest possible string that the computer will accept has 255 characters. Finally, add the lines below, changing lines 160 and 200 as shown. Then run the program.

```
160 extra$ = "AAA"
200 FOR count = 1 TO LEN(newword$)
220 PRINT LEFT$(newword$,count)
240 NEXT count
```

One last demonstration of the use of the LEN function concerns situations where there is a need to place a program heading, or something similar, in the centre of the screen. First remember that in Mode 7, the screen is 40 spaces wide, and suppose the heading is a string, A$. Then find the length of that string using LEN(A$). Then, subtract this from 40 to find the total number of spaces left. Divide this number by two to find how many of these extra spaces to put on each side of A$. We can now use the TAB function with this to move the cursor to the right spot. Type this in directly:

```
A$ = "HEADING" : PRINT TAB((40 - LEN(A$)) / 2) ; A$
```

The word COUNT

The reserved word COUNT is used to count how many symbols the cursor has printed across the screen. (This is not to be confused with the variable 'count', in lower case, which we have used quite a lot). If the cursor has been forced back to the beginning of a line by a new PRINT or by use of the RETURN key, then COUNT will equal zero. So we must use a semi colon to keep the cursor out along the line if we wish to use COUNT. Here is an example:

```
100 PRINT "AAAA";
120 PRINT COUNT
```

When this is RUN line 120 will print 4. Now remove the semi colon from line 100 and RUN it again. This time line 120 will cause the machine to print 0. We can use this technique to print a row of symbols across the screen like this:

```
100 REPEAT PRINT " ";
120 UNTIL COUNT = 40
```

We can now repeat in a similar way the exercise on page 174, where we wished to find the largest possible string that the computer can handle. Using COUNT it can be done more economically. First type in NEW and then this program:

```
100 REPEAT
120 word$ = word$ + "*"
140 PRINT word$;
160 PRINT COUNT''
180 Z = INKEY(20)
200 UNTIL FALSE
```

Now run this, and a sequence of strings made up entirely of stars will appear on the screen, followed on each occasion by the number of stars in the sequence. This numbering is done by using COUNT in line 160. The two apostrophes are there to make some space on the screen. Line 180 provides a short delay and makes the screen legible.

The RIGHT$ function

This is very similar to the LEFT$ function. The difference is obvious and implicit in the word. With LEFT$ we are able to select a part of the string, starting on the left: so with RIGHT$ we can select part of the string, starting on the right.

Some examples with the resulting printout are now shown.

Program	Printout
100 PRINT RIGHT$("Micro",1)	o
120 PRINT RIGHT$("Return",4)	turn
140 word$ = "ABCD" 160 FOR count = 1 TO 4 180 PRINT RIGHT$(word$, count) 200 NEXT count	D CD BCD ABCD

A short example now follows which illustrates the essential difference between the LEFT$ and RIGHT$ functions. It makes use of the beginning of a famous sentence that reads the same from left to right as it does from right to left. The sentence is ABLE WAS I ERE I SAW ELBA. Type in the program below and run it..

```
100 MODE 7
120 word$ = "ABLE WAS I"
140 FOR count = 1 TO LEN(word$)
160 PRINT LEFT$(word$,count), RIGHT$(word$,count)
180 NEXT count
```

The MID$ function

This is probably the most useful of the string formatting functions and is in some ways the most sophisticated. First, some examples. (Remember to type in NEW to remove the old program).

Program	Printout
100 PRINT MID$("DRONES",3,2)	ON
120 PRINT MID$("DRONES",3,4)	ONES
140 PRINT MID$("DRONES",4)	NES
160 B$ = "ZYXWV"	Y
180 FOR count = 1 TO 4	YX
200 PRINT MID$(B$,2,count)	YXW
220 NEXT count	YXWV

So a statement like this MID$(word$,4,6) means, "make a substring by beginning at the fourth character of word$, and make it six characters long.". The second of these numbers may be omitted as follows. Type this in and press RETURN

```
PRINT MID$("FERGAL", 3)
```

A slightly more complex use of this function is now described, line by line. The program accepts an input of a number from 1 to 7 where these numbers represent days of the week. Therefore Sunday is 1, Monday is 2, and so on. The program then translates the number you have input into the first three letters of the appropriate day.

```
100 MODE 7 : INPUT "Input day as a number "day
```

This line clears the screen and invites the input.

```
120 week$ = "..SUNMONTUEWEDTHUFRISAT"
```

This sets up a string made up of two dots, followed by a long word made up of the first three letters of each day. It is placed in the variable week$.

```
140 day$ = MID$(week$, 3 * day,3)
```

In line 140 the MID$ function is used to select the appropriate three letters from the long string week$. This is done in two stages, first by using the second or last 3 in the brackets, to specify a string three characters long. Then the middle part of the material inside the brackets, 3 * day, selects the appropriate starting point for the three-letter string to be printed.

When day = 1, we expect the outcome to be SUN. In this case 3 * day becomes 3, and the MID$ function becomes MID$(week$, 3, 3). This means begin at the third character and take three characters. The first two characters are dots, which are spacefillers, and the third character is the first letter S, of SUN. So SUN is selected and called day$. Finally, put in a print line.

```
160 PRINT day$
```

So the whole routine looks like this:

```
100 MODE 7 : INPUT "Input day as a number "day
120 week$ = "..SUNMONTUEWEDTHUFRISAT"
140 day$ = MID$(week$, 3 * day,3)
160 PRINT day$
```

You ought to be able to write a similar routine for the 12 months. The two routines can then be put together, and the program converted to translate as follows:

Day 3, 14th day of month 7, 1850

into

Tuesday, July 14th, 1850

The CHR$ function and VDU

In chapter 7, when discussing control operations we discovered that we could use VDU 7, 'to ring the bell' on the computer, and that an alternative to this was to use PRINT CHR$ 7. We are now going to discuss this string function CHR$ and its partner VDU in greater detail.

Many computers use the set of numbers from 0 to 255 to store control codes and characters like the letters of the alphabet, numerals and punctuation marks. On the BBC computer there is a further complication in that MODE 7 does this differently from the other modes and must be considered separately. So we will begin by discussing MODES 0 to 6, amd will have a separate section later on MODE 7.

The set of numbers 0 to 255 is used in MODES 0 to 6 to represent what are called ASCII codes (American Standard Code for Information Interchange). A diagram showing these is given on pages 490 and 491 of the User Guide and this is very useful for reference. (The total of 256 is used because 256 represents 2 to the power of 8 and is the total number of different combinations possible with 8 binary digits. An example of such a combination is 10001101, and this is 141 in base 10). In the BBC micro computer the numbers from 0 to 255 are used as follows:

Range	Description
0-31	Control codes. See pages 142 to 147 and also pages 377 to 389 of the User Guide.
32-126	The full set of characters. The meaning of this is looked at below in detail.
127	A control code.
128-223	Not used.
224-255	User defined characters. These are described in chapter 11, page 216.

For the purpose of this section we are interested in the 95 codes from 32 to 126 and we will now write some short programs to display a few of these. The first program invites the user to put in some numbers in this range (32 to 126). It then translates each one into a character from the character set and displays both the number and the character on the screen.

```
100 MODE 6
120 REPEAT
140 INPUT number
160 IF number < 32 OR number > 126 THEN 140
180 letter$ = CHR$ number
220 PRINT number, letter$
240 UNTIL FALSE
```

Type this in and run it and try putting in some numbers. For example the numbers 65 to 90 represent the capital letters while the numbers from 97 to 122 represent the lower case letters. For example check that 65 produces A. We can now add some lines to this program so that it cumulates a set of letters into a word as you feed in the appropriate numbers. Change or add the following lines.

```
120 FOR count = 1 TO 10
200 word$ = word$ + letter$
220 PRINT' word$
240 NEXT count
```

Line 200 cumulates the letters produced by line 180 into the string word$. During each circuit of the loop the complete word is printed on the screen by line 220. The apostrophe between PRINT and word$ makes a line space each time.

Suppose we wished to turn word$ into N. IRELAND. The numbers corresponding to these characters are as follows:

```
78 46 32 73 82 69 76 65 78 68
N  .     I  R  E  L  A  N  D
```

Now run the program and respond to the question mark by typing in the number for N, that is 78, and then pressing RETURN. Then type in the next number, that is 46, and press RETURN. Continue in this way.

We can do this a great deal more simply using VDU instead of CHR$. Just type in the following:

```
VDU 78, 46, 32, 73, 82, 69, 76, 65, 78, 68
```

and press RETURN. This prints the message immediately, but it leaves the cursor out at the end of the line. The number associated with pressing the RETURN key is 13. So use the COPY key to repeat this, but put the number 13 at the end. This time the cursor returns to the start of the line but does not go down to the next line. The number for dropping a line is 10, so repeat it again and put 10 at the end, after the 13. This time it works perfectly.

The next program will loop through the complete set of numbers and print them and the characters corresponding to them on the screen. It begins like this:

```
100 MODE 6
120 FOR count = 32 TO 126
140 PRINT count, CHR$ count
180 NEXT count
```

Type in and run it. This works in that the corresponding pairs are printed on the screen side by side, but they appear very quickly and without much spacing. To improve this type in a new version of line 140 as shown, and also a line to produce a small delay between each pair. In line 140 we use the word SPC. This is explained in Chapter 10.

```
140 PRINT count ; SPC(3) ; CHR$ count
160 Z = INKEY(50)
```

It will now present the information in a more leisurely and readable style. We can also write line 140 as:

```
140 PRINT count : VDU count
```

Normally it is easier to use VDU to print individual characters on the screen especially if there is no problem with spacing or presentation. But suppose you wished to print quotation marks on the screen during the run of a program. This can be done more easily using CHR$. For example, try this line. Remember to type in NEW first.

```
100 PRINT "My name is  " CHR$34 "PRENTICE HALL" CHR$34
```

Now type in RUN and press RETURN. The screen will now print this line.

```
My name is "PRENTICE HALL"
>-
```

This is of course because 34 is the number used to represent the quotation mark.

MODE 7 character set

We noted earlier that MODE 7 uses a different character set from the other modes and will now look at this separately. The set of characters and associated numbers just described for the other modes are almost identical to those used in MODE 7. The exceptions, with corresponding code numbers, are shown below.

MODE 7	Other MODES	Code
←	[	91
½	\	92
→	]	93
↑	^	94
¼	{	123

‖	:	124
¾	}	125
÷	~	126

But, in addition to these differences the whole range of numbers 0 to 255 is used differently in MODE 7.

There are in fact two character sets sharing the range of numbers, an alphanumeric and a graphics set. In places these overlap. The two tables on pages 486 to 489 of the User Guide can be used for more detail about this, but some comments follow:

1. The full character set is represented twice within the range. For example VDU 65 and VDU 193 both return Capital A.

2. The special MODE 7 color and other codes are in the range 128 to 159. Some of these have already been discussed in chapter 5.

3. The graphics codes are accessed by first printing one of the color graphics codes shown below:

145	Red graphics
146	Green graphics
147	Yellow graphics
148	Blue graphics
149	Magenta graphics
150	Cyan graphics
151	White graphics

Then the punctuation, numerical and lower case symbols become chunky graphics symbols as shown in the table in the User Guide, pages 488 and 489. For example, type this in and RUN it:

```
100 MODE 7
120 PRINT "ABCabc"
140 PRINT CHR$ 145 ; "ABCabc"
```

Line 120 will print the upper and lower case letters exactly as shown, but the CHR$ 145 in line 140 will print ABC properly (albeit in red) but abc will be changed into graphics characters.

The ASC function

This is the inverse or opposite of the CHR$ function. It translates the first letter of a string into its corresponding CHR$ number. As an example, remember that CHR$ 65 = A. Now type in this program:

```
100 A = ASC("A")
120 B = ASC("AT")
140 A$ = "ATE"
160 C = ASC(A$)
180 PRINT A,B,C,
```

Now run this. The result should be:

```
65     65     65
```

This means that the ASC function returned, in each case, the CHR$ number 65 associated with A. If we wished to have a record of the numbers associated with each letter of a string, and not just the first letter, we can use the MID$ function as follows:

```
100 name$ = "VALERIE"
120 FOR count = 1 TO LEN(name$)
140 B$ = MID$(name$,count,1)
160 A = ASC(B$)
180 PRINT B$,A
200 NEXT count
```

This produces the CHR$ numbers for the letters of VALERIE as shown.

```
V       86
A       65
L       79
E       69
R       82
I       73
E       69
```

The STR$ function

This function acts as the opposite of the VAL function. That is, it takes a number and translates it into a string. This will not change how the set of characters making up the number looks on the screen, but it allows you to manipulate it by means of the various string formatting functions described earlier in the chapter. To illustrate how STR$ works, type in this program:

```
100 number = 44.25
120 word$ = STR$(number)
140 FOR count = 1 TO LEN (word$)
160 letter$ = MID$(word$,count,1)
180 PRINT letter$
```

In line 100, the variable number represents a number. Line 120 converts it into a string. The next three lines apply string formatting techniques to this string, which results in each separate character being isolated and printed. Run it and see if it works.

Ordering strings

It is often very useful to be able to put strings in alphabetical order. This is very simple because strings can be compared in exactly the same way as numbers using the signs > , = and < . When we find that A$ < B$, it means that, according to alphabetical order, A$ comes before B$. Type in this program and try it.

```
100 A$ = "AABC"
120 B$ = "ABCD"
140 IF A$ < B$ THEN PRINT A$,B$ ELSE PRINT B$,A$
```

Run this program and it should put the two strings A$ and B$ in correct alphabetical order. Now change lines 100 and 120 as shown:

```
100 INPUT "First word "A$
120 INPUT "Second word "B$
```

Now run the program, and type in whichever two words you choose. The program will put them in alphabetical order and print them. A routine to sort a longer list of words into alphabetical order is shown in the answers to the problems in Chapter 13.

INSTR

This function allows us to know whether or not one string is contained within another. For example we can use it to test whether or not the string US is contained in the string HOUSE. To do this type the following in directly and press the RETURN key.

```
PRINT INSTR("HOUSE", "US")
```

The response will be the number 3. This means that the second string is indeed a substring of the first, but also that it begins at the third letter of the first. Now try one where the answer is no. Type this in and press RETURN.

```
PRINT INSTR("HOUSE", "YOU")
```

The response is 0 which is an indication that the second string is not a substring of the first. (Always make sure that the second string is shorter than the first as there is a bug in the operating system which can lead to difficulties). Of course it is possible for the substring to be made up of a single letter, like this:

```
PRINT INSTR("ENVELOPE", "E")
```

The response to this is obviously 1 since E is the first letter of the word envelope. But there are other Es in the word, the next one being the fourth letter. Suppose we knew that the letter or word or substring that we wanted was in the second half of the word. We can tell the computer not to start looking until, for example, the third letter. Type this in:

```
PRINT INSTR("ENVELOPE", "E", 3)
```

The response is 4, which means that the fourth letter of the word is an E also. Now try this:

```
PRINT INSTR("ENVELOPE", "E", 5)
```

This time the answer is 8. We can also use variables to hold the strings as follows. This time we use a program as follows. Type it in and run it. The result will be 1.

```
100 MODE 7
120 one$ = "ENVELOPE"
140 two$ = "E"
160 PRINT INSTR(one$, two$)
```

We will now adapt this so that it locates all the occasions when the second string occurs in the first. First type in NEW and then this program:

```
100 MODE 7
120 INPUT' " What is the first string  ", one$
140 INPUT' " What is the second string  ", two$
160 IF LEN(two$) > LEN(one$) THEN PRINT "Substring too
    long." : GOTO 140
180 FOR count = 1 TO LEN(one$)
200 PRINT INSTR(one$, two$, count)
220 NEXT count
```

Now run this and respond as before with ENVELOPE for the string held in one$ (line 120) and with E for the string held in two$ (line 140). The loop in lines 180 to 220 will look for the letter E in the word ENVELOPE starting at the first letter, then at the second, and so on. The response will be 1, 4, 4, 4, 8, 8, 8, 8. The 1 refers to the first incidence of E, the 4 to the second and the 8 to the third.

STRING$

This is a facility for duplicating strings or for making a long string by joining together duplicates of a small one. Type this in:

```
100 MODE 7
120 unit$ = "X"
140 whole$ = STRING$(40, unit$)
160 PRINT whole$
```

The effect of line 140 is to produce a long string, whole$, made up of forty Xs joined together; that is forty versions of unit$ joined together. Run it and check this. Now type in NEW and this program.

```
100 MODE 7
120 INPUT' " What string do you wish to copy ", unit$
140 INPUT' " How many duplicates ", many
160 whole$ = STRING$(many, unit$)
180 PRINT whole$
```

Run this a few times and try different strings and numbers. For example try OXO followed by 8. (Remember that the maximum length of a word is 255 characters).

Problems

1. Use random numbers to select, from a deck of 52 cards, two poker hands each with five cards. The two hands should be presented on the screen each time. Remember to write a routine to check that any particular card has not been 'dealt' already.

2. Write a program for crossword puzzlers to help them find the answer to clues where all but one or two letters are known. The program should print on the screen every possible word that can be made by putting all the letters of the alphabet in the appropriate spaces. It should also allow users to decide whether they wish to use all 26 letters of the alphabet or just the 5 vowels.

3. Write a program which allows you to put in a passage of prose and then counts the number of occurrences of each letter of the alphabet within the passage. Use the word GET$ as the input device and provide responses which allow you to:

(a) Indicate when you have completed a passage.
(b) Abort a piece of work and begin again.
(c) Delete a mistake.

Use CHR$ and ASC to allow you to edit out spaces and punctuation marks.

CHAPTER 10
FORMATTING

Formatting with PRINT

We have already shown (Chapter 2) how the use of commas and semi- colons can place numbers and strings in particular columns on the screen. We now want to look a bit more closely at the word PRINT and how it can be used to change formatting. In most circumstances we will be using PRINT in those modes where the screen is forty columns wide and in this case the screen can be thought of as divided into four bands each of width ten columns. Each of these bands is called a field. However if you are using MODE 5 or MODE 2 then the screen is only twenty columns wide and in this case the screen is divided into two bands each of width ten columns. Also in MODE 0 and 3 the screen is eighty columns wide and is made up of eight bands or fields each of width ten columns.

As a demonstration of this type in this program:

```
100 CLS
120 INPUT' "Which mode ",mode
140 MODE mode
160 PRINT'' 1, 2, 3, 4, 5, 6, 7, 8
180 PRINT'' 1; 2; 3; 4; 5; 6; 7; 8
200 PRINT'' ;1; 2; 3; 4; 5; 6; 7; 8
220 PRINT'' ;1, 2, 3, 4, 5, 6, 7, 8
```

Run this a few times and change the mode each time and look carefully at the results.

You can alter this formatting very easily using a variable with the very odd title of '@%'. This is the symbol for 'at' followed by the percentage sign. As usual we will demonstrate how this works by using a short program. Type this in:

```
100 MODE 4
120 @% = &0000000A
140 PRINT' "1234567890123456789012345678901234567890"
160 P = 12.317
180 Q = 5.4869
200 R = 0.35271
220 S = 0.0182
240 PRINT' P, Q
260 PRINT' R, S
```

We will change line 120 to a variety of other forms and, in this way, we will try to demonstrate how to print numbers in a variety of ways. (Notice the A at the end of line 120). For this reason we have used four quite different numbers for P, Q, R and S and in lines 240 and 260 have printed them on the screen. Line 140 just prints the numbers 1 to 9, and then 0 for 10, four times in succession across the screen so that we can use this as a guide to check our formatting.

Now RUN this program and it will print all four numbers P, Q, R and S with their last digits on column 10 and on column 20. This is the normal printing format. Now change line 120 as follows and RUN the program again.

```
120 @% = &00000008
```

This time the field width is changed to 8 so that the last digit of each of the numbers P, Q, R and S appears on either column 8 or column 16. We will now look at this number following the sign '@%' in more detail. It begins with the symbol '&' and this is followed by a set of eight digits. (We will explain how A is a digit in a moment). These are thought of in groups of two, and indeed can be thought of as 4 distinct two-digit numbers set side by side. We will refer to these as, from the left, pair 1, pair 2, pair 3, and pair 4. The two-digit number on the extreme right, called pair 4, is used to determine the width of the field for formatting. The sign & is an indication to the computer that the number which follows is written in base sixteen or, simply, in hex. If you have not met this idea before it is described in Appendix B. The only thing we need to know here is that in base sixteen the first fifteen numbers are written as 1, 2, 3, 4, 5, 6, 7, 8, 9, A, B, C, D, E, F. That is A means 10, B means 11 and so on up to F which means 15. We then write sixteen as 10, seventeen as 11 and so on.

So let us suppose that we wished to print our number in fields of width twelve characters. Remember that C means twelve. So change pair 4, the final two-digit number on line 120, as follows and run the program again.

```
120@% = &0000000C
```

This time you will find that the last digits of the numbers A, B, C and D are printed on columns 12 and 24. Throughout the rest of this section we will put pair 4 as 0C, as shown above. We now consider the second-last of these four two digit numbers from line 120, that is pair 3.

This second-last two digit number, that is pair 3, controls the number of significant figures used when printing a number. To demonstrate this change line 120 again as follows, and then run the program.

```
120 @% = &0000030C
```

The result will look like this.

```
1234567890123456789012345678901234567890

        12.3        5.49

       0.353     1.82E-2
```

Notice that in each case the number retains 3 significant figures, and this includes correct rounding. However, there is a complication about this in that the behaviour of this two-digit number, pair 3 which controls the number of significant figures is influenced by pair 2 of the four two-digit numbers in line 120, that is the one that is second from the left. At the moment it is set at 00. Pair 2 represents the way in which numbers are to be formatted. There are 3 possible formats and these are represented by the numbers 00, 01, and 02. We will give an example of each in a moment.

When pair 2 = 00 numbers are formatted in the normal way, that is in the way they appear when the computer is switched on. This is described in more detail in chapter 7.

When pair 2 = 01 all numbers are written in exponent form, sometimes called 'scientific notation'. So for example 12.3 becomes 1.23E1 which means 1.23 multiplied by one 10.

When pair 2 = 02 then all numbers are printed with a fixed number of decimal places. The actual number is determined by pair 3. At the moment it is set at 03.

To demonstrate these three formats, change line 120 in succession to each of the following and run the program.

Remember that the four numbers being printed each time are entered as :

P = 12.317

Q = 5.4869

R = 0.35271

S = 0.0182

A. Format 1. When pair 2 = 00. This is called G or general format. Notice that three figures are retrieved from each number P, Q, R, S.

120 @% = &0000030C

Result 12.3 5.49

0.353 1.82E-2

B. Format 2. When pair 2 = 01. This is called E or exponent format. Again notice that three figures are retained.

120 @% = &0001030C

Result 1.23E1 5.49E0

3.53E-1 1.82E-2

C. Format 3. When pair 2 = 02. This is called F or fixed format. The effect of this is to produce a fixed number of figures after the decimal point.

120 @% = &0002030C

Result 12.317 5.487

0.353 0.018

The last of the four two digit pairs called pair 1, on the extreme left, is normally equal to 00. If it is changed to 01 it means that the function STR$ will acknowledge the effect of line 120. Otherwise it will not. This is described in the User Guide on page 358. We can summarize the effects of line 120 as follows. The variable @% is put equal to an 8 digit base-sixteen number as follows:

@% = AA BB CC DD

AA is usually 00, unless you wish to use STR$.

BB can be 00, 01 or 02 depending on how you want to format the numbers.

CC is the number of digits printed and this depends partially on the format chosen in BB.

DD determines the width of the fields across the screen.

Therefore @% = &00020307 would produce a fixed format (from 02) of three decimal places (from 03) printed on fields 7 columns wide (from 07).

Formatting with TAB

There are occasions when the PRINT statement by itself will not format the words or numbers on the screen in the way that we want. We can then use TAB which is short for TABULATION and this is always used with PRINT or INPUT. This allows us to be very precise about where on the screen to begin writing. Here is an example.

```
100 MODE 7
120 PRINT "Name" ; TAB(25) ; "Score" ; TAB(32) ; "Rank"
140 PRINT "Kerry Dunn" ; TAB(25) ; 70 ; TAB(32) ; 4
```

The screen columns are numbered from the left, and the first one is numbered 0, the second one is number 1, and so on until the last column which will be numbered 19,39 or 79 depending on the mode. So in this example, line 120 prints the word Name on the left of the screen. It then uses TAB(25) to move the cursor out 25 columns from the left edge of the screen to column 24, and prints the word Score on columns 25 to 28. Finally it uses TAB(32) to move the cursor to column 31 and prints the word Rank in columns 32 to 35. The use of TAB(25) and TAB(32) again on line 140 makes sure that Kerry Dunn, the score 70, and the rank 4, are all printed starting on exactly the same columns, as the headings on the line above. Now add these lines to the program:

```
160 PRINT "Julie Forde" ; TAB(25) ; 90 ; TAB(32) ; 1
180 PRINT "Cathy Ferguson" ; TAB(25) ; 71 ; TAB(32) ; 3
```

Now RUN it again. You will notice that the names are aligned on the left. That is, the first letter of each name is lined up with the one above. It would be interesting on some occasions to have a technique to align them on the right with the last letters in the same column.

To do this we must find the length of each name, but because the lines get a bit cluttered we will first put each word and name in a variable, as follows. (First type in NEW, and then these lines):

```
100 MODE 7
120 a$ = "Name" : b$ = "Score" : c$ = "Rank"
140 n1$ = "Kerry Dunn"
160 n2$ = "Julie Forde"
180 n3$ = "Cathy Ferguson"
```

We will now find the lengths of the names as follows:

```
200 a = LEN(a$)
220 n1 = LEN(n1$)
240 n2 = LEN(n2$)
260 n3 = LEN(n3$)
```

We then use the TAB function to move the cursor out a fixed number of spaces, say 20, less the length of the string in question, here called either a, n1, n2, or n3. This will make each name start on such a column so that they all end on column 19. So the print part of the program now looks like this:

```
300 PRINT TAB(20-a); a$; TAB(25); b$; TAB(32); c$
320 PRINT TAB(20-n1); n1$; TAB(25); 70; TAB(32); 4
340 PRINT TAB(20-n2); n2$; TAB(25); 90; TAB(32); 1
360 PRINT TAB(20-n3); n3$; TAB(25); 60; TAB(32); 5
```

We can also use TAB to center a program heading, that is to place it in the centre of the top of the screen. This was discussed on page 44 . Remember that in MODE 7 there are 40 spaces across the top of the screen. First we use the LEN function to find the length of the heading. Then subtract this length from 40, and divide by two. Here is an example. (First type in NEW):

```
100 MODE 7
120 title$ = "**Formatting**"
140 PRINT TAB((40 - LEN (title$))/2); title$
```

We can use the TAB function to draw a sine curve as follows. The main axis lies down the middle of the screen, so if you wished to see this curve in the normal way, you would have to turn the monitor on its side. First we will type in the program and then discuss it line by line.

```
100 MODE 7
120 FOR X = 0 TO 4 * PI STEP .2
140 Y = SIN X
160 Y = 20 * Y + 20
180 PRINT TAB(Y) "*"
200 NEXT X
```

Line 100 clears the screen. Lines 120 and 200 together make a loop which takes X in small steps of 0.2 from 0 to 4 * PI. Line 140 puts Y equal to SIN X each time. However, you will remember that SIN X always lies between -1 and +1. That is the range looks like this:

- 1   - 0.5   0   + 0.5   + 1

If we now multiply each number in the range by 20 it looks like this:

- 20   - 10   0   + 10   + 20

Now add 20 to each of the numbers above and it looks like this:

0   10   20   30   40

which is almost exactly the range across the screen. (In fact the range is 0 to 39 but the error involved will make little if any difference when drawing curves). So line 160 scales up each value according to this pattern : that is, each value of Y is multiplied by 20 and then 20 is added to it. Line 180 then moves the cursor out Y spaces, using TAB(Y) and prints a star on the next space.

Now run this program a few times to see what happens. Remember that the range from 0 to 4 * PI in line 120 represents two full cycles of the curve. You can experiment with this by changing the range and by changing the step used. To do this, change line 120 as shown and type in lines 50 and 60.

```
50  INPUT' " Number of PI ", number
60  INPUT' " Step to be used ", step
120 FOR X = 0 TO number * PI STEP step
```

Now run the program, and when 'Number of PI' appears on the screen, type in 2. Then when 'Step to be used' appears, type in 0.1. Run it a number of times, and each time try different numbers.

It is also possible to use TAB with the word INPUT as well as the word PRINT. In fact the rules governing spacing and formatting with INPUT are more or less identical to those with PRINT. Here is an example.

```
100 MODE 7
120 INPUT TAB(10) "Put in a number "; number
140 PRINT TAB(10) "The number is   "; number
```

All the work done so far with TAB has been in MODE 7 where the screen is 40 columns wide. This is true also of MODES 1, 4 and 6. It is as well to remember that in MODES 2 and 5 the screen is only 20 columns wide and that in MODE 0 and 3 the screen is stretched to 80 columns wide. Apart from the need to remember that the numbers are different, TAB does not behave in any way differently in these other modes.

TAB(column, row)

Another form of TAB allows the user to specify not just the column but also the row on the screen where a word or number is to be placed. Here is an example. (First type in NEW to remove the last program).

```
100 MODE 7
120 PRINT TAB(5,0); "This is the top."
140 PRINT TAB(5,12); "This is the middle."
160 PRINT TAB(5,24); "This is the bottom."
```

Now type in RUN and press RETURN and look what happens. Notice that the top row of the screen is now numbered 0 and the bottom row is numbered 25 (or 31). Now type in NEW again and then this program.

```
100 MODE 7
120 PRINT "First line."
160 PRINT TAB(0,0) "Short time"
```

Now type in RUN and press RETURN. The words 'Short time' will appear at the top left corner of the screen, but the words 'First line' will seem not to appear at all. To demonstrate what is happening, put in an extra line:

```
140 Z = GET
```

Now run the program again. First the screen will clear, then the words 'First line' will appear, from line 120. Now press the space bar (line 140) and watch the screen carefully. The words 'Short time' (line 160) will replace 'First line'. RUN this a few times until you are clear about what is happening. Remember that TAB(0,0) makes sure that the words appear at the top left corner.

SPC function

This function can be very useful in formatting because it allows us to make a specified space between two columns. Most of the things that it does can be achieved using the special forms of PRINT, but sometimes this is simpler. It is most useful when you have a set of numbers arranged in a set of fixed columns with all the numbers in each column containing the same number of digits. Here is an example:

```
100 CLS
120 FOR num = 10 TO 24
140 PRINT num ; SPC(5) num + 100; SPC(5) num + 1000
160 NEXT num
```

Type this in and try it. This technique is only useful if we are dealing with numbers that are of a specified width. For example, if we are dealing with examination results, expressed as percentages, we might assume that they would all lie between 10 and 99. Then, if we want to list the results with the marks on the left and the names on the right, the SPC function is a very useful way of formatting these results. However, it has to be typed in along with each line, so it can be a bit cumbersome. Type in the example below, first remembering to clear the old program:

```
100 MODE 7
120 PRINT 34; SPC(8) "Scullion, F."
140 PRINT 35; SPC(8) "McGouran, G."
```

Extending decimal places

We have already shown how the computer writes decimals to at most nine significant figures. It is sometimes necessary, especially in some mathematical investigations, to know a great many more figures than this. The following program divides a number X by a number Y, and gives as many decimal figures as you wish. First type it in and then read the explanation below.

```
100 MODE 7
120 INPUT' "What is the top line ", top
140 INPUT' "What is the bottom line ", bot
160 INPUT' "how many decimal places ", dec
180 num = top DIV bot
200 PRINT TAB(0,12) ; num ; ".";
220 top = top MOD bot
240 FOR count = 1 TO dec
260 top = 10 * top
280 IF top = 0 THEN count = dec : GOTO 340 : REM end of
    loop
```

```
300 num = top DIV bot
320 top = top MOD bot
340 PRINT num;
360 NEXT count
```

Lines 100 to 160 clear the screen, input top and bot for the fraction and input dec for the number of decimal figures required. Lines 180 and 200 produce the number to be written in front of the decimal point and write it down with the decimal point. Lines 240 and 360 make a loop to produce the required number of decimal points. Lines 260, 300 and 320 combine to find the next decimal figure and to find the new value of top ready for the next loop. If the division has been exact, this is checked by line 280.

Now run the program and input the fraction 15/13. That is, input 15 for top and 13 for bot. Then input 20 for dec. It would be interesting to adapt this program to check when a full cycle has been completed and the true decimal representation of the fraction has been achieved.

VDU 5 and underlining

We have already shown how to use VDU 5 to make the two cursors, text and graphics, come together. Two of the side effects of using VDU 5 are that the screen does not scroll up as normal, and when an attempt is made to write on a line that already contains symbols, these are overwritten and not removed. Here is an example. Type it in and try it:

```
100 MODE 4
120 VDU 5
140 MOVE 100, 700
160 PRINT "llllllll" : REM lower case L
180 MOVE 100, 700
200 PRINT "--------" : REM same key as =
220 VDU 4
```

We can use this to underline a sentence. Change the above program as follows:

```
160 PRINT "This sentence is underlined."
200 PRINT "____________________________" : REM same key as
```

Problems

1. Using some of the formatting techniques, write a program to allow you to input successive items from a shopping list or

bill. For each item, there should be three other inputs: that is, price of each; percentage discount; number of each. The program should calculate a totals column and a final overall total. The complete set of information should be presented in formatted columns on the screen.

2. Write a stock-keeping program which allows you to create a list of items in stock, the number of each in stock, and the number at which reordering is necessary. This information should be presented on the screen after each entry in a suitably tabulated form. There should be a further routine to allow you to update the number of each item and this should include a message about the extent to which each item is above or below the reorder number. Finally, it should be possible to save and recover the list with a tape.

CHAPTER 11
GRAPHICS AND COLOR

Introduction

We have tried to develop introductory ideas about graphics and color in many of the preceding chapters. In this chapter we will try to organise these ideas and develop graphics and color a bit further. For most of this work we will use the PLOT statement. The great variety of ways in which this can be used was described in detail on page 129, but in order to develop a systematic approach we will use only seven of these. Essentially these allow us to do the following:

> Move the cursor.
> Plot a point and remove a point.
> Plot a line and remove a line.
> Draw a triangle filled with color and remove the triangle again.

In order to remove points, lines and triangles we will simply redraw them in the screen background color.

PLOT

The seven forms of the PLOT statement are now described in turn:

(a) Move the cursor. PLOT 4,X,Y or MOVE X,Y. This moves the cursor to the point (X, Y) but puts no mark on the screen. It is used so often that the special word MOVE can be used as a substitute for PLOT 4.

(b) Draw a line. PLOT 5,X,Y or DRAW X,Y. This draws a straight line from the last point plotted to the point (X, Y). It too has a special word DRAW which can be used in place of PLOT 5.

(c) Remove a line. PLOT 7,X,Y. This does exactly the same as PLOT 5,X,Y but it does it in the screen background color and so removes any line already there.

(d) Plot a point. PLOT 69,X,Y. This moves the cursor to the point (X, Y) and plots a point there.

(e) Remove a point. PLOT 71,X,Y. This moves the cursor to the point (X, Y) - exactly the same as PLOT 69,X,Y - but the point is plotted in the screen background color and so the effect is to remove any point already there.

(f) Draw a triangle. PLOT 85,X,Y. This uses the two previously plotted points along with (X,Y) to produce a colored triangle.

(g) Remove a triangle. PLOT 87,X,Y. This does exactly the same as PLOT 85,X,Y but since it uses the screen background color, it effectively removes any triangle already there.

We will now write a short program which demonstrates each of these in turn. It begins as follows:

```
100 MODE 5
120 PLOT 4, 800, 100 : REM same as MOVE
140 PLOT 5, 100, 800 : REM same as DRAW
```

Type this in and run it. Line 120 moves the cursor to the point (800,100) and line 140 joins this point to the point (100,800). We now want to remove this line, so add those lines to the program.

```
160 PRINT TAB(1,1); "Press a key" : Z = GET
180 PLOT 4, 800, 100
200 PLOT 7, 100, 800
```

Now run this. It will first draw the line, and then when you press a key lines 180 and 200 will remove the line again. Notice that we have used PLOT 4 and PLOT 5 here instead of MOVE and DRAW. In the future however we will use MOVE and DRAW.

We now want to change this program a little so that it will plot a point at (100,800) and then remove the point. We need only change two lines, as follows:

```
140 PLOT 69, 100, 800
200 PLOT 71, 100, 800
```

(For this exercise we do not need line 180, but we will need it in a moment so do not remove it). Run this new version and line 140 will plot a point and line 200 will remove it again.

Finally we want to draw a triangle and remove it. This time we must change four lines as follows:

```
120 MOVE 100, 100 : MOVE 800, 100
140 PLOT 85, 100, 800
180 MOVE 100, 100 : MOVE 800, 100
200 PLOT 87, 100, 800
```

In lines 120 and 180 we must specify the first two corners of the triangle, so that in line 140 the third corner is used to complete the triangle. Run this and check that it works.

Graphics color

We wish to use color in this section so we will use MODE 5 which has four colors. This means that what follows can be used with both Model A and Model B versions of the computer. All of this can be easily adapted for other modes with color and, in particular, MODE 2 with its sixteen colors will be discussed by itself at the end of the chapter.

The word used to generate color for work with graphics is GCOL and this is short for Graphics Color. It can be used to set both foreground and background colors and we will demonstrate this with some examples. First type in the following.

```
100 MODE 5
180 FOR forecol = 0 TO 3
200 GCOL 0, forecol
220 MOVE 100, 100
240 DRAW 1000, 700
260 PRINT TAB(1,1); "Press a key"
280 Z = GET
300 NEXT forecol
```

Lines 180 and 300 use the variable forecol (that is, foreground color) to set up a loop which changes the colour number from 0 through to 3. Remember that 0 is black, 1 is red, 2 is yellow and 3 is white. Line 200 used GCOL 0, forecol to establish the foreground graphics color each time. The first number after GCOL is almost always zero, and the second is the number of the color that we wish to use to draw lines. (This first number after GCOL is discussed in greater detail on page 224). The two lines 220 and 240 draw a line from the point (100, 100) to the point (1000, 700). Run the program and check that the color of the line changes each time. It begins as black so nothing shows the first time.

Now we wish to change the background color as well. For this we use GCOL followed by zero again; but the second number is 128 for black, 129 for red, 130 for yellow and 131 for white. To demonstrate this add these lines to the program.

```
120 FOR backcol = 128 TO 131
140 GCOL 0, backcol
160 CLG
320 NEXT backcol
340 MODE 7
```

We use lines 120 and 320 together to loop through the background colors which are in the variable backcol. Line 140 establishes this color each time and line 160 changes the whole screen to this color. Finally line 340 brings the screen back to normal. Run it and check that it works.

Plotting points

First of all we will look at plotting points. Later we will look at lines and triangles. The first example allows us to use the four arrowed keys on the keyboard to move a point about the screen left, right, up and down. This effectively turns the screen into a sketch pad. We begin as follows. First type in NEW to remove any old program and then type this in.

```
100 MODE 4
140 X=500 : Y=500 : REM starting point.
320 PLOT 69, X, Y
```

Line 140 establishes the starting point in roughly the middle of the screen and line 320 plots this first point. Remember from page 133 that PLOT 69 puts a single point on the screen. We now need a line which will accept input from the keyboard but will not stop and wait for this. We showed on page 125 that the word to be used to do this is INKEY (number) where the variable number is an indication of how long the computer will wait for an input from the keyboard. In this case we will use INKEY(0). So the line looks like this:

```
200 point = INKEY(0)
```

We now wish to test the input from the keyboard for one of the four arrow keys. The table on page 497 of the User Guide shows all the codes associated with the keyboard. The numbers for the four arrow keys are:

```
Left        136
Right       137
Down        138
Up          139
```

But, in order to stop these keys simply moving the cursor about - which is their normal role - we must use one of the FX statements. (See User Guide, page 418). To turn off normal cursor movements we need *FX4,1 and to turn it on again we need *FX4,0. So we now add these lines:

```
120 *FX4,1 : REM enables direction keys.
220 IF point = 136 THEN X = X - 4 : REM move left.
240 IF point = 137 THEN X = X + 4 : REM move right.
260 IF point = 138 THEN Y = Y - 4 : REM move down.
280 IF point = 139 THEN Y = Y + 4 : REM move up.
360 *FX4,0 : REM returns direction keys.
```

This of course only moves the point once and we want to move it repeatedly, so we need a loop and a test to know when we are finished. So we add these lines which are explained in the next paragraph.

```
160 test = 0 : REM to test later for end of program.
180 REPEAT
300 IF point = 83 OR point = 115 THEN test = 1 : REM
program ends.
340 UNTIL test = 1
380 PRINT "Now finished."
```

Line 160 introduces the variable test which will be checked for the program ending. Line 300 checks if the letter S for STOP (capital S is 83 and lower-case s is 115) has been pressed. If it has then the variable test becomes one. Lines 180 and 340 make a loop which ends when test is one. Type all this in and then use the arrowed keys to draw patterns on the screen. The complete program looks like this:

```
100 MODE 4
120 *FX4,1 : REM enables direction keys.
140 X = 500 : Y = 500 : REM starting point.
160 test = 0 : REM to test later for end of program.
180 REPEAT
200 point = INKEY(0)
220 IF point = 136 THEN X = X - 4 : REM move left.
240 IF point = 137 THEN X = X + 4 : REM move right.
260 IF point = 138 THEN Y = Y - 4 : REM move down.
280 IF point = 139 THEN Y = Y + 4 : REM move up.
300 IF point = 83 OR point = 115 THEN test = 1 : REM
    program ends.
320 PLOT 69, X, Y
340 UNTIL test = 1
```

```
360 *FX4,0 : REM returns direction keys.
380 PRINT "Now finished."
```

We can change this program quite dramatically by adding two further lines to it, as follows:

```
210 oldx = X : oldy = Y : REM retains old values of X and Y
330 PLOT 71, oldx, oldy : REM removes old point
```

Type these in and run the program. This time the point moves about the screen but does not leave a trace behind it. That is, it moves like a ball. This gives an indication, which we will develop further later, of how to make objects move about the screen. This one moves rather slowly and we could speed it up by changing the number 4 on each of the lines 220, 240, 260 and 280 to 8 or 12, or even larger. Try some of these.

Drawing a circle

The program for drawing a circle is slightly more mathematical than usual and so a little bit of extra explanation is necessary; but even if you don't understand all of it you can type it in and see if it works. You can then change bits of the program to make the circle smaller or bigger, or with a different center.

To draw a circle we need to know the following things:

(a) Where is its center? We can choose this: and because we want, on this occasion, to draw as big a circle as possible we will put the center of the circle near the center of the screen, so the first line to consider is:

```
140 xcenter = 640 : ycenter = 512
```

where xcenter is the number we go across and ycenter is the number we go up to get the center of the circle. This is not the first line of the program. We will add bits to this as we go along.

(b) What is the length of the radius? This, of course, depends on where we put the center. Remember that the screen is 1024 units high so the maximum possible value for the radius is 512. To be on the safe side we will make it a bit smaller:

```
160 radius = 500
```

(c) The line making up the actual outline of the circle will not be a continuous line, but a series of dots. We must choose the number of dots to use. This is a matter of trial and error, and for our large circle we chose 200 and call it nopoints, that is number of points.

```
120 nopoints = 200
```

(d) With the usual introductory lines, the program so far looks like this:

```
100 MODE 4
120 nopoints = 200
140 xcenter = 640 : ycenter = 512
160 radius = 500
```

Make sure that your version on the screen looks like this. The next bit involves some trigonometry. Each point on the circumference of a circle can be located with reference to the center of the circle as shown in this diagram.

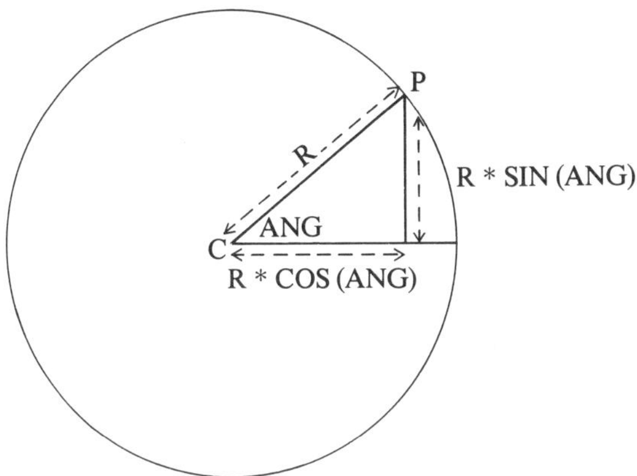

We have chosen the center in line 140, and the radius in line 160. The angle will be different for each of the 200 points. The length of the two lines which determine the position of P from the center are shown as radius*COS(angle) and radius * SIN(angle). So if we can compute these two lengths for each of the 200 positions, and in each case add them to the centre numbers, then we can use PLOT 69 to put a dot on each. Fortunately the computer does this for us.

The number of points, i.e. 200 has been stored in nopoints, so we can set up a loop:

```
180 FOR count = 1 TO nopoints
```

Now we need the angle size (called angle) which changes for each point. Since an angle of 2 * PI means one full revolution (that is a circle) then the angles we want will be one twohundredth of this, and then two twohundredths of this, and then three, and so on up to 200 twohundredths (that is a full circle) have been calculated. (For an explanation of PI see page 318 of the User Guide).

```
That is (2 * PI) * (1/200)
and     (2 * PI) * (2/200)

down to

        (2 * PI) * (200/200)
```

Now since count runs from 1 to 200 (in line 180) and since nopoints is 200, we can express all this as:

```
200 angle = (2 * PI) * (count / nopoints)
```

We then compute the coordinates of the points corresponding to each angle:

```
220 X = radius * COS(angle)
240 Y = radius * SIN(angle)
```

We then plot each point, remembering to add the coordinates of the center (xcenter,ycenter) to each point.

```
260 PLOT 69, X + xcenter, Y + ycenter
```

Finally we close the loop:

```
280 NEXT count
```

So the second part of the program looks like this:

```
180 FOR count = 1 TO nopoints
200 angle = (2 * PI) * (count/nopoints)
220 X = radius * COS(angle)
240 Y = radius * SIN(angle)
260 PLOT 69, X + xcenter, Y + ycenter
280 NEXT count
```

List your program and check it with this. Now run it to see if it works. Remember that you can change the center, the radius and the number of points.

PLOT and lines

Do not type in NEW to remove this program as we are now going to adapt it so that it can be used to demonstrate how to make a circle by drawing lines rather than by plotting points.

```
260 PLOT 5, X + xcenter, Y + ycenter
```

(Remember that DRAW is an alternative to PLOT 5). Run this and note that the first line is drawn from the bottom left of the screen. This suggests a way of using complete lines to draw the circle. Put in this extra line:

```
250 MOVE xcenter, ycenter
```

Now run the program again and this time the program joins the center of the circle to each point each time so that the circle looks like a wheel with a great many spokes.

We now add a few more changes so that this spoked circle is drawn in different colors. Change line 100 to MODE 5 as shown and add the other lines.

```
100 MODE 5
170 FOR col = 1 TO 4
175 GCOL 0, col
300 NEXT col
```

Disappearing lines

We now want to illustrate how lines can be drawn and then disappear again so that a different sort of movement is involved. The program begins like this:

```
100 MODE 4
120 X = 0 : Y = 500 : REM starting point.
140 inc = 200 : REM change in Y.
160 MOVE X, Y
180 X = X + 50 : Y = Y + inc : REM new position.
200 DRAW X, Y : REM first line.
```

Type this in and run it. It draws the first line on the screen, and it runs, at an angle from the left middle of the screen, up a short distance. We now want it to come down again and over, and so zig-zag across the screen. So we need a loop as follows:

```
220 REPEAT
260 inc = -inc : REM change Y direction to down.
280 MOVE X, Y
300 X = X + 50 : Y = Y + inc
340 DRAW X, Y
400 UNTIL X > 1280
```

Run this and it will produce the required zig-zag line across the screen. We now want to remove each section of the line as soon as we have drawn the next one. To do this we must add lines to the program as follows:

```
240 oldx = X : oldy = Y : REM remember old positions.
360 MOVE X - 100, Y + inc : REM moves to beginning of last
   line.
380 PLOT 7, oldx, oldy : REM removes last line.
```

This does what we wish but it does it very quickly so we finally put in a delay as follows:

```
320 Z = INKEY(50)
```

Type in RUN and watch the section of the line move across the screen.

PLOT and triangles

We will now use a similar routine to draw a square in the bottom left corner of the screen and then move it diagonally up towards the top right corner. First type in NEW to remove the old program. This program begins like this:

```
100 MODE 4
120 X = 0 : Y = 0
140 incx = 100 : incy = 100
200 MOVE X, Y : MOVE X + incx, Y
220 PLOT 85, X, Y + incy : PLOT 85, X + incx, Y + incy
```

Run this and it should produce a white square in the bottom left corner. This square is made up of two triangles both produced by the line 220. We now add these lines to make this square move:

```
160 REPEAT
240 X = X + incx : Y = Y + incy
340 UNTIL Y > 1200
```

Type this in and the program will now make a staircase of white squares along the diagonal of the screen. All that remains is to remove each square before drawing the next so as to produce the illusion of movement.

```
300 MOVE X - incx, Y - incy : MOVE X, Y-incy
320 PLOT 87, X - incx, Y : PLOT 87, X, Y
```

When this is run the program works, but too quickly, so enter this delay line.

```
260 Z = INKEY(20) : REM short delay
```

Finally add a couple of REM lines and the program is complete as shown below.

```
100 MODE 4
120 X = 0 : Y = 0
140 incx = 100 : incy = 100
160 REPEAT
180 REM draw square.
200 MOVE X, Y : MOVE X + incx, Y
220 PLOT 85, X, Y + incy : PLOT 85, X + incx, Y + incy
240 X = X + incx : Y = Y + incy
260 Z = INKEY(20) : REM short delay
280 REM remove square.
300 MOVE X - incx, Y - incy : MOVE X, Y - incy
320 PLOT 87, X - incx, Y : PLOT 87, X, Y
340 UNTIL Y > 1200
```

Drawing bar graphs

We will now use the PLOT facilities and the graphics colors to write a program to produce bar graphs. We need to use all of the following three procedures.

(a) A procedure called PROCinputdata that allows us to input the data that will be used to draw the bar graph. The questions we need to ask include:

(i) How many bars will the graph have? We will use this information tocalculate the width of a bar by dividing it into the width of the screen. We will also use it in a FOR loop to invite the input of all the data.

(ii) What is the largest of the data inputs? We will divide the height of the screen by this so that we can have a height-unit. Then each data input will be multiplied by this height-unit. In this way we will make full use of the height of the screen each time we draw a graph.

(iii) What is the name of each bar? This is needed so that we can label it.

(b) A procedure called PROCdrawgraph to draw the graph. This will use PLOT 85, which produces triangles, and each bar will be made of two triangles placed side by side. We must now decide whether or not we wish to use color. This depends to some extent on whether we are using Model A or Model B of the computer. Consider each in turn:

(i) Using Model A means that, for color, we must use MODE 5. But in this mode the text screen is only 20 columns wide, so each text character is very wide and so labelling a graph is surprisingly difficult. This means that if we want color we must use MODE 5 and although we will label the graph, it will not look very well. If we are more interested in the labelling than in the color then we should use MODE 4. The program that we write will allow the user to choose between these.

(ii) Using Model B there is no problem. For color with good labelling use MODE 1. For colour with less good labelling use MODE 2 and have sixteen colors available. For black-and-white use MODE 0 or MODE 4.

The program will be written for the Model A machine to begin with, but later we will show how to adapt it for a Model B. For color we will use GCOL.

(c) A procedure called PROClabelgraph that allows us to label the graph.

The program begins as follows. We have used REM statements here and there to help us remember what each part is doing, but you can leave these out if you wish.

```
100 DIM data(20), label$(20)
120 MODE 7
140 INPUT'' "Which MODE (4 or 5)  ",mode
160 IF mode <> 4 OR mode <> 5 THEN 140
180 PROCinputdata
200 MODE mode
220 PROCdrawgraph
240 PROClabelgraph
260 END
```

These introductory lines describe the complete program and make it very clear what we are doing. We will look at it line by line.

Line 100 books space for twenty pieces of data and for twenty labels, one for each bar of the graph.

Line 120 clears the screen and allows all the screen writing and input work to be done in this clear mode.

Line 140 invites the user to choose between modes 4 and 5 and the answer is stored in the variable mode.

Line 160 ensures that either MODE 4 or MODE 5 is chosen.

Line 180 calls the input-data procedure which will invite the user to put into the computer the data necessary to draw the graph.

Line 200 uses MODE to change to either MODE 4 or MODE 5. This statement is put here and not inside the graph-drawing procedure because it is not permitted to change a MODE inside a PROCEDURE.

Line 220 calls the graph drawing procedure.

Line 240 calls the graph labelling procedure.

Line 260 ends the program.

We must now write the three procedures described above. These are:

(1) to input the data;
(2) to draw the graphs;
(3) to label the graph.

Bar graph procedures

We now look at each of these three procedures in turn. The first one is called PROCinputdata. In this we use the TAB function to place the questions on the screen. We also use a number of variables for the first time in this procedure. They are as follows:

bars	This represents the number of bars to be drawn in the graph.
data	The data to be used in drawing the bars will be stored in this array.
count	This is used in loops to count the number of cycles.
big	This is used to hold the value of the largest piece of data. It is used for scaling purposes.
label$	The labels to be printed on each bar will be stored in this array.

The procedure begins like this:

```
280 DEF PROCinputdata
300 CLS
320 PRINT TAB(0,4); "How many bars will the graph have?"
340 PRINT TAB(15,6); : INPUT bars
350 IF bars < 1 OR bars > 20 THEN 300
360 PRINT TAB(0,8); "Input the data for the bars 1 at a
    time"
380 FOR count = 1 TO bars
400 PRINT'' "Bar no.  "; count; : INPUT "  ",data(count)
420 NEXT count
```

This is all fairly straightforward. Line 400 uses spaces to make the screen more legible in a couple of places. (For example, after the words Bar no.). The rest of this procedure looks like this.

```
440 INPUT''' "What is the largest of the data  ",big
460 PRINT'' "Input labels for the bars 1 at a time."
480 FOR count = 1 TO bars
500 PRINT'' "Bar no.  "; count; : INPUT "  ", label$(count)
520 NEXT count
540 ENDPROC
```

This is almost a rerun of the first part except that on this occasion we are putting in labels. The COPY key is very useful when typing lines like this .

The next procedure actually draws the graph. It tries to ensure that the whole screen is used for the graph no matter how large or small or varied the data is; it leaves a left margin for the axes so that appropriate numbers can be put along the side; finally it leaves space along the bottom for the labels.

In order to ensure that the whole screen is used we divide the number of bars into the screen width, which we take to be 1000, and call the result width. This number will in fact be used for the width of each bar on the graph. This means that no matter how many bars there are they will all have the same width. Obviously the more bars there are the narrower each will be. We use the integer division symbol DIV for this since decimals are not needed. We then than turn to the height of the screen. This is a slightly more complicated procedure. We want the largest of the bars to stretch from the top to the bottom of the screen (more or less). We take this total height to be 900 and divide this by big the variable representing the largest bar as produced by line 440. We use normal division this time because the result, which we call heightunit, will be used to multiply each data value so as to scale each from 0 to 900. The procedure begins as follows:

```
560 DEF PROCdrawgraph
580 width = 1000 DIV bars : REM width of a bar
600 heightunit = 900 / big : REM one unit of height
620 count = 0 : REM counts bars
640 col = 0 : REM used with GCOL for colors
```

Each bar is produced by drawing two triangles. The technique used to do this is demonstrated in the diagram below.

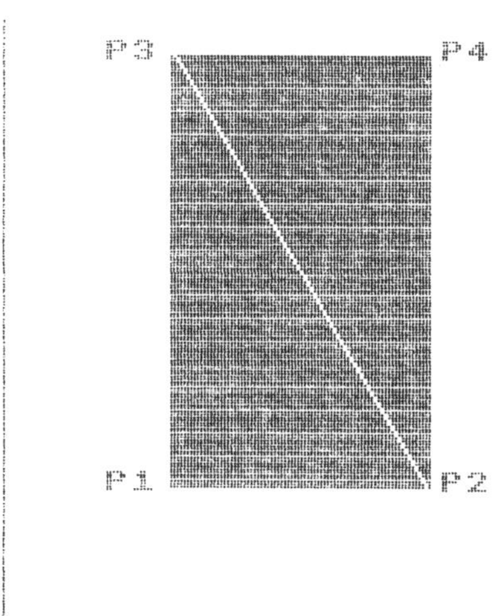

The four corners of the diagram are labelled P1, P2, P3 and P4. and this represents the order in which we plot them. The program lines look like this.

1. MOVE to P1

2. MOVE to P2

3, PLOT 85 with P3

4. PLOT 85 with P4

We will also ensure that there is a left margin by adding 150 to each value of X and so moving everything over 150 points to the right. This part of the procedure looks like this. (We have left some lines out for the monent).

```
660 FOR X = 150 TO 150 + (bars - 1) * width STEP width
680 count = count + 1 : REM counts bars
780 MOVE X + 10, 50 : REM the point P1
800 MOVE (X + width) - 10, 50 : REM the point P2
820 PLOT 85, X + 10, 50 + heightunit * data(count) : REM
    the point P3
840 PLOT 85, (X + width) - 10, 50 + heightunit *
    data(count) : REM the     point P4
860 NEXT X
880 ENDPROC
```

This looks complicated but it is really quite simple. The +10 and -10 that appear on lines 780 to 840 are there to make sure that there is a space between each bar. The Y value of 50 represents the space at the bottom of the screen for labels.

Some lines were left out to avoid confusion and are now shown below. They must now be typed in with the rest.

```
700 col = col + 1 : REM changes the color of each bar
720 IF col = 4 THEN col = 1 : REM avoids black on black
740 IF mode = 4 THEN 780 : REM no color
760 GCOL 0, col : REM produces color
```

This program should now work in that it will draw the bars of the graph if the data is fed in. But we still have to write the procedure for labelling the graph. It begins as follows:

```
900  DEF PROClabelgraph
920  VDU 5 : REM joins two cursors
940  count = 0 : REM counts bars
960  FOR X = 0 TO (bars-1) * width STEP width
980  count = count + 1
1000 MOVE X + 160, 100 + heightunit * data(count) : REM
     tops of bars
1020 PRINT; data(count) : REM labels bars with numbers
1040 MOVE X + 160, 30 : REM bottoms of bars
1060 PRINT label$(count) : REM labels bars with words
1080 NEXT X
```

This part of the procedure prints the numbers on the top of the bars and the labels along the bottom. In line 920 VDU 5 is used to join the two cursors and make this labelling easier. The last part of the procedure looks like this:

```
1100 FOR Y = 0 TO 10
1120 MOVE 0, 50 + Y * 90 : REM moves up left side.
1140 PRINT; INT(Y * big / 10) : REM labels left side with
     numbers.
1160 NEXT Y
1180 VDU 4 : REM separates cursors again.
1200 ENDPROC
```

This simply divides the left side of the screen, that is the Y axis into ten divisions and labels them with numbers ranging in equal steps from 0 to big. The complete program looks like this

```
100  DIM data(20), label$(20)
120  MODE 7
140  INPUT'' "Which MODE (4 or 5)  ",mode
160  IF mode <> 4 AND mode <> 5 THEN 140
180  PROCinputdata
200  MODE mode
220  PROCdrawgraph
240  PROClabelgraph
260  END
280  DEF PROCinputdata
300  CLS
```

```
320  PRINT TAB(0,4); "How many bars will the graph have"
340  PRINT TAB(15,6); : INPUT bars
350  IF bars < 1 OR bars > 20 THEN 300
360  PRINT TAB(0,8); "Input the data for the bars 1 at a
     time"
380  FOR count = 1 TO bars
400  PRINT'' "Bar no.  "; count; : INPUT "  ",data(count)
420  NEXT count
440  INPUT''' "What is the largest of the data  ",big
460  PRINT'' "Input labels for the bars 1 at a time."
480  FOR count = 1 TO bars
500  PRINT'' "Bar no.  "; count ; : INPUT "  ",
     label$(count)
520  NEXT count
540  ENDPROC
560  DEF PROCdrawgraph
580  width = 1000 DIV bars : REM width of a bar
600  heightunit = 900 / big : REM one unit of height
620  count = 0 : REM counts bars
640  col = 0 : REM used with GCOL for colors
660  FOR X = 150 TO 150 + (bars - 1) * width STEP width
680  count = count + 1 : REM counts bars
700  col = col + 1 : REM changes the color of each bar
720  IF col = 4 THEN col = 1 : REM avoids black on black
740  IF mode = 4 THEN 780 : REM no color
760  GCOL 0, col : REM produces color
780  MOVE X + 10, 50 : REM the point P1
800  MOVE (X + width) - 10, 50 : REM the point P2
820  PLOT 85, X + 10, 50 + heightunit * data(count) : REM
     the point P3
840  PLOT 85, (X + width) - 10, 50 + heightunit *
     data(count) : REM the point P4
860  NEXT X
880  ENDPROC
900  DEF PROClabelgraph
920  VDU 5 : REM joins two cursors
940  count = 0 : REM counts bars
960  FOR X = 0 TO (bars-1) * width STEP width
980  count = count + 1
1000 MOVE X + 160, 100 + heightunit * data(count) : REM
     tops of bars
1020 PRINT; data(count) : REM labels bars with numbers
1040 MOVE X + 160, 30 : REM bottoms of bars
1060 PRINT label$(count) : REM labels bars with words
1080 NEXT X
1100 FOR Y = 0 TO 10
1120 MOVE 0, 50 + Y * 90 : REM moves up left side
1140 PRINT; INT(Y * big / 10) : REM labels left side with
     numbers
1160 NEXT Y
1180 VDU 4 : REM separates cursors again
1200 ENDPROC
```

Character generation

On page 179 when we were discussing character sets and ASCII codes we indicated that the numbers from 240 to 255 had been left available to be used for the creation or the generation of characters, shapes, drawings and so on by the user. We will now show you how to set about designing your own characters.

To begin with we need some squared paper and on this we draw an eight by eight grid like the one shown below. Then we use a felt pen or something similar and fill in the squares so as to create a picture. We have done it below and tried to make a cartoon face.

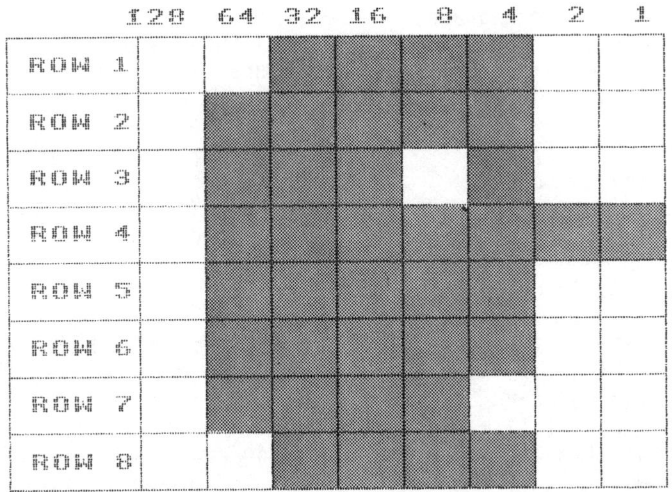

Notice that we have numbered the rows from the top as Row 1, Row 2, down to Row 8. For each of these rows we will generate a number so that we end up with eight numbers. We do this by looking at the numbers along the top. These are, reading from the right,1, 2, 4, 8, 16, and so on up to 128. (These are the powers of two and indicate that we are in fact dealing with binary numbers or numbers in base two).

Now look at the diagram carefully and consider Row 1 to begin with. The squares that have been coloured are situated below the numbers 64, 32, 16, and 8. These add up to 120 and so the number for Row 1 is 120. Then row 2 involves the numbers 128, 64, 8, 4, 2 and 1. These add up to 207. Continue in this way all the way down as shown on the right side of the grid. In this way we produce the eight numbers shown there.

We now allocate these eight numbers to one of the set of available codes from 240 to 255. It does not matter which, so long as we do not use the same number for two different characters. We will use 240 for this example so we then put it all together with the statement VDU 23:

```
VDU 23, 240, 120, 207, 248, 224, 248, 248, 248, 112
```

Notice that VDU is followed by ten numbers. The 23 is always necessary. The 240 is chosen by us from the range 240 to 255. The last eight numbers come from the grid as we have just shown. This line makes the code 240 represent the cartoon face. It does not actually print the face. To achieve this we must print CHR$ 240. So we now need a program to put this cartoon face on the screen.

```
100 MODE 4
120 VDU 23, 240, 120, 207, 248, 224, 248, 248, 248, 112
160 PRINT TAB(10,10); CHR$ 240
```

Type this in and run it. Now change it slightly so that it prints a row of faces across the screen.

```
140 FOR count = 1 TO 12
160 PRINT TAB(3 * count, 10); CHR$240
180 NEXT count
```

Larger characters

From this it is clear that we could quite quickly design and produce a range of characters and shapes to be used in games and as illustrations. You will however have discovered that the shape on the screen, when produced in this way, is a bit small. But we could design the left half of a shape as one new character and the right half as another new character and then draw them side by side. Or we could design a pattern or shape spread over a two by three grid, and so on. In order to demonstrate this we have designed a skull-face on a two-by-two grid like this

A	B
C	D

We have produced four sets of numbers in this way and have located these in the ASCII codes 240 for A, 241 for B, 242 for C, and 243 for D. We will put these into a program so that the appropriate lines look like this:

```
120 VDU 23, 240, 7, 15, 31, 57, 113, 113, 255, 254
140 VDU 23, 241, 224, 240, 248, 156, 142, 142, 255, 127
160 VDU 23, 242, 126, 31, 12, 12, 14, 15, 7, 3
180 VDU 23, 243, 126, 248, 112, 48, 112, 240, 224, 192
```

Type these in carefully. We will now use CHR$ to put them together into one string which we can then print whenever we wish on the screen.

```
200 lt$ = CHR$ 240 : REM left-top
220 rt$ = CHR$ 241 : REM right-top
240 lb$ = CHR$ 242 : REM left-bottom
260 rb$ = CHR$ 243 : REM right-bottom
```

We also need to use the control characters for down and left. This is, because we print the character for box A (in the diagram above) and then print beside it the character for box B, we must then move the cursor down one line and back left two spaces before we can print the character in box C, below box A. So we add these lines.

```
280 down$ = CHR$ 10
300 left$ = CHR$ 8
```

Now we can combine all of these into one string which we call skull$ as follows:

```
320 skull$ = lt$ + rt$+ down$ + left$ +left$ + lb$ + rb$
```

Now when we print the string 'skull$', if we have done it properly, it will make a skull on the screen. Add these lines and RUN the program.

```
100 MODE 4
460 PRINT skull$
```

This should work, but we will add a few more lines and cover the screen with skulls.

```
340 VDU 5 : REM joins cursors
360 FOR X = 100 TO 1000 STEP 100
380 FOR Y = 100 TO 1000 STEP 100
440 MOVE X, Y
480 NEXT Y
500 NEXT X
540 VDU 4
```

Type this in and RUN the program again. As a final refinement we can try to add colour and a message to this rather grisly screen display.

```
100 MODE 5
400 col = RND(4) : REM choose color randomly
420 GCOL 0, col
520 MOVE 0, 530 : PRINT "CURSE OF THE SKULLS"
```

If you have a Model B machine change line 100 to MODE 1 - or change it to MODE 2 and also change line 400 to col = RND(16).

This program could be developed further into a very interesting game, but we will leave it there.

Using VDU for character

However do not use NEW to remove the skulls program as yet because we now want to demonstrate how we can simplify and shorten some of this if we use VDU instead of CHR$. (We discussed the equivalence of these two words on page 178). Remember that the four parts of the skull are now represented by the ASCII numbers 240, 241, 242 and 243 and that down is 10 and left is 8. We can put the combination of these (which we used to produce skull$ above) into one VDU statement as follows. Notice that it replaces the PRINT skull$ line in the program as well:

```
460 VDU 240, 241, 10, 8, 8, 242, 243
```

So, as a result of this simplification we no longer need skull$ and therefore we can remove all the lines from 200 to 320, as follows : DELETE 200,320. Now try it again. The final simpler version of the program looks like this:

```
100 VDU 5
120 VDU 23, 240, 7, 15, 31, 57, 113, 113, 255, 254
140 VDU 23, 241, 224, 240, 248, 156, 142, 142, 255, 127
160 VDU 23, 242, 126, 31, 12, 12, 14, 15, 7, 3
180 VDU 23, 243, 126, 248, 112, 48, 112, 240, 224, 192
340 VDU 5
360 FOR X = 100 TO 1000 STEP 100
380 FOR Y = 100 TO 1000 STEP 100
400 col = RND(4)
420 GCOL 0,col
440 MOVE X, Y
460 VDU 240, 241, 10, 8, 8, 242, 243
480 NEXT Y
500 NEXT X
520 MOVE 0, 530 : PRINT "CURSE OF THE SKULLS"
540 VDU 4
```

Text and graphics windows

It is possible to define two different parts of the screen to represent separately a text window and a graphics window. This means that, when you write text, it appears only in the text window; and when you draw shapes using graphics words, these shapes appear only in the graphics window. The best way to do this is to use a sheet of squared paper and draw on it a rectangle representing the screen. Then draw two other separate rectangles inside this large one. Here is an example.

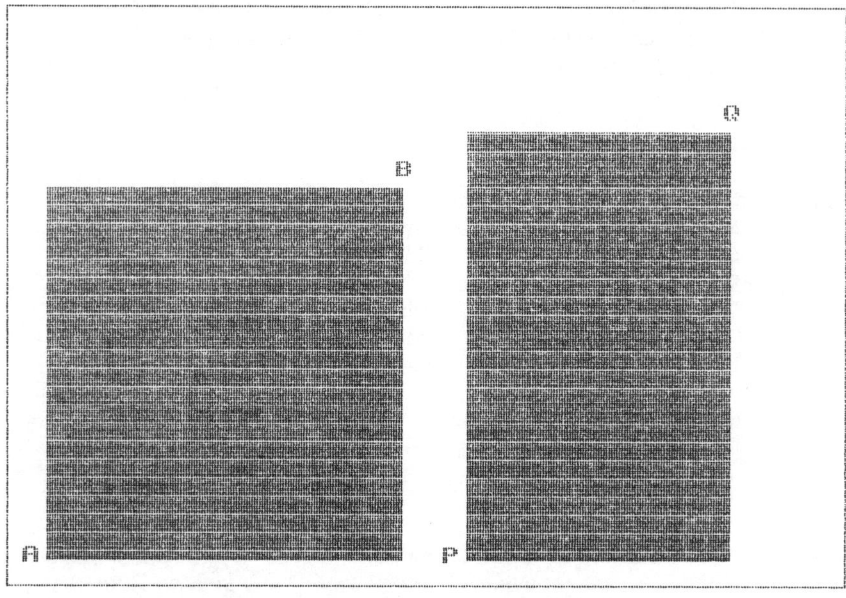

We will assume for the moment that we are going to use MODE 4. Notice that the two graphics axes are measured from the bottom left-hand corner and run across from 0 to 1279 and up from 0 to 1023. On the other hand the text axes are measured from the top left and run across from 1 to 40 and down from 1 to 32. (Remember also that these text axes numbers change for other modes. This is discussed below).

Now we will define the graphics window. To do this we use VDU 24 followed by four numbers. These are the coordinates of the two corners of the graphics window marked A and B. It is up to the user to think about where these should be placed. We have put A at (60, 50) and B at (600, 700). So the appropriate line in a program would be:

```
140 VDU 24, 60; 50; 600; 700;
```

Notice the semicolons, including the one at the end of the line and also the order in which these numbers occur. The beginning of the program looks like this.

```
100 MODE 4
120 COLOUR 129 : CLS
```

This last line makes the complete screen white. We do this so that we can make the windows black. We will now define the text window in a similar way this time using VDU 28, again followed by four numbers. These are the coordinates of the two corners of the text window marked P and Q. Remember that the text axes are numbered quite differently so again we must carefully choose what the coordinates of this P and Q are. We have chosen P to be (22,30) and Q to be (38,5). So the line for this is:

```
160 VDU 28, 22, 30, 38, 5
```

Notice that this time we use commas and we do not put one at the end of the line. (The reason for the semi-colons and commas is to do with the size of the numbers involved. When they are likely to be bigger than 255, as they are with graphics, then we must indicate this to the computer by using semi-colons).

We also wish to move the graphics origin to the point A, and we can do this with VDU 29 followed by the coordinates of A. Notice that once again we must use semi colons.

```
180 VDU 29, 60; 50;
```

Now we must make the existence of these two windows obvious by changing their color to black. To do this we use these two lines.

```
200 COLOUR 128 : CLS
220 GCOL 0, 128 : CLG
```

Now run this program and the two windows will become clear. However it will make the point even better if we print something - this will appear in the text window - and then draw or plot something - and this will appear in the graphics window. First type in the following lines, and run the program to check the text window.

```
240 PRINT "This is the text"
260 PRINT "screen.  It is"
280 PRINT "now very small."
```

Now type in the following lines. The first line uses the MOVE statement to establish two corners of a triangle. The next line uses PLOT 85 to complete the triangle.

```
300 MOVE 30, 30 : MOVE 500, 200
320 PLOT 85, 250, 500
```

Run this program and make sure that it works properly. Finally we can return the screen to its normal disposition by using VDU 26 or by using CTRL and Z.

In this case we have used MODE 4. Had we chosen to use MODE 5 we would have had access to other colors but we would have had to adjust the text window since, in this mode, the screen is only twenty columns wide. This means that line 160 must be changed as follows. Notice that the second and fourth numbers have been halved:

```
160 VDU 28, 11, 30, 19, 5
```

A further consequence of changing to MODE 5 is that the text letters are now twice as broad. For this reason lines 240, 260, and 280 need to be changed also.

Color variety

Do not use NEW to remove the last example as we will now use it to develop further the use of color. In this last program we used MODE 4 which has two colors only, that is black and white. The way to use and access these was described on page 44. However, although we remain limited to two colors, we can choose our two colors from the sixteen that are available to the computer. So, for example, instead of black and white, we could have yellow and blue. In the example that we now develop we will use only the first eight of these colors numbered 0 to 7. These are the eight non-flashing colors.

The colors black and white in MODE 4 have the numbers 0 and 1, like this:

```
Black    --    0
White    --    1
```

The eight colors that we are going to choose from are numbered as follows:

```
0   --   Black
1   --   Red
2   --   Green
3   --   Yellow
4   --   Blue
5   --   Magenta
6   --   Cyan
7   --   White
```

We can use VDU 19 to change either of the two colors, black and white, to any that we choose from the list above. Suppose for example we wanted to change black to yellow and white to blue. This is now shown with the numbers in brackets after each color.

Black (0) to become Yellow (3)

White (1) to become Blue (4)

This change is brought about as follows using VDU 19. Remember these lines are added to the program already in the memory.

```
420 VDU 19, 0, 3, 0, 0, 0 : REM changes black to yellow
440 VDU 19, 1, 4, 0, 0, 0 : REM changes white to blue
```

After VDU 19 we put the original color (in this case either 0 or 1). After this we put the new color (in this case 3 or 4). Finally we put three zeros as shown. These have no function in the statement at the moment but are available for extensions. These three zeros can be replaced by ; 0 ;. In other words the whole of line 420 can look like this:

```
420 VDU 19, 0, 3; 0;
```

Before running this to illustrate the color changes we need a delay so that we can see both the original colors and the new colours. Type in this delay line and then run the program:

```
340 time = TIME : REPEAT UNTIL  TIME - time > 200
```

We can illustrate the whole range of possible two color combinations by using two loops and changing lines 420 and 440 as follows. Type these in and then RUN the program and watch the color combinations.

```
360 FOR back = 0 TO 7
380 FOR fore = 0 TO 7
400 CLS
420 VDU 19, 0, back, 0, 0, 0
440 VDU 19, 1, fore, 0, 0, 0
460 time = TIME : REPEAT UNTIL TIME - time > 200
480 NEXT fore
500 NEXT back
```

We can use exactly similar techniques to ring the color changes in a four color or a sixteen color mode. For example, in MODE 5 there are four colors, so that if we wished to change all four of these we would need four VDU statements representing the four colors. These four colors and their numbers are as shown below. Suppose we wished to change each of these to the corresponding color shown on the right.

```
Black (0)    ---   Blue (4)
Red (1)      ---   Green (2)
Yellow (2)   ---   Magenta (5)
White (3)    ---   Yellow (3)
```

Note that since the machine is in MODE 5 the four colors and the numbers by which they are known are on the left. However the new colors, that is the ones to which we wish to change are taken from the MODE 2 sixteen color set and these are numbered differently. For example note above that yellow is numbered 2 in MODE 5 but 3 in MODE 2. So the four VDU statements necessary to effect the above change would be. (Remember to type in NEW first).

```
220 VDU 19, 0, 4, 0, 0, 0 : REM black to blue
240 VDU 19, 1, 2, 0, 0, 0 : REM red to green
260 VDU 19, 2, 5, 0, 0, 0 : REM yellow to magenta
280 VDU 19, 3, 3, 0, 0, 0 : REM white to yellow
```

So we will build a short and rather artificial program round these four VDU statements to illustrate this. It begins like this.

```
100 MODE 5
120 MOVE 10, 10 : MOVE 50, 800
140 GCOL 0, 1 : PLOT 85, 400, 30 : REM red triangle
160 GCOL 0, 2 : PLOT 85, 600, 900 : REM yellow triangle
180 GCOL 0, 3 : PLOT 85, 900, 10 : REM white triangle
200 Z = INKEY(200) : REM short delay
```

Remember that the screen background is black so this complete program will illustrate how we can simultaneously change four colors.

GCOL and Boolean operators

So far we have used GCOL, always followed by the number zero, to define graphics colors. (See page 201). In MODE 5, for example, if we wished to draw triangles in yellow we would use GCOL 0, 2. The 2 represents yellow, and we have up to now always used 0 as the other number. This way of using GCOL allows us to produce any of the available graphics colors, and, in a sense, we do not need to go beyond this for most things.

However it is possible to use the numbers 1, 2, 3, 4 (as well as 0) after GCOL, with effects we will now try to explain.

First of all, when we switch the machine on the screen is black. If we wish to change this black to another color we use:

GCOL 0, first.

Here first is a variable in the range 0, 1, 2, 3, (for MODE 5). Type in this program and we will add further lines to it as we go along.

```
100 MODE 7
120 PRINT"Choose the first color.  This will be"
140 PRINT"called first, and will be used with"
160 PRINT"GCOL 0, first and the word PLOT to"
180 PRINT"product a colored rectangle."
200 INPUT'"      ", first
220 REM draw first rectangle
240 MODE 5
260 GCOL 0, first
280 MOVE 0,0:MOVE 1000,0
300 PLOT 85,0,600:PLOT 85, 1000,600
```

Now run this and try some numbers in the range 0 to 3 to represent the variable first in line 200. This is a color number. We can now use GCOL again, like this:

```
GCOL 2,3
```

The second of these numbers, in this case it is 3, is also a color number; but the first number, in this case 2, is not a color number, but refers to a way of connecting or combining or operating on the two color numbers (first used in line 200 of the program, and 3 in the statement GCOL 2,3) to produce a new color number.

We can put this more generally as follows. First use GCOL 0, first. Then use GCOL boole, second. The variable boole is the operator which combines the two colour numbers called first and second. To demonstrate this add these lines to the program.

```
320 PRINT"Press the space bar.":Z=GET
340 MODE 7
360 PRINT"We will now use GCOL boole,second"
380 PRINT"To combine the colors represented"
400 PRINT"by first and second.  We will then draw"
420 PRINT"a smaller rectangle inside the first one."
440 INPUT"Input a value for boole "boole
460 INPUT"Input a value for second "second
480 REM draw first rectangle again
500 MODE 5
520 GCOL 0, first
540 MOVE 0,0:MOVE 1000,0
560 PLOT 85,0,600:PLOT 85, 1000,600
580 REM draw second rectangle
600 GCOL boole, second
```

```
620 MOVE 100,100:MOVE 600,100
640 PLOT 85,100,300:PLOT 85,600,300
```

In lines 200, 440 and 460 we choose values for first, boole and second. Then line 520 uses GCOL 0, first to establish the first color. Immediately after this a rectangle is drawn colored according to the number first (lines 540 and 560). Line 600 uses GCOL boole, second to effect the combination of first and second. Immediately after this another rectangle is drawn inside the first so that the effect on the color of this combination can be seen. Type this in and then run the program and try various combinations. A table can then be made showing the results. Here is an example of such a table.

```
First color is yellow using GCOL 0, 2
boole is 1
GCOL 1, 0 produces yellow on yellow
GCOL 1, 1 produces white  on yellow
GCOL 1, 2 produces yellow on yellow
GCOL 1, 3 produces white  on yellow
```

The meaning of this variable boole is now given for each of its four possible values.

(a) When boole = 1 than the color is 'first OR second'. This is the Boolean OR described on page 68 and refers here to a mathematical operation on the binary numbers representing first and second.

(b) When boole = 2 then the color is 'first AND second'. Again this is the Boolean AND.

(c) When boole = 3 then the color is 'first EOR second'.

(d) When boole = 4 then the color first is inverted and it does not matter what the second is. To invert a color means to interchange the first color for the last, the second color for the second last, and so on.

Problems

1. Write a program, using high resolution graphics, which will make a ball bounce repeatedly from the top of the screen to the bottom and, at the same time, move slowly across from left to right.

2. Write a program which draws a grid of hexagons on the screen, using high resolution graphics.

3. Write a program so that two players can play the game 'Counters'. A set of 40 counters are placed on the screen. Each player in turn 'removes' one, two or three of them. The player to take the last counter loses. This means that when a player presses the keys 1, 2, or 3, an appropriate number of counters disappears from the screen. The shape of the counter should be designed using the character generation technique described on page 216.

CHAPTER 12
THE SOUND OF MUSIC

Introduction

The music generating facilities on the BBC microcomputer are very extensive and very complex. It would not be possible to cover all the variations in one chapter so we will try using some examples to initiate processes which can be developed by the user over time. The two new words involved are SOUND and ENVELOPE and we will begin by dealing with SOUND.

SOUND

This word SOUND is used by the BBC microcomputer to produce music and sound effects. In order to demonstrate the range of musical sounds available we will begin with a short program which will play through a series of octaves. An octave is made up of twelve semi-tones so that if we started, for example, at C and played this and the twelve succeeding semi-tones we would arrive at C again only an octave higher. We can demonstrate this as follows.

Begin at	C,	C#,	D,	D#,	E,	F,	F#,	G,	G#,	A,	A#,	B,	C
	1	2	3	4	5	6	7	8	9	10	11	12	13

Notice that the first note is C and the 13th note is C. Each of the notes is given a number by the computer and, beginning at the lowest possible C which the computer can play, the twelve notes in an octave with their numbers are shown below.

C	C#	D	D#	E	F	F#	G	G#	A	A#	B	C
5	9	13	17	21	25	29	33	37	41	45	49	53

To go up a semitone means therefore that four is added and so to go up a full octave, say from C(5) to C(53), we add on 48 that is 12 times 4. This also means that the computer can play notes which differ by a quarter of a semitone. Each of the whole numbers from 0 to 255 can be used. Here is a program to demonstrate this. It begins with a few lines of explanation about what the program is going to do.

```
100 MODE 7
120 PRINT' "This program will sound each of the 12"
140 PRINT' "semitones in an octave. Then when you"
160 PRINT' "press the space bar it will play the"
180 PRINT' "12 semitones of the next octave up"
200 PRINT' "and so on."
```

We are going to play a sequence of octaves so we need an outside loop which counts these. We will use the variable octave for this. Then we need an internal loop to count the notes. The first note to be played has the number 5 and the last has the number 49, and a full octave goes up in steps of 4 by a total of 48. So that in the next octave the first note is 5 + 48 and the last note is 49 + 48. So the first and last notes for the succeeding octaves are:

first	5	5 + 48	5 + 2 * 48	5 + 3 * 48
last	49	49 + 48	49 + 2 * 48	49 + 3 * 48

We can therefore generalise this, using the variable 'octave', as follows:

```
220 FOR octave = 0 TO 5
240 PRINT'' "This is octave number  "; octave + 1
260 first = 5 + 48 * octave
280 last = 49 + 48 * octave
300 FOR note = first TO last STEP 4
```

Line 240 simply puts a message on the screen. Lines 260 and 280 represent the pattern of numbers just described and these are used in the beginning of the loop which will play the twelve notes of the octave.

Now for the critical line which actually makes the computer play the notes. This uses the words SOUND and, of course, uses the variable note from line 300. It looks like this:

```
320 SOUND 1, -15, note, 10
```

The other three numbers in line 320 will be discussed in detail on page 000 so, in order to finish the program and hear the music, we will not discuss them here. The rest of the program looks like this.

```
340 NEXT note
360 PRINT''' "When it stops press the spacebar."
380 Z = GET
400 NEXT octave
420 PRINT'' "That was the last one."
```

Type this in and then run the program a few times. There are a couple of things to notice about what happens when you do run the program. The message on line 360 should not appear until after the full 12 notes have been played in the preceeding loop. However you will find that it appears on the screen not long after the octave begins to play. Run the program again and check this. This means that the computer puts the music to be played into a queue inside and then simply goes on with the rest of the program. This could be a very useful facility when playing games or when interacting with the computer in any way.

The second thing to notice is that, in the last or sixth octave, the notes stop going up and start again at the bottom. This happens when the numbers go beyond 255. In this case the number 256 is treated by the computer exactly like the number 1.

Playing a tune

We will now write a program to play a short tune or melody. The tune we have chosen is called Fanny Power and it was written in Ireland in the eighteenth century. We use the first part only and it has 38 notes. Each note in a tune has two numbers associated with it. The first is a measure of the pitch of the note and the second number is a measure of how long the note lasts. This is called the duration of the note. So, to begin with, we must declare two arrays to hold these numbers as follows. (Remember to use NEW to remove the last program).

```
100 DIM pitch(38), dur(38)
120 MODE 7
```

We will then place the number representing the notes in four data lines as follows. The letters representing the notes are placed in REM lines above the data lines.

```
180 REM next four data lines : pitches of 38 notes
200 REM   D, G, D, G, A, B, C, B, A, G
220 DATA 109, 129, 109, 129, 137, 145, 149, 145, 137, 129
240 REM   G, F#, E, D, F#, D, F#, G, A, C
260 DATA 129, 125, 117, 109, 125, 109, 125, 129, 137, 149
280 REM   B, A, G, B, C, D, E, A, A, G
300 DATA 145, 137, 129, 145, 149, 157, 165, 137, 137, 129
320 REM   G, F#, E, D, G, F#, G, G
340 DATA 129, 125, 117, 109, 129, 125, 129, 129
```

Later we will describe where these numbers came from, but for the moment type them in so that we can demonstrate how to make the computer turn them into music.

The second set of numbers associated with notes represent their duration and this is contained in a corresponding set of four data lines shown below. The numbers here represent the relative lengths of the notes and are at their shortest possible. In a moment we will introduce a scaling factor for these numbers to make the notes last longer.

```
360 REM next four data lines : duration of notes
380 DATA 1, 2, 1, 1, 1, 1, 2, 1, 2, 1
400 DATA 1, 1, 1, 1, 1, 1, 2, 1, 2, 1
420 DATA 1, 1, 1, 1, 1, 1, 2, 1, 2, 1
440 DATA 1, 1, 1, 1, 1, 1, 3, 3
```

We now store these two sets of numbers in their appropriate arrays using READ

```
460 FOR count = 1 TO 38 : READ pitch(count) : NEXT count
480 FOR count = 1 TO 38 : READ dur(count) : NEXT count
```

Now that we have stored the notes of the tune as two arrays of numbers we can begin to use the SOUND command. This is used as shown below, that is it is followed by four numbers. Type this in directly and press RETURN.

```
SOUND 2, -15, 129, 40
```

A sound or a note will be made in response to this which will last for two seconds. The four numbers are now taken one at a time.

(a). The first number here is 2. This can be any number from the set 0, 1, 2, 3. The number 0 produces what is called noise and this is used for special effects rather than for music. The other three numbers 1, 2, 3 each provide a channel for producing more-or-less pure musical notes. Until we use other programming techniques to introduce variations on the sounds, there is no very obvious difference between these, so for our melody we can choose any one of the three.

(b). The second number represents the loudness of the music and this varies from -15, which is the loudest possible, to 0 which is silence.

(c). The third number is the pitch of the note. In this example it is 129 which represents the note G. We have 38 of these available in our program waiting to be used. They are also stored in the array-variable pitch. The numbers available range from 0 to 255.

(d). The fourth number, 40 in this example, represents the length or duration of the note. Again we have 38 of these available in our program, stored in the array-variable dur. However we must scale these duration numbers up as they are currently as small as is possible. This allows us to choose how fast or how slow the tune should sound. Twenty represents about one full second, forty represents two seconds, and so on.

So we now need a loop which uses this SOUND command, as follows.

```
520 FOR count = 1 TO 38
540 SOUND 1, - 15, pitch(count), factor * dur(count)
560 NEXT count
```

Line 540 uses SOUND; the first number is 1, so it uses channel 1; the second number puts the volume at maximum, that is -15; the third number is the pitch; the fourth number is the duration, but multiplied by a scale factor called factor. We now need a line which invites the user to input a value for this variable factor.

```
160 INPUT'' "Choose a speed between 2 (fast) and 10 (slow)"
    ,factor
```

Now run the program and try different values for the variable factor until the tune plays at a speed which you find pleasing. We can now add two further lines to make the computer play the tune more than once.

```
500 FOR repeat = 1 TO 3
580 NEXT repeat
```

There are further refinements which it is possible to add to this; for example we can make the computer play the tune in a quite different octave. The numerical inter-relationships have already been described to some extent, and you will remember that the numerical difference between two identical notes, one an octave up on the other, is 48. This means that normally if we add 48 to each note number, or subtract 48 from each note number, then we move the tune up a full octave or down a full octave. In fact the range of notes in this particular tune means that it does not go outside two octaves, and because of the range of notes available this means that the tune can be played at four different levels. That is the one in which it is currently written and three others all below it. We can achieve this very easily by adding one new line and changing an existing one. We use the variable 'oct' to stand for the octave change.

```
140 INPUT'' "Choose an octave (1 -4) ",oct
540 SOUND 1,-15, pitch(count) + 48 * (oct -3), factor *
    dur(count)
```

This completes the program, and it should now look like this :

```
100 DIM pitch(38), dur(38)
120 MODE 7
140 INPUT'' "Choose an octave (1-4) " oct
160 INPUT'' "Choose a speed between 2(slow) and 10(fast)"
    ,factor
180 REM next four data lines : pitches of 38 notes
200 REM   D, G, D, G, A, B, C, B, A, G
220 DATA 109, 129, 109, 129, 137, 145, 149, 145, 137, 129
240 REM   G, F#, E, D, F#, D, F#, G, A, C
260 DATA 129, 125, 117, 109, 125, 109, 125, 129, 137, 149
280 REM   B, A, G, B, C, D, E, A, A, G
300 DATA 145, 137, 129, 145, 149, 157, 165, 137, 137, 129
320 REM   G, F#, E, D, G, F#, G, G
340 DATA 129, 125, 117, 109, 129, 125, 129, 129
360 REM next four data lines : duration of notes
380 DATA 1, 2, 1, 1, 1, 1, 2, 1, 2, 1
400 DATA 1, 1, 1, 1, 1, 1, 2, 1, 2, 1
420 DATA 1, 1, 1, 1, 1, 1, 2, 1, 2, 1
440 DATA 1, 1, 1, 1, 1, 1, 3, 3
460 FOR count = 1 TO 38 : READ pitch(count) : NEXT count
480 FOR count = 1 TO 38 : READ dur(count) : NEXT count
500 FOR repeat = 1 TO 3
520 FOR count = 1 TO 38
540 SOUND 1, - 15, pitch(count) + 48 * (oct - 3), factor *
    dur(count)
560 NEXT count
580 NEXT repeat
```

We can change the program once more so that the tune is played on all three channels at once but in different octaves. First remove the choice line 140 and then change line 540 and add two other lines so that it looks like this.

```
540 SOUND 1, -15, pitch(count), factor * dur(count)
545 SOUND 2, -15, pitch(count)-48, factor * dur(count)
550 SOUND 3, -15, pitch(count)-96, factor * dur (count)
```

Run this again. The tune is played this time with three voices more or less, if not exactly, simultaneously. Save this program on cassette or disk because we will be referring to it again a few pages on when we deal with the exact synchronization of three voices, and then again later when we deal with the word ENVELOPE.

Musical notes

We have already discussed the way in which the pitch of musical notes is developed. The range on the computer is over five full octaves and the addition of 1 to the numerical representation of a note raises it by one quarter of a semitone. The way in which the numbers are allocated to notes is shown in the tables below and over the page. These numbers can be allocated to the notes on a normal musical staff in a variety of ways and a possible allocation would be as shown over the page:

	OCTAVE					
Note	1	2	3	4	5	6
A#	45	93	141	189	237	
A	41	89	137	185	233	
G#	37	85	133	181	229	
G	33	81	129	177	225	
F#	29	77	125	173	221	
F	25	73	121	169	217	
E	21	69	117	165	213	
D#	17	65	113	161	209	
D	13	61	109	157	205	253
C#	9	57	105	153	201	249
C	5	53	101	149	197	245
B	1	49	97	145	193	241

Notes outside this range, and sharps and flats, can now be easily found and used in the SOUND command. The duration numbers run from -1 to 254. Each unit represents a twentieth of a second so 0 represents silence and 20 represents one second. -1 is used to make a note last indefinitely. This can of course be stopped using the ESCAPE key, or by more sophisticated methods as described later. To demonstrate how the timing works type in and run this program and then count the seconds as notes change. The pitch of the notes is being chosen randomly.

```
100 MODE 7
120 PRINT' "The notes will change every second....."
140 PRINT' ".....starting....NOW."
160 REPEAT
180 SOUND 1,-15,RND(255),20
200 UNTIL FALSE
```

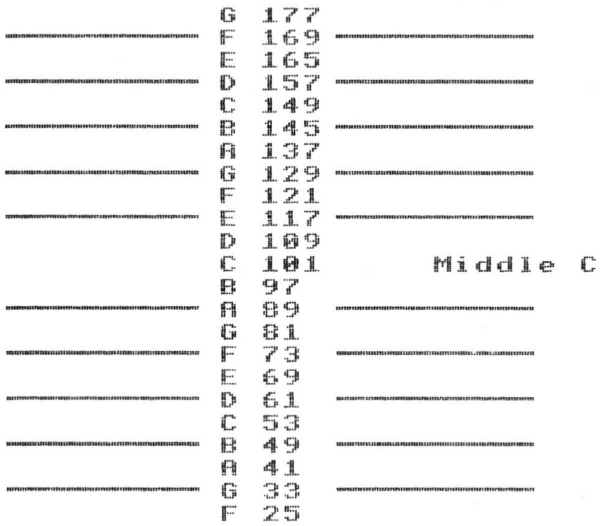

```
G 177
F 169
E 165
D 157
C 149
B 145
A 137
G 129
F 121
E 117
D 109
C 101        Middle C
B 97
A 89
G 81
F 73
E 69
D 61
C 53
B 49
A 41
G 33
F 25
```

Chords

The existence of three different voices or channels means that we can play chords, simply by using the sound command three successive times, using a different channel number each time. First type this in and try it. Notice that the channel number after the word SOUND is different for each note.

```
100 SOUND 1, -15, 129, 40 : REM G on channel 1
120 SOUND 2, -15, 145, 40 : REM B on channel 2
140 SOUND 3, -15, 157, 40 : REM D on channel 3
```

This is a chord made up of three notes G, B and D. However it sounds just a bit fuzzy because the notes are beginning to sound a little moment of time after each other. We need some technique for making them all begin to sound at exactly the same moment. We can do this by changing the channel number on each line so as to tell the computer to wait and play this note and the next two notes simultaneously : that is we can tell the computer to synchronize the three notes. Line 100 at the moment looks like this.

```
100 SOUND 1, -15, 129, 40
```

The channnel number is the 1 after the word SOUND and it is permitted to change this to a four-digit number in base sixteen. (See Appendix B for further information about base sixteen). With this computer we always indicate that we are dealing with a base sixteen number by putting the symbol '&' in front of it, and the number we are going to use this time is &0201. So the new lines 100 to 140 look like this:

```
100 SOUND &0201, -15, 129, 40
120 SOUND &0202, -15, 145, 40
140 SOUND &0203, -15, 157, 40
```

Change these lines in this way and run the program again. This time the chord will sound much more clean and together.

To explain this we will look more closely at line 100 and at this number 0201. The first and third digits are usually zero and the meaning to be attached to them is described in more detail below. For the moment we will concentrate on the other digits, that is the 2 and the 1. The 1 represents the channel number and, as before on line 100, this is still 1. The 2 is the critical number when we are interested in the synchronization of music. It means, play three notes all at once: that is, this note on line 100, and the next two notes. The next two notes are on other channels and they also have this 2 in the same position. Look at lines 120 and 140. So we can use this technique to play chords of any sort.

We can also use it to make sure that whenever we use three channels or voices the notes are synchronised. We can go back now to the program for playing a tune which we finished discussing on page 233. There we asked you to save this on a disk or cassette. If you did this, load it again now and then list the three lines 540 to 550.

```
540 SOUND 1, -15, pitch(count), factor * dur(count)
545 SOUND 2, -15, pitch(count) -48, factor * dur(count)
550 SOUND 3, -15, pitch(count) -96, factor * dur(count)
```

Run this program again and listen to it and then change the lines as follows:

```
540 SOUND &0201, -15, pitch(count), factor * dur(count)
545 SOUND &0202, -15, pitch(count) -48, factor * dur(count)
550 SOUND &0203, -15, pitch(count) -96, factor * dur(count)
```

Then run it again and this time it will be much smoother and crisper.

The extended SOUND statement

We must now look in more detail at the meanings to be attached to the four base-sixteen digits which we used above. In general form we can write these as &HSFC and we will consider each in turn.

1). H represents the first digit and stands for the word HOLD. It will be either 0 or 1 and is usually 0. If it is 1 then the SOUND command does not actually produce a note at all. Its effect is to allow the preceeding note to continue to sound, that is to HOLD the preceeding note.

2). S represents the second digit and this is used for SYNCHRONIZATION of notes as described above. For our purposes S will be 0, 1, or 2. If it is 0, then notes play in their normal unchanged order. If it is 1 then this note and the next note appearing on another channel with a 1 in this spot will be played together. So this note will be held up until then. If it is 2 then this note and the next note appearing on each of the the two other channels will be played together. If any other notes appear on the list of notes to be played, before a set of properly synchronized notes have occurred, then this other note will be played first.

3). F represents the third digit and it stands for the word FLUSH. It can be 0 or 1 and it is usually 0. If it is 1 then this note is played at once before any other waiting in the queue on that channel. The other waiting notes are Flushed out and lost.

4). C represents the fourth digit and stands for CHANNEL. It can be 0, 1, 2 or 3 and this represents the Channel number.

The noise channel

In the normal or unextended SOUND statement we have shown how it is possible to have three sound channels or voices numbered 1, 2 and 3. But it is also possible to use the number 0 to produce noises or sounds which are of a random or unstructured character and are not therefore to be described as music. However this facility has a great range of possible sound effects available to it and these can be very useful for certain kinds of programs. For example type this in directly, and press RETURN.

```
SOUND 0, -15, 4, 40
```

The sound is rather like car radio interference or even a rough sea. To try out all of them type in this short program and listen to each in turn. Below the program we have made an attempt to describe what the noise sounds like to us, although this seems to change over time!

```
100 FOR pitch = 0 TO 7
120 SOUND 0, -15, pitch, 40
140 PRINT'' "This is pitch number  "; pitch
160 PRINT' "Press spacebar." : Z = GET
180 NEXT pitch
```

When pitch is 0 the noise is like a fairly high pitched continuous door-bell.

When pitch is 1 the noise is rather like the last one but lower, like a train horn or the buzzer of a cooker.

When pitch is 2 the noise is still like 0 or 1 but lower still, sometimes like a cow lowing.

When pitch is 3 the noise is like a creaky door closing. This noise is changed by the pitch setting on channel 1.

When pitch is 4 the noise is like radio interference on a car radio.

When pitch is 5 the noise is like a machine gun firing very quickly or a pneumatic drill.

When pitch is 6 the noise is like that made at 5, but lower.

When pitch is 7 the noise is like the noise made when the pitch is 4 - radio inferference again.

To some extent these descriptions are fanciful but you must make your own choice. However putting these into loops which change the pitch or the duration in a regular way can produce interesting sound effects. Here is an example of a siren-sound. Type it in and try it.

```
100 FOR count = 1 TO 10
120 SOUND 0, -15, 0, 10
140 SOUND 0, -15, 2, 10
160 NEXT count
```

ENVELOPE

This word is used by the computer to vary the music or noise produced by the SOUND command. It does not make any sound itself, but it changes the effects of the word SOUND. Remember that SOUND is followed by four numbers, like this:

```
SOUND 2,-15,129,40
```

The second of these numbers, in this case -15, is used to represent the loudness of the music and it can range from 0, which is silence, to -15 which is the loudest possible. But it can also be one of the four positive numbers 1,2,3 or 4. If it is one of these then it refers to a corresponding ENVELOPE. For example the line:

```
SOUND 2,3,129,40
```

refers to, or calls on, an envelope numbered 3. The appropriate ENVELOPE then, when it appears, will be numbered 3, and this will be the first number following the word. For example, it would begin like this

```
ENVELOPE 3,.........
```

The word ENVELOPE is followed by fourteen numbers each of which has a specific function. But we can demonstrate the effects of an envelope by using the program for playing a tune which we saved on tape or disk earlier. Load this again now and then proceed as follows. First remove lines 545 and 550 as we wish to concentrate on one channel only. Then change line 540 as follows:

```
540 SOUND 1, 1, pitch(count), factor * dur(count)
```

Notice that we have changed the second number from -15 to 1, because we wish to call up an envelope numbered 1. We will put the envelope on line 450 before the loops begin. It is shown below. Copy it in carefully even though it does not as yet make much sense. The first number is of course 1, as this is the envelope number which is being called by the SOUND command.

```
450 ENVELOPE 1,3,  2,1,1,1,1,1,  121,-10,0,-5,120,120
```

Now run the program and listen to the new sound. It is as though the tune was being played on a rather tinny organ. It is interesting to remove line 450 and listen to the tune without the envelope, and then again with it. The envelope described in line 450 is called each time by the SOUND command in line 540 and changes each note of the tune in exactly the same way.

The fourteen numbers

A total of fourteen numbers, each responsible for a little bit of the change in each note is very formidable but we will not in fact pay equal attention to all of them. They can be divided into three sets as follows:

```
ENVELOPE  N,T,  P1,P2,P3,NS1,NS2,NS3,  A,D,S,R,AE,DE
```

SET 1 N,T. These are concerned with the envelope number and with time.

SET 2 P1,P2,P3,NS1,NS2,NS3. These are concerned with what is called a Pitch Envelope.

SET 3 A,D,S,R,AE,DE. These are concerned with what is called an Amplitude (or Loudness) Envelope.

First consider SET 1 which contains only two numbers, called N and T. N stands for the envelope Number and, as already described, can be any one of the four numbers 1,2,3 or 4. This is the connection between SOUND and ENVELOPE. T stands for time and this is measured in hundredths of a second. The total length of each note played by the SOUND command is divided into hundredths of a second and T represents how many of these hundredths will be considered as a unit by the envelope. More about this in a moment. Because we are going to be more concerned with it, we will consider SET 3 before considering SET 2. SET 3 is made up of six numbers as follows:

A	D	S	R	AE	DE
Attack	Decay	Sustain	Release	Attack End	Decay End

These describe an Amplitude envelope and they affect the loudness of each individual note so that the note does not have the same amplitude or loudness all the way through. They can be demonstrated graphically as follows over the page:

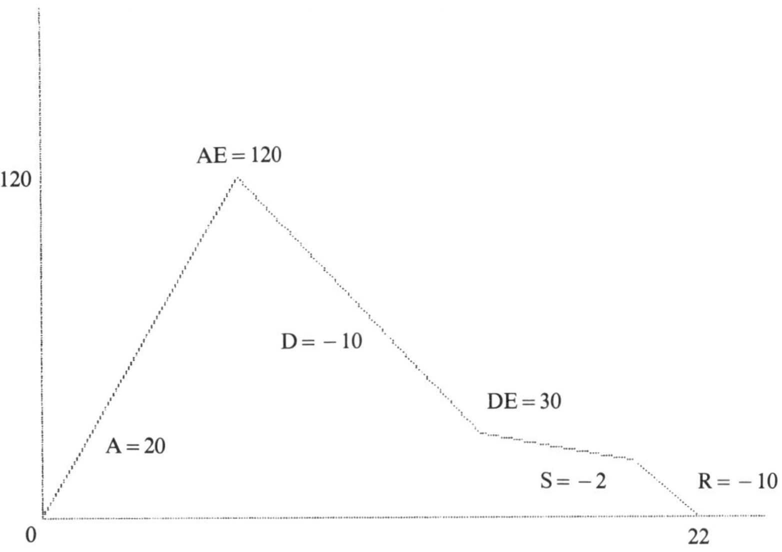

This is a note which lasts for 20 hundredths of a second, that is for one fifth of a second. In this case the second number in the first set, that is T, is equal to one. These twenty divisions of the note are shown along the bottom. During the first six of these the amplitude of the note rises from zero or silence, to 120. This is represented by the first section of the line on the graph. The amount that the line goes up during each hundredth of a second is called the Attack rate, that is A, and in this case it is 20. One example of this is shown in the diagram. Since the amplitude goes from 0 to 120 in 6 hundredths of a second, then A must be 20. Also AE must be 120.

The second section of the line drops from 120 to 30 a total drop of 90. This is the Decay phase and it lasts from the 6th hundredth of a second point to the 15th, that is for 9 hundredths of a second. So the decay rate must be -10. This is also shown on the diagram. So D = -10 and DE = 30. (The decay line need not actually go down, that is to say, D could be positive, and DE could be greater than AE).

The third line represents what is called the Sustain phase. This lasts until the end of the note, that is for 5 hundredths of a second. During this time the amplitude drops from 30 to 20 a total of -10. So the sustain rate, S, is -2. The Release phase normally affects only the final note of the tune and always ends when the amplitude is back to zero again. In this case it takes 2 hundredths of a second to go from an amplitude of 20 to zero, so the release rate, R, is -10.

So far for this amplitude envelope the six numbers are:

A	D	S	R	AE	DE
20	-10	-2	-10	120	30

In a few moments we will give some examples of how to use this envelope to produce particular kinds of sounds. But first we must mention the second set of numbers. These constitute the Pitch envelope and this is used to change the pitch of a note during its duration, in a similar way to the way we have just shown how to change its amplitude. However, for normal musical sounds it is unlikely that the pitch would in fact change in any significant way and so we will not go into details of its use. For those who are interested the User Guide gives a good survey of the meaning of each of the six numbers involved in the Pitch envelope. We will always put six zeros for this envelope, and so the full envelope command for the example we showed would be like this:

```
ENVELOPE 1,1,  0,0,0,0,0,0,  20,-10,-2,-10,120,30
```

Musical instruments

Different musical instruments have quite distinctive amplitude envelopes and an attempt can be made to produce copies of some of these using the envelope command. The three types of sound we will consider are produced by hitting, plucking and blowing. For example a piano makes its notes by hitting or striking a stretched string with a hammer. Its envelope looks approximately like this:

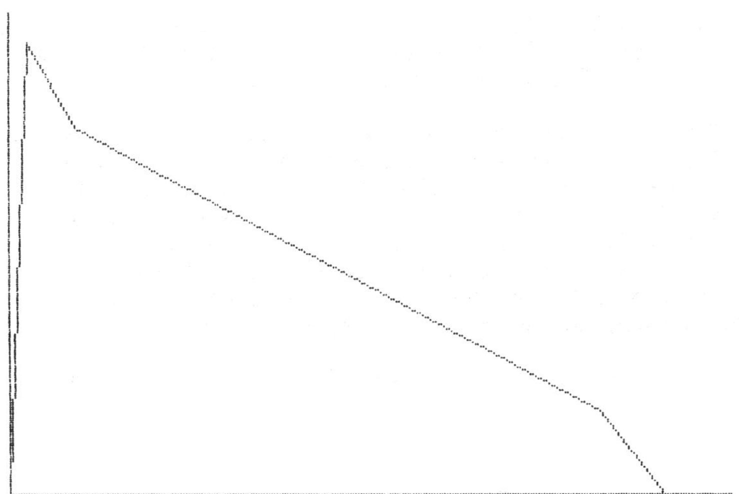

So a possible numerical representation of the envelope for a piano-like sound is as follows:

```
ENVELOPE 1,1,  0,0,0,0,0,0,  120,-6,-1,-1,126,66
```

A similar envelope can be used to produce the sound of a glockenspiel or a set of musical bells, since they also produce their sound by hitting or striking.

```
ENVELOPE 1,1,  0,0,0,0,0,0,  20,-3,0,-1,120,20
```

A harpsichord produces its sound by plucking stretched strings, and in this respect it is comparable to a guitar or a mandolin. A plucked sound produces an envelope like this:

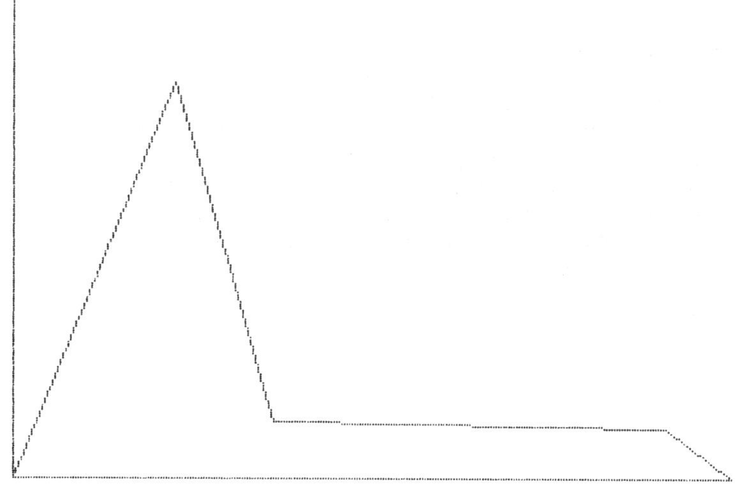

Based on this an envelope for a harpsichord could be as follows:

```
ENVELOPE 1,1,  0,0,0,0,0,0,  120,-6,0,-1,126,80
```

A much more tinny plucked sound, a bit like an overstretched mandolin is produced like this:

```
ENVELOPE 1,1,  0,0,0,0,0,0,  120,-10,0,-1,126,20
```

Organs, flutes, and reeded instruments produce sounds by blowing air against edges or reeds. The envelope for this kind of sound looks like this:

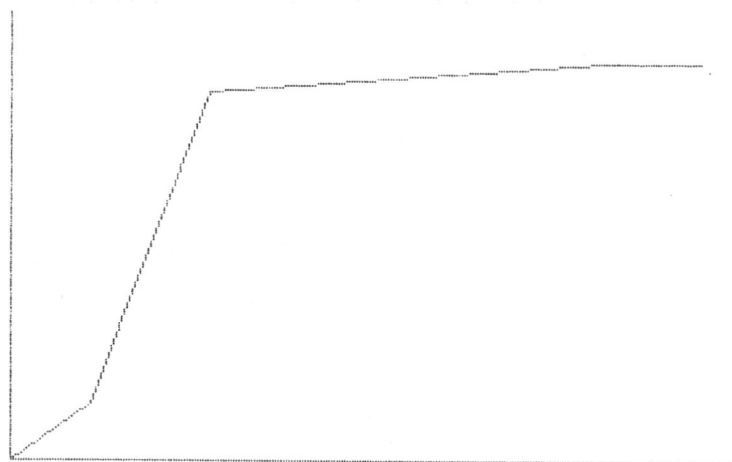

An envelope for a sound like a flute is as follows:

```
ENVELOPE 1,1,  0,0,0,0,0,0,  4,6,0,-1,20,120
```

And a sound something like an organ can be produced by this envelope:

```
ENVELOPE 1,1,  0,0,0,0,0,0,  60,10,0,-60,60,120
```

Problem

1. Use the program written in this chapter for playing a tune as the basis for the development of a full 'Melody Maker' program. It should allow you to input a tune, save it on disk, play the tune, and so on.

CHAPTER 13
A STRUCTURED PROGRAM

Introduction

In this chapter we will make use of many of the techniques of structuring which much of the rest of this book has been trying to develop. We will begin by designing a program on paper. The main body of this program will consist of a sequence of simple statements each representing a major task. These tasks will be performed using a procedure for each. It is not necessary at this initial stage to write the procedures. It is enough to decide what procedures are necessary. They can then be written later.

The program we will write is a game program. We choose this because, along with the structuring techniques involved, it allows us to make use of some of the graphics facilities we have developed earlier, particularly in chapter 11.

The game

The game is a fairly simple bat and ball game, but it will be easy to add new procedures to it so that it can become quite complicated. First of all we draw three walls, one at the top of the screen, one on the left of the screen and one on the right of the screen. Then we have a bat made up of a single short horizontal line, and we move this back and forward across the bottom of the screen. Then we have a moving ball which bounces off the three walls when it hits them, but disappears into the bottom of the screen. So the game involves moving the bat about and trying to stop the ball from disappearing into the bottom of the screen.

First, we will try to design the game on paper. To play the game we need to do the following things, in this order.

1. Set up the variables to be used in the program.

2. Draw the three walls on the screen.

3. Draw the ball for the first time.

4. Draw the bat.

5. Move the ball one step.

6. Check if the ball hits a wall or the bat, and if it does, make it change direction.

7. Check if the ball has gone off the screen. If it has, change the score, put a message on the screen, and draw a new ball.

8. Check the keyboard to see if the player is trying to move the bat. If so the move the bat one step.

9 Go back to number 4.

Almost all of these can be written as procedures and some of them will be cycled round again and again as indicated by number 9. So, although we have not actually written any of the routines yet, the beginning of the program will probably look something like this. (Don't type it in yet). Note that we have chosen to work in MODE 5, which gives us 4 colors.

```
100 MODE 5
120 PROCsetupvariables
140 PROCsetupscreen
160 PROCnewball
180 REPEAT
200 PROCdrawbat
220 PROCmoveball
240 PROCcheckkeyboard
260 UNTIL FALSE
```

Writing the program

We will now begin to write the program based on this structure. It is of course unlikely that a preliminary design like this will come out exactly right in normal circumstances, but even if it does not, it is a good idea to try to think the problem through in this way before starting. Then you have some kind of plan to build around and the finished program is likely to be more coherent and to contain fewer mistakes. At each stage in what follows type in RUN and try the program out. To begin with we need line 100, that is we must decide which MODE to use. We have chosen MODE 5, but you must think about this. A full description of the various modes and their properties appears on page 134. Note that we cannot put this MODE statement inside a procedure. So the first line in our program is:

```
100 MODE 5
```

Type it in and press RETURN. Now, according to the plan we need a procedure to set up the variables. At this stage we don't really know much about the variables we are going to use. These will be developed as we go along, but since it is a game we will make the background color of the screen red. We can do this with the statement GCOL 0, 181 followed by CLG. These words are described in full on page 201. So, part of this procedure looks like this. (Note that the line numbers are a bit irregular because these lines are part of a long completed program which we are working towards).

```
300 DEF PROCsetupvariables
400 GCOL 0,181 : CLG
420 ENDPROC
```

We now call this procedure on line 120, as follows:

```
120 PROCsetupvariables
260 END
```

Line 260 is a temporary line which will be changed later. Type this in and run the program. It will make the whole screen red.

The next part of the plan involves setting up the screen for the game. This means drawing walls across the top and on the left and right. It begins as follows where the left wall is created by lines 520 and 540. (Since the screen is now red you may wish to type in MODE 7 and press RETURN):

```
460 DEF PROCsetupscreen
500 REM LEFT
520 MOVE 30,300 : MOVE 50,300
540 PLOT 85,30,800 : PLOT 85,50,800
700 ENDPROC
```

Now call this procedure as follows, and then run the program:

```
140 PROCsetupscreen
```

The left wall is drawn in white because we have not specified a foreground color, and white is assumed to be the foreground color unless the computer is instructed differently. This is called the default color. Remember that the number 85 after the word PLOT on line 540 means draw a triangle, and the two PLOT statements on line 540 together produce a rectangular wall.

This way of drawing triangles is described on page 208. The right wall is made in exactly the same way, as follows:

```
560 REM RIGHT
580 MOVE 1230,300 : MOVE 1250,300
600 PLOT 85,1230,800 : PLOT 85,1250,800
```

The top wall is created in a different color for decorative reasons, but also because later on when the ball is hitting walls on the screen we will want to distinguish the top wall from the two side walls, and this is done by using color. So the routine for the top wall looks like this:

```
620 REM TOP
640 GCOL 0,2
660 MOVE 30,780 : MOVE 1250,780
680 PLOT 85,30,800 : PLOT 85,1250,800
```

Line 640 makes the color yellow, and lines 660 and 680 are much like the lines used for the walls. The procedure to set up the screen is now complete and looks like this:

```
460 DEF PROCsetupscreen
500 REM LEFT
520 MOVE 30,300 : MOVE 50,300
540 PLOT 85,30,800 : PLOT 85,50,800
560 REM RIGHT
580 MOVE 1230,300 : MOVE 1250,300
600 PLOT 85,1230,800 : PLOT 85,1250,800
620 REM TOP
640 GCOL 0,2
660 MOVE 30,780 : MOVE 1250,780
680 PLOT 85,30,800 : PLOT 85,1250,800
700 ENDPROC
```

The ball-court has now been drawn so we must now draw the ball. At the beginning of each game the ball ought to appear at a different spot across the screen, otherwise the game will be predictable. It is not necessary however for the distance up the screen to vary. We will use the variables X and Y for these starting points. To begin with, Y will always be set at 400, but the value of X will be allocated randomly, as follows:

```
740 DEF PROCnewball
780 X = RND(1171) + 54 : Y = 400
820 ENDPROC
```

The random number function RND has been described on page 126. For our purpose here it is enough to remember that RND(1171) produces a whole number randomly from the range 1 to 1171. So when, as in line 780, 54 is added each time to this, the range becomes 55 to 1225. These limits ensure that the ball appears somewhere between the two walls. We then call this procedure with the line:

```
160 PROCnewball
```

Our next task is to draw the bat. This is simple since the bat is just a horizontal line across the screen. However we will wish to move the bat, so its two ends will vary even though its distance from the bottom of the screen will not. So we need to declare two variables as follows. Note that these are placed in the appropriate procedure, that is in PROCsetupvariables.

```
340 batleft = 600 : batright = 700
```

Then the procedure for drawing the bat looks like this:

```
860 DEF PROCdrawbat
900 MOVE batleft,320 : DRAW batright,320
920 ENDPROC
```

We call this procedure with the line:

```
200 PROCdrawbat
```

The next part of the program is probably the most important. This is the procedure which moves the ball and checks for walls and scores. The ball is moved by increasing the values of X and Y and so we need two new variables to represent the increases. We will declare these variables first in the procedure for setting up variables, as follows. Retype line 340

```
340 incX = 8 : incY = 8 : batleft = 600 : batright = 700
```

Then the new procedure begins like this:

```
 960 DEF PROCmoveball
1020 X = X + incX : Y = Y + incY
1120 PLOT 69,X,Y
1140 ENDPROC
```

Line 1120 uses the number 69 with PLOT to plot a single point rather than a line. Now call this procedure as follows:

```
220 PROCmoveball
```

If you now run this program you will find that although the ball moves, it also leaves a path or trace behind it. So we need a line to remove the last position of the ball when we have drawn the next.

```
1000 PLOT 71,X,Y
```

This should work because the number 71 means plot the point in the same color as the screen, which of course makes it disappear. Now that we have established a way of making the ball move we can go back for a second to the new ball procedure and put in this line:

```
800 incY = 8
```

This ensures that, when the ball appears for the first time, it moves up the screen. We must now test for the ball hitting a wall. To do this we use the words IF and THEN and the new word POINT. This word is used as follows. Type in the line and we will discuss it.

```
1060 IF POINT(X,Y) = 3 THEN X = X - incX : Y = Y - incY :
incX = -incX
```

In the phrase IF POINT(X,Y) = 3 the 3 refers to the color of the screen at the point X,Y. The four colors are numbered:

0 -- Black
1 -- Red
2 -- Yellow
3 -- White

So the phrase means, 'if the point X,Y is colored white'. We have used 3 or white because the walls on the left and right are white. The rest of line 1060 moves the point back a space if the color is white using X = X -incX and Y = Y - incY. If this is not done, the ball takes a bite out of the wall. The final statement on the line is, incX = -incX. This changes the direction of movement of the ball from left-right to right-left or vice versa.

The next line is almost identical except that it checks for contact with the top wall or with the bat, both of which are colored yellow. The number for yellow is 2.

```
1080 IF POINT(X,Y) = 2 THEN X = X - incX : Y = Y - incY :
incY = -incY
```

Notice also that this time we change incY to -incY because we want the movement of the ball to change from up to down or vice-versa. Finally we need to check when the ball has gone off the screen. The number for this is set at -1. If it has gone off the screen then we need to do two things. One, call on a scoring procedure, and then call on the new ball procedure. So the line looks like this:

```
1100 IF POINT(X,Y) = -1 THEN PROCscore : PROCnewball
```

Remember that PROCscore has not yet been written. The completed routine now looks like this, with the inclusion of a REM line.

```
 960 DEF PROCmoveball
1000 PLOT 71,X,Y
1020 X = X + incX : Y = Y + incY
1040 REM CHECK WALLS AND SCORE
1060 IF POINT (X,Y) = 3 THEN X = X - incX : Y = Y - incY :
     incX = -incX
1080 IF POINT (X,Y) = 2 THEN X = X - incX : Y = Y - incY :
     incY = -incY
1100 IF POINT (X,Y) = -1 THEN PROCscore : PROCnewball
1120 PLOT 69,X,Y : REM DRAW BALL
1140 ENDPROC
```

Before we can run this we need a procedure called PROCscore. This will count the number of balls used, measure the length of time that the player manages to keep a ball on the screen, and print messages on the screen to let the player know how he or she is getting on. It begins by using the statement VDU5. This brings the graphics cursor and the text cursor together and allows us, using the statement MOVE, to write wherever we like on the graphics screen. This is put in the procedure for setting up variables as follows:

```
360 VDU 5
```

We have enough room at the top of the screen for messages, so we use MOVE 100,1000 for one line of text, and MOVE 100,950 for the second. So the procedure begins like this:

```
1180 DEF PROCscore
1280 MOVE 100,1000
1440 ENDPROC
```

We will use the variable balls to count the number of balls and we will begin with eight of them. So this variable is also declared in line 360 of the procedure for setting up variables. Retype it as follows:

```
360 balls = 8 : time = TIME : VDU 5
```

We have also used this line to establish a variable time equal to the built-in function TIME. (See page 121). We will use this to measure how long a ball is kept on the screen. We now add the following lines to the score procedure.

```
1260 balls = balls - 1
1300 PRINT "Balls left "; balls
1380 MOVE 100,950
1400 PRINT "Time spent "; TIME - time
1420 IF balls = 0 THEN END
```

Type this in and run the program. Although it will work you will find that there are problems about the numbers. First the numbers become steadily more unreadable because they are being printed on top of each other: and second the time measure is very large because it is in hundredths of a second. The first can be cured by typing beforehand a repeat of the lines 1300 and 1400, but changing the color of the writing to red, so that the last message is wiped out before the next one goes in. This is done as follows:

```
1220 MOVE 100,1000
1240 GCOL 0,1 : PRINT "Balls left "; balls : GCOL0,2
```

Line 1220 makes sure that we are on the right line. In line 1240, GCOL0,1 makes the color red, and then GCOL0,2 turns it back to yellow. In a similar way we have:

```
1320 MOVE 100,950
1340 GCOL 0,1 : PRINT "Time spent "; TIME - time : GCOL0,2
```

We can change the number given for the time from hundredths of a second to seconds by dividing by 100 as follows. We will use the variable 'scoretime' for this, and put it in the early procedure for setting up variables.

```
380 scoretime = (TIME - time) DIV 100
```

We must then change lines 1340 and 1380 as follows:

```
1340 GCOL 0,1 : PRINT "Time spent ";scoretime; "secs" :
     GCOL 0,2
1400 PRINT "Time spent ";scoretime; "secs"
```

We must also put in a line to update the scoretime after each run, as follows. This is identical to line 380:

```
1360 scoretime = (TIME - time) DIV 100
```

The complete procedure now looks like this:

```
1180 DEF PROCscore
1220 MOVE 100,1000
1240 GCOL 0,1 : PRINT "Balls left ";balls : GCOL 0,2
1260 balls = balls - 1
1280 MOVE 100,1000
```

```
1300 PRINT "Balls left ";balls
1320 MOVE 100,950
1340 GCOL0,1 : PRINT "Time spent ";scoretime; "secs" : GCOL
     0,2
1380 MOVE 100,950
1400 PRINT "Time spent  ";scoretime; "secs"
1420 IF balls = 0 THEN END
1440 ENDPROC
```

Moving the bat

If we now run the program, everything should work, except that we cannot move the bat along the bottom of the screen. To do this we need a procedure which allows the player to press some letter on the keyboard to make the bat go left, and another letter to make it go right. For this we have chosen N and M because they are beside each other about the middle of the bottom row of keys. You can choose others if you wish. We have called the procedure 'checkkeyboard' and within this we call up one of two other procedures to move LEFT or RIGHT.

```
1480 DEF PROCcheckkeyboard
1520 A$ = INKEY$(0)
1540 IF A$ = "N" OR A$ = "n" THEN PROCleft
1560 IF A$ = "M" OR A$ = "m" THEN PROCright
1580 ENDPROC
```

The word INKEY$ means that the computer accepts a single character input from the keyboard. The number in brackets (0 in this case) is a measure of how long it should wait for this input. Lines 1540 and 1560 test whether the input is N or M (in either upper or lower case) and directs the program to an appropriate procedure. If there is no keyboard input, the program continues immediately without stopping. This means that the ball will continue to move whether the bat moves or not. (In fact, as you will find, it moves slightly more quickly). This procedure is called in line 240 as follows:

```
240 PROCcheckkeyboard
```

Now we must write the two procedures which move the bat left or right. Since we have already written a procedure to draw the bat, based on two variables representing its ends, batleft and batright, all we need to do here is wipe out the bat, move the values of the two ends over to the left a bit, and then it will be redrawn in the new position. This will happen each time the letter N is pressed, and it will happen quite quickly, so the bat will appear to move. It begins as follows

```
1620 DEF PROCleft
1680 batright = batright - 20
1700 batleft = batleft - 20
1760 ENDPROC
```

We have chosen to move the end 20 units to the left, but you can speed up the movement of the bat by increasing this 20, or slow it down by decreasing it. Now we need a line to remove the extra bit of bat left out on its right. To do this we use GCOL, 0,1 to change the color to red, and then, later, change it back to yellow with GCOL 0,2. The line looks like this:

```
1720 GCOL 0,1
1740 MOVE batright,320 : DRAW batright + 20,320 : GCOL 0,2
```

The procedure to move right is almost identical and the two complete procedures are now shown below.

```
1620 DEF PROCleft
1660 IF batleft < 70 THEN batleft = batleft + 20 : batright
     = batright + 20
1680 batright = batright - 20
1700 batleft = batleft - 20
1720 GCOL 0,1
1740 MOVE batright,320 : DRAW batright + 20,320 : GCOL 0,2
1760 ENDPROC
1800 DEF PROCright
1840 IF batright > 1210 THEN batleft = batleft - 20 :
     batright = batright - 20
1860 batleft = batleft + 20
1880 batright = batright + 20
1900 GCOL 0,1
1920 MOVE batleft,320 : DRAW batleft - 20,320 : GCOL 0,2
1940 ENDPROC
```

The main program

The program is now almost complete. All the necessary procedures have been written and the lines necessary to call these. The main body of the program, that is the first lines, currently look like this:

```
100 MODE 5
120 PROCsetupvariables
140 PROCsetupscreen
160 PROCnewball
200 PROCdrawbat
220 PROCmoveball
240 PROCcheckkeyboard
260 END
```

The procedures then follow. The only thing that remains to be done is the loop round the last three procedure calls. To do this we use the words REPEAT UNTIL as follows (see page 90).

```
180 REPEAT
260 UNTIL FALSE
```

Type these in and the program should now run properly. This use of the word FALSE is described on page 93. The complete program listing now looks like this. It is exactly as we have described it except that we have added a lot of REM statements to assist readability.

```
100 MODE 5
120 PROCsetupvariables
140 PROCsetupscreen
160 PROCnewball
180 REPEAT
200 PROCdrawbat
220 PROCmoveball : REM checks walls and score
240 PROCcheckkeyboard : REM checks for bat movement
260 UNTIL FALSE
280 REM ******************************************
300 DEF PROCsetupvariables
320 REM ******************************************
340 incX = 8 : incY = 8 : batleft = 600 : batright = 700
360 balls = 8 : time = TIME : VDU 5
380 scoretime = (TIME - time) DIV 100
400 GCOL0,181 : CLG
420 ENDPROC
440 REM ******************************************
460 DEF PROCsetupscreen
480 REM ******************************************
500 REM  LEFT
520 MOVE 30,300 : MOVE 50,300
540 PLOT 85,30,800 : PLOT 85,50,800
560 REM  RIGHT
580 MOVE 1230,300 : MOVE 1250,300
600 PLOT 85,1230,800 : PLOT 85,1250,800
620 REM  TOP
640 GCOL 0,2
660 MOVE 30,780 : MOVE 1250,780
680 PLOT 85,30,800 : PLOT 85,1250,800
700 ENDPROC
720 REM ******************************************
740 DEF PROCnewball
760 REM ******************************************
780 X = RND(1171) + 54 : Y = 400 : REM ball starting point
800 incY = 8 : REM ensure new ball moves up
820 ENDPROC
840 REM ******************************************
860 DEF PROCdrawbat
```

```
 880 REM ********************************************
 900 MOVE batleft,320 : DRAW batright,320
 920 ENDPROC
 940 REM ********************************************
 960 DEF PROCmoveball
 980 REM ********************************************
1000 PLOT 71,X,Y : REM remove ball
1020 X = X + incX : Y = Y + incY : REM next ball position
1040 REM check walls and score
1060 IF POINT(X,Y) = 3 THEN X = X - incX : Y = Y - incY :
     incX = -incX
1080 IF POINT(X,Y) = 2 THEN X = X - incX : Y = Y - incY :
     incY = -incY
1100 IF POINT(X,Y) = -1 THEN PROCscore : PROCnewball
1120 PLOT 69,X,Y : REM draw ball
1140 ENDPROC
1160 REM ********************************************
1180 DEF PROCscore
1200 REM ********************************************
1220 MOVE 100,1000
1240 GCOL 0,1 : PRINT "Balls left "; balls : GCOL 0,2
1260 balls = balls - 1
1280 MOVE 100,1000
1300 PRINT "Balls left "; balls
1320 MOVE 100,950
1340 GCOLO,1 : PRINT "Time spent  "; scoretime; " secs " :
     GCOL 0,2
1360 scoretime = (TIME - time) DIV 100
1380 MOVE 100,950
1400 PRINT "Time spent  "; scoretime; " secs "
1420 IF balls = 0 THEN END
1440 ENDPROC
1460 REM ********************************************
1480 DEF PROCcheckkeyboard
1500 REM ********************************************
1520 A$ = INKEY$(0)
1540 IF A$ = "N" OR A$ = "n" PROCleft
1560 IF A$ = "M" OR A$ = "m" PROCright
1580 ENDPROC
1600 REM ********************************************
1620 DEF PROCleft
1640 REM ********************************************
1660 IF batleft < 70 THEN batleft = batleft + 20 : batright
     = batright + 20
1680 batright = batright - 20
1700 batleft = batleft - 20
1720 GCOLO,1
1740 MOVE batright,320 : DRAW batright + 20,320 : GCOL 0,2
1760 ENDPROC
1780 REM ********************************************
1800 DEF PROCright
1820 REM ********************************************
```

```
1840 IF batright > 1210 THEN batleft = batleft - 20 :
     batright = batright - 20
1860 batleft = batleft + 20
1880 batright = batright + 20
1900 GCOLO,1
1920 MOVE batleft,320 : DRAW batleft - 20,320 : GCOL 0,2
1940 ENDPROC
1960 REM ******************************************
```

Problems

1. Write a bibliography program which allows you to input a list of books. Each entry should include the author's name, the title of the book, the publisher and the year of publication. The menu should allow the following options:

BEGIN	a new list
READ	a current list
ALPHABETIZE	the list
ADD	a name to the list
DELETE	a name from the list
CHANGE	any specified entry
SAVE	the list on tape
RECOVER	the list from tape
FINISH	for now

As well as the subroutines necessary for these, it should also include a routine for holding the screen.

2. Write a test standardization program. This should allow the input of names and scores of a class, and should then calculate the mean and standard deviation of these scores. The user should then be invited to choose a new mean and a new standard deviation and the program should then calculate a new score for each name. The data should be displayed on the screen in three columns, i.e. names, scores, standardized scores. There should be routines for saving on tape, recovering from tape, putting in alphabetical order, adding and taking away names, changing all the scores, and so on.

CHAPTER 14
IN THE CLASSROOM

Introduction

This section tries to describe a set of activities which a teacher might use in introducing the computer into his or her classroom. Although these activities are presented in a particular order, this does not mean that we think that this order is very important. In certain circumstances changes in the ordering would be sensible and even necessary. As well as this it has been assumed that, for some of these activities, suitable software is available or can be constructed. This is certainly overoptimistic now but a great quantity of software is under development for this machine. The quality is improving all the time so we hope that this book will help teachers and others to become more expert at both writing software and improving or revising bought software.

The ideas that follow are meant as a very general guide and no special kind of school or range of school ages is specified. Many of the suggestions would work very well in a primary school for example, but are generally not intended exclusively for that age. We would also wish to add that we do not consider all of them to have equal educational potential. We are very clear, however, that all school subjects can benefit from using the machine. That is to say, we would not support at all the notion that mathematics and the sciences have a better case than the other disciplines. In particular, the sophisticated string-handling and word-processing capacity of the machine makes it as capable of dealing with words as with numbers. Add to this the very sophisticated graphics, color and music facilities and a great part of the curriculum is within range.

We also believe that the potential of machines like this is very great and that as time goes on the range and complexity of the tasks that they can accomplish successfully will be greatly extended. In practical terms, therefore, we believe that all users should join a Users' Club either locally or nationally so as to keep in touch with developments in software and add-on hardware (see Appendix D).

The computer as a games-player

To begin with, it is necessary to overcome any inhibitions and anxieties that children may have about playing with the computer. They must become adept at setting the machine up, loading programs from tape or disk, pressing keys, using the RETURN, and CTRL and ESC keys, and so on.

Games, probably bought from a software house to begin with, are the ideal introduction. Not only do they act as an immediate stimulus but they build up a degree of motivation and interest that is hard to acquire in any other way. It is even likely, after some experience, that children will take on the onerous task of typing in long game programs from books and magazines, even before they have had any experience of programming.

Although many of the most popular games are arcade type games, like Starwars, not all games that can be played on the computer are trivial or unintellectual. Many of these, such as Mastermind or Noughts and Crosses (or Tic-Tac-Toe), have a logical or mathematical dimension that is important educationally. This is not to mention complex games like Draughts, Chess and Go.

The computer as a calculator

The first chapter of this book shows how to begin to use the computer as a simple calculator. This usually involves the use of the word PRINT. At a very elementary level children can go to the computer to check answers to arithmetical calculations. One effect of this is to put some emphasis on the importance of the 'ordering' of calculations and on the ambiguity of statements like:

```
20 - 10 - 4
```

For example, we can compare the answer to:

```
PRINT (20 - 10) - 4
```

with the answer to:

```
PRINT 20 - (10 - 4)
```

and discuss why these are different. It is also an interesting and important mathematical notion to be able to store numbers in variables. This can be done on the computer and, at the same time, a simulation of the process can be developed in the classroom. For example, we can input the following lines, remembering to press the RETURN key after each.

```
first = 4
second = 5
add = first + second
product = first * second
PRINT first, second, add, product
```

Alongside this we can have a set of small cardboard boxes labelled first, second, add and product. The first line 'first = 4' can be represented visually by putting four counters in the box labelled first. This process is then continued for each of the other boxes. This sort of exercise allows children to develop some kind of mental imagery about the internal processes of the machine. A similar activity is possible with strings. Suppose the school is called 'St. John's Academy'. Then:

```
one$ = "St."
two$ = " John's"
three$ = " Academy"
total$ = one$ + two$ + three$
PRINT total$
```

(Note: there is a space before the quotation marks and the J and the A in lines 2 and 3 above). Boxes can be used again to represent the memory units and this time will be labelled one$, two$, and so on.

The computer as a teacher

At a very elementary level it is possible to write a little program to allow children to practice addition. Suppose, for example, we wish to add two two-digit numbers each time. First, we can create the numbers with these two lines:

```
100 top = RND(99)
120 bottom = RND(99)
```

We then find the answer with:

```
140 answer = top + bottom
```

We then display the problem and invite an answer from the child:

```
160 PRINT SPC(10); top
180 PRINT SPC(9); "+" bottom
200 PRINT SPC(8); "----"
220 INPUT SPC(10); result
```

Then check if the answer is correct.

```
240 IF answer = result THEN PRINT "Correct" ELSE PRINT
    "Sorry that is     not correct."
260 PRINT "Do you want to try another?"
```

and so on.

This is just the bones of a program and a great deal can be done to dress it up and present it in an interesting and fascinating way. What about using graphics to make the screen 'explode' when a correct answer is given! Of course, this program can easily be adapted for subtraction, multiplication, division and so on. It can also, with very little extra thought, become a word-completion or sentence-completion program.

These are simple examples of Computer Assisted Learning (shortened to CAL). It is possible to develop these into a quite complex suite of such programs and, as time goes on, most teachers will do this. But the alternative is to buy commercial versions of such programs and adapt these to your own needs.

For older primary children more complex problems become possible, such as completing sequences, plotting points, visual representations of fractions, completing symmetrical shapes, rotations, solving simple equations, and many more. For high school children the possibilities are even greater and are limited only by the imagination of the teacher or programmer.

The program that follows is an example which is more complex both in its content and in the amount of programming necessary to make it work. It uses two random numbers, generated in lines 120 and 140, to produce linear sequences of numbers. A set of six numbers in a linear sequence is then written on the screen with a bar, equal in length to each number, drawn beside each number. The user is then invited to put in the next two numbers in the sequence.

```
100 MODE 7
120 first = RND(6) : REM first term
140 differ = RND(7) : REM term difference
160 FOR count = 1 TO first : PRINT"*"; : NEXT count
180 PRINT TAB(36);first
200 FOR term = 1 TO 5
220 next = first + term * differ
240 FOR count = 1 TO next : PRINT"*"; : NEXT count
```

```
260 PRINT TAB(36);next
280 NEXT term
300 INPUT'' "Put in the next number "result
320 IF result = first + 6 * differ THEN 360 ELSE 340
340 PRINT'' "Hard luck.  Try again." : GOTO 300
360 PRINT'' "Well done."
```

The computer as a manager

There are a number of ways in which the computer can be used to store and generate records of class activities. An example of this is the 'Test Standardize' program in the problems attached to Chapter 13. This allows a teacher to store and, perhaps more importantly, to standardize any set of scores generated by a class.

Let us take another example. Suppose a teacher has created a set of mathematics workcards (called C1, C2, etc.) which has a complex organizational structure. A very small subset of this structure is shown below:

```
Stage 1. Choose one of: C1 C2 C3
Stage 2. Do C4 - which includes short test
Stage 3. If score is equal to 50 or is less than 50, do C5
         If score is greater than 50, do C6
Stage 4. After C5, do C7 and C8
         After C6 do C9
Stage 5. Do card 10
```

It would be a relatively simple task to write a program which would 'advise' each pupil about which card to use next. The first few steps in such a program are shown below. To begin with, the child is asked to indicate whether or not he/she is a beginner. If he/she is a beginner then the problem is immediately solved: do C1, C2 or C3. If the child is not a beginner then further information is necessary:

```
100 MODE 7 : PRINT "Are you a beginner?"
120 INPUT ans$ : IF ans$ = "YES" OR ans$ = "yes" THEN
    PROCbegin ELSE     PROCcont
140 END
160 DEF PROCbegin
180 PRINT' "Choose one of the cards numbered"
200 PRINT "C1, C2, C3"
220 ENDPROC
240 DEF PROCcont
260 PRINT "What card have you just completed?"
280 INPUT reply$
300 IF reply$ = "C1" OR reply$ = "C2" OR reply$ = "C3" THEN
    320 ELSE 340
320 PRINT '"The next card must be chosen from...."
340 ENDPROC
```

Again, commercial programs for purposes of this sort will often be available, and will certainly become available as time goes on.

In more general terms the machine can be used to manage or advise about or control any complex set of educational decisions or structures. In this sort of system the machine acts simply as a recordkeeper and patternkeeper and so is able, very quickly, to compare individual performances or courses or patterns with a more general established or expected set.

The computer as an aid in simulations

The programs on 'tossing a coin' and on 'tossing a die' in Chapter 7 are elementary examples of simulation programs. Instead of actually throwing a die or a coin 200 times, it is possible to get the computer to simulate this process and produce a set of likely outcomes. Clearly the random number function will allow it to be used to produce figures of this sort for any such problem.

There are many situations in subjects like biology and geography where such random number techniques are useful in that they allow a complex set of natural phenomena linked by probabilistic relationships to be observed and studied in the classroom. Usually the real complexity of the situation and the interrelationships have to be severely oversimplified but, nonetheless, their structure and the processes through which they operate can be partially retained even in an oversimplified simulation model. An example now follows.

A factory is about to employ a new workforce of 1000 people. Some of these will be junior managers and some will be shopfloor workers. No exact figures are decided upon, but it is expected that the probability of becoming a junior manager is 1/4 or 0.25, so that the probability of working on the shopfloor is therefore 3/4 or 0.75.

After three years there will be a promotions exercise. Of the junior managers some will become senior managers, and the probability of this is about 1/10 or 0.1. The other junior managers will remain junior managers, and the probability of this is therefore about 9/10 or 0.9. Of those working on the shopfloor some will be promoted to foremen. The probability of this is reckoned to be 1/3 or 0.33. The other shopfloor workers will remain on the shopfloor, and so the probability of this is 2/3 or 0.67.

Use a simulation exercise based on random numbers to see how many of the 1000 workers might end up in each of the four employment categories. These are:

1. Senior management.
2. Junior management.
3. Foremen.
4. Shopfloor workers.

Admittedly this problem is fairly easily solved using simple arithmetic and the rules of probability. But that would leave out the random element, to some extent, and the real-life notion that the probabilities quoted are not precise.

Here is a program which can be used. As always, it is fairly unadorned and a great deal more can be done with it, but at the end it produces figures of those actually in each of the four categories.

```
100 MODE 7
120 INPUT "Input total number of workers  "total
140 sm = 0 : REM senior management.
160 jm = 0 : REM junior management.
180 fm = 0 : REM foremen.
200 sf = 0 : REM shopfloor workers.
220 FOR count = 1 TO total
240 first = RND(4) : REM management or workers.
260 second = RND(10) : REM management promotion
280 third = RND(3) : REM worker promotion.
300 IF first = 1 THEN PROCmanagement ELSE PROCworkers
320 NEXT count
340 PRINT'' "Senior management  "sm
360 PRINT' "Junior management  "jm
380 PRINT' "Foremen            "fm
400 PRINT' "Shopfloor workers  "sf
420 END
440 DEF PROCmanagement
460 IF second = 1 THEN sm = sm + 1 ELSE jm = jm + 1
480 ENDPROC
500 DEF PROCworkers
520 IF third = 1 THEN fm = fm + 1 ELSE sf = sf + 1
540 ENDPROC
```

Learning programming

This aspect of the computer's potential use in school can easily be forgotten in all the other more obviously functional and applied uses which we have described. But for those children who wish to learn how to program and who may do examinations in computer science, or similar subjects, then a machine like this is most valuable.

In the past, learning to program was often a paper exercise with long delays between writing the program and testing it. With this computer there is an immediate feedback and any attempt at programming can be tested on the spot. A great deal can be done with a very limited set of BASIC statements and commands and, once these have been understood there is tremendous scope for experiment and practical work.

There are also many side-effects from this kind of exercise. These range from the development of physical skills, like typing, to the logical skills necessary to predict the consequences of a series of simple statements and commands.

Appendix A Disk drives

Introduction

There are a number of disk systems available for use with the BBC microcomputer but we will deal only with the system manufactured by the makers of the computer, that is to say we will deal with the standard system.

You can purchase either a single disk drive or a pair of drives. These are light colored metal boxes about 24 by 9 by 15¢ cms. The front is black with the BBC owl motif and a small flap door which closes over a thin letter box style opening into which the disk is placed. A flat ribbon cable and a power cable are attached at the back and these are both connected directly to the computer. To see where, you must lift the computer over and look at its underside. There is no separate power line running from the disk drive to an independent power source, so the power comes directly to the disk drive from the computer. This means that, when you buy a disk drive, you must also buy a disk interface which has to be fitted to the computer. Finally there is also provided a Disk System User guide and a Utilities Disk. (If you have any difficulty getting the system connected together, the Disk System User Guide shows the process very clearly).

Disk drives and disks

In chapter 6 we described in detail how to use a tape-recorder with tape cassettes to store and retrieve programs and data files. Disk drives and floppy disks are used like tape-recorders and cassettes, but they have the great advantage that they work very much more quickly. The disks (sometimes called discs or diskettes) are used as a storage system and are completely blank when purchased.

Formatting a disk

Before a new blank disk can be used it must be formatted. This is done using a special program stored on the Utilities Disk supplied with the system. It divides the circular disk up, first of all, into 40 rings called tracks. Then it divides each of these tracks into ten sectors, each sector being part of a ring, i.e. shaped rather like a letter C. Each sector can hold 256 bytes of information, or one quarter of a kilobyte. So the whole disk holds 40 x 10 x 1/4 or 100 kilobytes.

Switch on the system and put the Utilities Disk into the drive. (The correct way round for the disk is shown in the User Guide). The screen now looks like this:

```
BBC Computer 32K

Acorn DFS

BASIC

½-
```

DFS stands for Disk Filing System and is an indication that the disk drive system has been properly connected up.

Now type in *FORM40 and press RETURN. (If you have a dual drive system then type in *FORM80 instead of *FORM40). Notice that this command begins with a star. Many of the disk operating words begin with a star. Immediately the red light on the front of the disk will go on and a whirring noise will come from the disk unit. Then this message will be printed on the screen. (Except that ABC will be replaced by a number, which may vary depending on the exact system being used).

```
Disk formatter ABC

Format which drive? -
```

Now take out the Utilities Disk. This is most important since formatting completely clears a disk so that any programs already on it are totally lost. (On every disk there is a little notch cut into one of the sides. This can be covered with an adhesive tab and if this is done the disk cannot be overwritten. This should now be done with the Utilities Disk).

Now insert a new blank disk into the drive and close the door. Then respond to the question on the screen with 0, (that is zero, since the single drive or the first of a pair is numbered 0). The computer will then print:

```
Do you really want to format drive 0?
```

This is just a precaution to give you another chance to make sure you have put in the correct disk. Type in Y (for Yes) and the disk drive responds at once. The light comes on and the whirring sound begins. On the screen the words 'Formatting drive 0' appear and then the numbers for each sector as it is formatted. There are 40 sectors and the numbers are written in hex or base sixteen, so they appear on the screen as follows:

```
00 01 02 03 04 05 06 07 08 09

0A 0B 0C 0D 0E 0F 10 11 12 13

14 15 16 17 18 19 1A 1B 1C 1D

1E 1F 20 21 22 23 24 25 26 27
```

This is followed by the message:

```
Disk formatted - repeat (Y/N) ?
```

Respond to this with N for No and the program ends.

Now type in *CAT (short for CATALOGUE)and press RETURN. The screen message will look something like this:

```
  (00)
Drive 0                 Option 0 (off)
Directory : 0.$         Library : 0.$

>-
```

This means that we are using drive 0 and there are currently no programs on the disk. The other information need not concern us for the moment.

Saving a program

We will now write a short program and then save it on the disk, just to demonstrate the technique.

```
100 CLS
120 PRINT "This is a test program"
140 PRINT "to be saved on the disk."
```

When you have done this type in the following and press RETURN:

```
SAVE "Testpro"
```

The word 'Testpro' is made up by the user to identify the program being saved and must not be more than 7 characters long. The disk will whirr gently for a few seconds with the red light on and the program will then be saved. To test this, use the *CAT command again, and when the listing appears on the screen, the title 'Testpro' will be there as evidence that the program has been saved.

Loading a program

Now type in NEW to remove this program from memory and then type in

```
LOAD"Testpro"
```

Then type in LIST and check that the program has been recovered.

You will notice that these two words, LOAD and SAVE, are used in exactly the same way with the disk system as they were with the tape system. The only differences are those of speed, and the fact that the disk system does not need to be switched on and off like the tape. The two words and their format are identical. This similarity of operation is also true of the word *CAT.

Data files

There is no need for a special section on saving data files as the words and syntax used in chapter 6 for loading data files onto tape also work with disks. So any programs which you have written using tapes for data saving and recovery will work without modification. The only change you may wish to make may be in the screen messages which you have included, like 'Data now being saved on tape'.

Transfer from tape to disk

If you have been using a tape system and have just bought a disk system, it is a simple matter to transfer programs.

(a) First make sure that both systems are attached to the computer.

(b) Type in *TAPE. This transfers the system from disk to tape operation.

(c) Now use LOAD to recover your program from the tape.

(d) Type in *Disk. This transfers the system back from tape to disk. It does not affect the program in memory.

(e) Now use SAVE to save the program on the disk.

Other commands

There are a number of techniques available on disk systems such as copying files, copying complete disks, locking files, dividing the catalogue up into independent sections, and so on. These are all described in the Disk System User Guide.

Appendix B Base sixteen numbers

Introduction

We have mentioned on several occasions that the computer sometimes handles numbers in base sixteen rather than base ten and that we may need to translate numbers from base ten to base sixteen and vice versa. In order to describe properly the whole idea of bases in arithmetic and the particular importance of base sixteen in computing we would need much more space than we have available here. We can, however, try to make the actual translation process as simple and direct as possible. We do this now in two ways, firstly by describing the process and secondly by using reference tables.

Base sixteen

Our number system is based on two important practices. Firstly, we use a limited or finite number of symbols to represent our numbers. In our normal counting we need only use ten symbols, that is the set: 0, 1, 2, 3, 4, 5, 6, 7, 8, 9. We know that we can represent any number by using these ten symbols in various combinations and repetitions. This raises the second practice, which is that the meaning or value of each symbol depends on its position with respect to the other symbols. For example we know that the four in 347 means four tens because the seven must mean seven units. So in base ten arithmetic we need ten symbols and we know what they mean by looking at where they are placed.

This means that in base sixteen, we need sixteen symbols and to make up the full set we make use of letters of the alphabet as follows:

Base sixteen	0	1	2	3	4	5	6	7	8	9	A	B	C	D	E	F	10
Base ten	0	1	2	3	4	5	6	7	8	9	10	11	12	13	14	15	16

We have written the same numbers in base ten for comparison. Note that in base ten when we reach 9, the next number, i.e. ten, uses the symbols 0 and 1 again like this, 10, meaning one ten and zero units. So in base sixteen in parallel to this, when we reach F (or 15), then the next number, i.e. sixteen, uses the symbols 0 and 1 again in the same way. Therefore in base sixteen, 10 means one sixteen and zero units. Similarly 20 means two sixteens and zero units (that is 32 in base ten), and so on. This also means that the base ten number 99 - which means nine tens and nine units - is paralleled in base sixteen by FF - which means fifteen sixteens and fifteen units. In both cases the next number is 100 which means ten tens in base ten, and sixteen sixteens in base sixteen. The process continues in this way.

Reference tables

We now present two tables which allow us to translate directly, from and to base sixteen, all base sixteen numbers from 00 to FF.

Table B1 translates from base sixteen to base ten. It is used as follows. Suppose we wish to change C7 into base ten. We start on the left, where it says First digit, and find the row with a C. Then move along this row to the column with 7 at the top where it says Second digit. The number you will find there is 199. So C7 in base sixteen is equivalent to 199 in base ten.

Table B2 does the translation from base ten to base sixteen. Start on the left where it says First digit and find the row with a 12. Then move along this row to the column with a 7 at the top where it says last digit. The number you will find is 7F. So 127 in base ten becomes 7F in base sixteen.

Table B1 Base sixteen to base ten

SECOND DIGIT

		0	1	2	3	4	5	6	7	8	9	A	B	C	D	E	F
	0	000	001	002	003	004	005	006	007	008	009	010	011	012	013	014	015
	1	016	017	018	019	020	021	022	023	024	025	026	027	028	029	030	031
	2	032	033	034	035	036	037	038	039	040	041	042	043	044	045	046	047
	3	048	049	050	051	052	053	054	055	056	057	058	059	060	061	062	063
	4	064	065	066	067	068	069	070	071	072	073	074	075	076	077	078	079
	5	080	081	082	083	084	085	086	087	088	089	090	091	092	093	094	095
	6	096	097	098	099	100	101	102	103	104	105	016	107	108	109	110	111
	7	112	113	114	115	116	117	118	119	120	121	122	123	124	125	126	127
FIRST DIGIT	8	128	129	130	131	132	133	134	135	136	137	138	139	140	141	142	143
	9	144	145	146	147	148	149	150	151	152	153	154	155	156	157	158	159
	A	160	161	162	163	164	165	166	167	168	169	170	171	172	173	174	175
	B	176	177	178	179	180	181	182	183	184	185	186	187	188	189	190	191
	C	192	193	194	195	196	197	198	199	200	201	202	203	204	205	206	207
	D	208	209	210	211	212	213	214	215	216	217	218	219	220	221	222	223
	E	224	225	226	227	228	229	230	231	232	233	234	235	236	237	238	239
	F	240	241	242	243	244	245	246	247	248	249	250	251	252	253	254	255

Table B2 Base ten to base sixteen

SECOND DIGIT

FIRST DIGIT	0	1	2	3	4	5	6	7	8	9
0	00	01	02	03	04	05	06	07	08	09
1	0A	0B	0C	0D	0E	0F	10	11	12	13
2	14	15	16	17	18	19	1A	1B	1C	1D
3	1E	1F	20	21	22	23	24	25	26	27
4	28	29	2A	2B	2C	2D	2E	2F	30	31
5	32	33	34	35	36	37	38	39	3A	3B
6	3C	3D	3E	3F	40	41	42	43	44	45
7	46	47	48	49	4A	4B	4C	4D	4E	4F
8	50	51	52	53	54	55	56	57	58	59
9	5A	5B	5C	5D	5E	5F	60	61	62	63
10	64	65	66	67	68	69	6A	6B	6C	6D
11	6E	6F	70	71	72	73	74	75	76	77
12	78	79	7A	7B	7C	7D	7E	7F	80	81
13	82	83	84	85	86	87	88	89	8A	8B
14	8C	8D	8E	8F	90	91	92	93	94	95
15	96	97	98	99	9A	9B	9C	9D	9E	9F
16	A0	A1	A2	A3	A4	A5	A6	A7	A8	A9
17	AA	AB	AC	AD	AE	AF	B0	B1	B2	B3
18	B4	B5	B6	B7	B8	B9	BA	BB	BC	BD
19	BE	BF	C0	C1	C2	C3	C4	C5	C6	C7
20	C8	C9	CA	CB	CC	CD	CE	CF	D0	D1
21	D2	D3	D4	D5	D6	D7	D8	D9	DA	DB
22	DC	DD	DE	DF	E0	E1	E2	E3	E4	E5

Table B2 (continued)

		SECOND DIGIT									
	23	E6	E7	E8	E9	EA	EB	EC	ED	EE	EF
FIRST DIGIT	24	F0	F1	F2	F3	F4	F5	F6	F7	F8	F9
	25	FA	FB	FC	FD	FE	FF				

Appendix C Answers to Problems

Chapter 1

1

```
(a) PRINT 4.27 + 31.28 + 173.1        RET
    208.65
(b) PRINT 13452/12                    RET
    1121
(c) PRINT (6.5/100)*73216             RET
    4759.04
(d) PRINT 12345 + (11/100)*12345      RET
    13702.95
(e) PRINT 5 - (1.34 + 1.78 + .69)     RET
    1.19
```

2

```
A = 650 : B=.02 : C = 71              RET
D = A + B*A - C : PRINT D             RET

592
D = D + B*D - C * PRINT D             RET

532.84
472.4968
410-946736
348.165671
```

3 The result is that eventually there are nearly four complete rows made up entirely of the letter A.

The result this time is that four rows fill up more quickly with repetitions of 12345.

4

```
MODE 5                                RET

MOVE 100,100                          RET

DRAW 1200,500                         RET

DRAW 400,800                          RET

DRAW 900,50                           RET

DRAW 1000,1000                        RET

DRAW 100,100                          RET
```

Chapter 2

1
```
100 CLS
120 REM names and bank balances
140 PRINT"Input 6 names.  In each case put in"
160 PRINT"the name and then put in the balance."
180 INPUT name1$
200 INPUT money1
220 INPUT name2$
240 INPUT money2
260 INPUT name3$
280 INPUT money3
300 INPUT name4$
320 INPUT money4
340 INPUT name5$
360 INPUT money5
380 INPUT name6$
400 INPUT money6
420 PRINT name1$,money1
440 PRINT name2$,money2
460 PRINT name3$,money3
480 PRINT name4$,money4
500 PRINT name5$,money5
520 PRINT name6$,money6
```

2
```
100 CLS
120 DATA socks,ties,shirts,shorts,coats,dresses
140 DATA 2,4,10,14,65,50
160 READ item1$
180 READ item2$
200 READ item3$
220 READ item4$
240 READ item5$
260 READ item6$
280 READ price1
300 READ price2
320 READ price3
340 READ price4
360 READ price5
380 READ price6
400 PRINT item1$,price1
420 PRINT item2$,price2
440 PRINT item3$,price3
460 PRINT item4$,price4
480 PRINT item5$,price5
500 PRINT item6$,price6
```

3

```
100 CLS
120 PRINT"Input four names and addresses. In each"
140 PRINT"case put the name in and"
160 PRINT"then the address in three lines."
180 PRINT"First one."
200 INPUT A1$,B1$,C1$,D1$
220 PRINT"Next one."
240 INPUT A2$,B2$,C2$,D2$
260 PRINT"Next one."
280 INPUT A3$,B3$,C3$,D3$
300 PRINT"Last one."
320 INPUT A4$,B4$,C4$,D4$
340 REM printout begins
360 PRINT A1$,B1$
380 PRINT C1$
400 PRINT D1$
420 PRINT A2$,B2$
440 PRINT C2$
460 PRINT D2$
480 PRINT A3$,B3$
500 PRINT C3$
520 PRINT D3$
540 PRINT A4$,B4$
560 PRINT C4$
580 PRINT D4$
```

4

```
100 REM standard letter
120 CLS
140 PRINT"            Standard letter"
160 PRINT"Put in today's date."
180 INPUT date$
200 PRINT"Now put in letter recipient."
220 INPUT person$
240 PRINT"Now put in reason for meeting."
260 INPUT reason$
280 PRINT"Now date when you will be available."
300 INPUT date2$
320 PRINT"Now time when you will be available."
340 INPUT time$
360 PRINT"Now where you will be available."
380 INPUT where$
400 PRINT"Education centre,"
420 PRINT"New University of Ulster,"
440 PRINT"Coleraine, N.Ireland."
460 PRINTdate$
480 PRINT"Dear "person$
500 PRINT"          I would like to arrange a"
520 PRINT"meeting to discuss:"
540 PRINT reason$
560 PRINT"I would be available on "date2$
580 PRINT"in "where$" at "time$
600 PRINT"I would be grateful if you could"
620 PRINT"come at this time."
640 PRINT"             Yours sincerely"
660 PRINT"             Fergal Dunn."
```

Chapter 3

1
```
100 CLS
120 PROCintroduction
140 PROCconversion
160 END
180 DEF PROCintroduction
200 CLS
220 PRINT"       WEIGHT  CONVERSION"
240 PROCspace(2)
260 PRINT'"This program converts pounds weight"
280 PRINT'"into grams.  One pound is taken to be"
300 PRINT'"equal to 435.592 grams."
320  PRINT'"When you see the question-mark"
340  PRINT'"put in the number of pounds you "
360  PRINT'"wish to convert."
380 PROCspace(2)
400 PROCholdscreen
420 ENDPROC
440 DEF PROCconversion
460 PROCspace(3)
480 PRINT"Now input the number and press RETURN."
500 PROCspace(2)
520 INPUTpounds
540 grams=pounds*435.592
560 PROCspace(2)
580 PRINT"The number of pounds is  ";pounds
600 PRINT"The number of  grams is  ";grams
620 PROCspace(2)
640 ENDPROC
660 DEF PROCspace(number)
680 FOR count=1 TO number
700   PRINT
720   NEXT count
740 ENDPROC
760 DEF PROCholdscreen
780 PRINT"     Press the space-bar."
800 ZZ=GET
820 ENDPROC
```

2
```
100 CLS
120 PROCintro
140 PROCinput
160 END
180 DEF PROCintro
200 PRINT"         AVERAGING"
220 PROCspace
240 PRINT"This program accepts a set of numbers."
260 PRINT'"finds their total and calculates"
280 PRINT'"an average.  Put them in one at a time"
300 PRINT'"After the last one put in -99."
320 PROCspace
340 PROCholdscreen
360 ENDPROC
380 DEF PROCinput
400 count=0:total=0
420 PROCspace
440 INPUT number
460 IF number=-99 THEN 560
480 count=count+1
```

continued

```
500 total=total+number
520 PROCspace
540 GOTO 420
560 average=total/count
580 PROCspace
600 PRINT'"You put in          "count" numbers"
620 PRINT'"The total is        "total
640 PRINT'"The average is      "average
660 ENDPROC
680 DEF PROCspace
700 PRINT:PRINT
720 ENDPROC
740 DEF PROCholdscreen
760 PRINT'"     Press the space-bar"
780 ZZ=GET
800 ENDPROC
```

3

```
100 CLS
120 PROCintro
140 PROCinput
160 PROCconversion
180 END
200 DEF PROCintro
220 PRINT"          MONEY CONVERSION"
240 PROCspace
260 PRINT'"This program accepts a sum of money"
280 PRINT'"in one currency and converts it"
300 PRINT'"into the equivalent amount in four"
320 PRINT'"other currencies.  You choose the other"
340 PRINT'"currencies and input the "
360 PRINT'"rate of exchange for each."
380 PROCholdscreen
400 ENDPROC
420 DEF PROCinput
440 PRINT'"Input the name of the first of the"
460 PRINT'"four currencies that you wish to convert"
480 PRINT'"your own money into."
500 INPUT'',currency1$
520 PRINT'"Now the name of the second currency."
540 INPUT'',currency2$
560 PRINT'"Now the name of the  third currency."
580 INPUT'',currency3$
600 PRINT'"Now the name of the fourth currency."
620 INPUT'',currency4$
640 PROCspace
660 PRINT'"Now input the current exchange rate"
680 PRINT'"for each of these currencies."
700 PRINT' currency1$,:INPUT rate1
720 PRINT' currency2$,:INPUT rate2
740 PRINT' currency3$,:INPUT rate3
760 PRINT' currency4$,:INPUT rate4
780 PRINT'"Now input the number of units of"
800 PRINT'"your own currency that you wish"
820 PRINT'"to have converted to the other four."
840 PROCspace
860 INPUT money
880 ENDPROC
900 DEF PROCconversion
```

continued

```
 920 newmoney1=rate1*money
 940 newmoney2=rate2*money
 960 newmoney3=rate3*money
 980 newmoney4=rate4*money
1000 PROCspace
1020 PRINT'"The amount given is  ";money
1040 PRINT'"The exchange values are:-"
1060 PRINT'currency1$,newmoney1
1080 PRINT'currency2$,newmoney2
1100 PRINT'currency3$,newmoney3
1120 PRINT'currency4$,newmoney4
1140 ENDPROC
1160 DEF PROCspace
1180 PRINT:PRINT
1200 ENDPROC
1220 DEF PROCholdscreen
1240 PRINT''"     Press the space bar."''
1260 ZZ=GET
1280 ENDPROC
```

Chapter 4

1
```
100  DIM numbers(10),left(10),middle(10),right(10)
120  CLS
140  PRINT "Input 10 numbers, one at a time."
160  count1 = 1 : count2 = 1 : count3 = 1
180  FOR count = 1 TO 10
200    PRINT'' "This is number ";count;:
       INPUT"   " numbers(count)
220    IF 10*numbers(count) MOD 10 = 0 THEN 240 ELSE
       PRINT'"   TRY AGAIN ";:GOTO 200
240    IF numbers(count)<10 THEN left(count1) =
       numbers(count) : count1 = count1 + 1
260    IF numbers(count)>9 AND numbers(count)<20 THEN
       middle(count2) = numbers(count) : count2 = count2 + 1
280    IF numbers(count)>19 THEN right(count3) =
       numbers(count) : count3 = count3 + 1
300    NEXT count
320  count1 = count1 - 1 : count2 = count2 - 1 : count3 =
     count3 - 1
340  PRINT' "The numbers less than 10 are:-"
360  PRINT
380  FOR count = 1 TO count1
400    PRINT left(count)
420    NEXT count
440  PRINT
460  PRINT' "The numbers between 10 and 20 are:-"
480  PRINT
500  FOR count = 1 TO count2
520    PRINT middle(count)
540    NEXT count
560  PRINT
580  PRINT' "The numbers greater than 20 are:-"
600  PRINT
620  FOR count = 1 TO count3
640    PRINT right(count)
660    NEXT count
```

2
```
100 CLS
120 INPUT'"What is the first number ",num1
140 INPUT'"What is the second number ",num2
160 PRINT''"Choose one of these numbers:-"
180 PRINT'"          1....Add"
200 PRINT'"          2....Subtiply"
220 PRINT'"          3....Multiply"
240 PRINT'"          4....Divide"
260 INPUT TAB(10,18),choice : IF choice<1 OR choice>4
    THEN 260
280 IF choice=1 THEN ans=num1+num2: GOTO 360
300 IF choice=2 THEN ans=num1-num2: GOTO 360
320 IF choice=3 THEN ans=num1*num2: GOTO 360
340 IF choice=4 THEN ans=num1/num2: GOTO 360
360 PRINT''"The answer is  "ans
```

Chapter 5

1
```
100 CLS
120 FOR count = 10 TO 100 STEP 10
140     PRINT ';count,SQR(count)
160     NEXT count
```

```
100 CLS
120 count=0
140 REPEAT
160   count=count+10
180   PRINT ';count,SQR(count)
200   UNTIL count=100
```

```
100 DIM month$(12),day(12)
120 DATA January,February,March,April,May,June,July,August
140 DATA September,October,November,December
160 DATA 31,28,31,30,31,30,31,31,30,31,30,31
180 FOR count=1 TO 12
200   READ month$(count)
220   NEXT count
240 FOR count=1 TO 12
260   READ day(count)
280   NEXT count
300 PRINT''
320 FOR count=1 TO 12
340   PRINT';month$(count),day(count)
360   NEXT count
```

```
100 MODE 7
120 PRINT CHR$129;CHR$157;CHR$130;CHR$141;"    A HAPPY CHRISTMAS"
140 PRINT CHR$129;CHR$157;CHR$130;CHR$141;"    A HAPPY CHRISTMAS"
160 PRINT CHR$128;CHR$157;CHR$141;"  "
180 PRINT CHR$128;CHR$157;CHR$141;"  "
200 PRINT CHR$128;CHR$157;CHR$141;"  "
220 PRINT CHR$128;CHR$157;CHR$141;"  "
240 PRINT CHR$132;CHR$157;CHR$131;CHR$141;"  TO ALL OUR READERS"
260 PRINT CHR$132;CHR$157;CHR$131;CHR$141;"  TO ALL OUR READERS"
280 PRINT CHR$132;CHR$157;CHR$141" "
300 PRINT CHR$132;CHR$157;CHR$141" "
320 PRINT CHR$130;CHR$157;CHR$141" "
340 PRINT CHR$130;CHR$157;CHR$141" "
360 PRINT CHR$128;CHR$157;CHR$130;"        FROM"
380 PRINT CHR$130;CHR$157;CHR$141;"   "
400 PRINT CHR$130;CHR$157;CHR$141;"   "
420 PRINT CHR$134;CHR$157;CHR$129;CHR$141;"  DUNN  AND  MORGAN"
440 PRINT CHR$134;CHR$157;CHR$129;CHR$141;"  DUNN  AND  MORGAN"
460 PRINT CHR$132;CHR$157;CHR$131;CHR$141;"        AND"
480 PRINT CHR$132;CHR$157;CHR$131;CHR$141;"        AND"
500 PRINT CHR$131;CHR$157;CHR$141;"  "
520 PRINT CHR$131;CHR$157;CHR$141;"  "
540 PRINT CHR$131;CHR$157;CHR$132;CHR$141;"   PRENTICE  HALL"
560 PRINT CHR$131;CHR$157;CHR$132;CHR$141;"   PRENTICE  HALL"
```

Chapter 6

1
```
 100 CLS
 120 PROCintro
 140 MODE 7:REM menu
 160 PRINT"Choose one of the following:-"
 180 PRINT'"     1....Read the list."
 200 PRINT'"     2....Save it on tape."
 220 PRINT'"     3....Recover it from tape."
 240 PRINT'"     4....Finish for now."
 260 Z=GET:IF Z<49 OR Z>52 THEN 260
 280 Z=Z-48
 300 ON Z GOTO 340,360,380,400
 320 GOTO140
 340 PROCread:GOTO 140
 360 PROCsave:GOTO 140
 380 PROCrecover:GOTO 140
 400 PRINT''"Thank you.":END
 420 DEF PROCintro
 440 CLS
 460 PRINT'"This program saves and recovers from"
 480 PRINT'"tape the set of numbers 1 to 100."
 500 PROCholdscreen
 520 ENDPROC
 540 DEF PROCread
 560 FOR count=1 TO 100
 580   PRINTcount
 600   NEXT count
 620 PROCholdscreen
 640 ENDPROC
 660 DEF PROCsave
 680 CLS
 700 X=OPENOUT("numbers")
 720 PRINT'"Data now being saved on tape."
 740 FOR count=1 TO 100
 760   PRINT#X,count
 780   NEXT count
 800 CLOSE#X
 820 PRINT'"Data now saved on tape."
 840 PROCholdscreen
 860 ENDPROC
 880 DEF PROCrecover
 900 CLS
 920 PRINT'"Data now being recovered from tape."
 940  X=OPENIN("numbers")
 960 FOR count=1 TO 100
 980   INPUT#X,count
1000   PRINT'"Data now recovered from tape."
1020   PROCholdscreen
1040   ENDPROC
1060   DEF PROCholdscreen
1080   PRINT''"   Press the space bar."
1100   ZZ=GET
1120   ENDPROC
```

2

```
100 DIM name$(4,100)
120 CLS
140 PROCintro
160 MODE 7:REM menu
180 PRINT"Choose one of the following:-"
200 PRINT'"     1....Input data"
220 PRINT'"     2....Read the list."
240 PRINT'"     3....Save it on tape."
260 PRINT'"     4....Recover it from tape."
280 PRINT'"     5....Finish for now."
300 Z=GET:IF Z<49 OR Z>53 THEN 300
320 Z=Z-48
340 ON Z GOTO 380, 400,420,440,460
360 GOTO160
380 PROCinput:GOTO 160
400 PROCread:GOTO 160
420 PROCsave:GOTO 160
440 PROCrecover:GOTO 160
460 PRINT''"Thank you.":END
480 DEF PROCintro
500 CLS
520 PRINT"         MAILING LIST"''
540 PRINT'"This program allows you to input data"
560 PRINT'"and to save and recover it from tape."
580 PROCholdscreen
600 ENDPROC
620 DEF PROCinput
640 CLS
660 INPUT'"How many names will be on the list  ",total
680 FOR count = 1 TO total
700   PRINT''
720   INPUT'"First the name ",name$(1,total)
740   INPUT'"Now the 1st address line ",name$(2,total)
760   INPUT'"Now the 2nd address line ",name$(3,total)
780   INPUT'"Now the 3rd address line ",name$(4,total)
800   NEXT count
820 ENDPROC
840 DEF PROCread
860 CLS
880 FOR count=1 TO total
900   PRINT'"This is number ";count'
920   FOR line = 1 TO 4
940     PRINT name$(line,total)
960     NEXT line
980   PROCholdscreen
1000   NEXT count
1020 PROCholdscreen
1040 ENDPROC
```

continued

```
1060 DEF PROCsave
1080 CLS
1100 X=OPENOUT("numbers")
1120 PRINT'"Data now being saved on tape."
1140 FOR count=1 TO total
1160   FOR line = 1 TO 4
1180     PRINT#X,name$(line,count)
1200     NEXT line
1220   NEXT count
1240 CLOSE#X
1260 PRINT'"Data now saved on tape."
1280 PROCholdscreen
1300 ENDPROC
1320 DEF PROCrecover
1340 CLS
1360 PRINT'"Data now being recovered from tape."
1380  X=OPENIN("numbers")
1400 FOR count=1 TO total
1420   FOR line = 1 TO 4
1440     INPUT#X,name$(line,count)
1460     NEXT line
1480   NEXT count
1500 PRINT'"Data now recovered from tape."
1520 PROCholdscreen
1540 ENDPROC
1560 DEF PROCholdscreen
1580 PRINT''"    Press the space bar."
1600 ZZ=GET
1620 ENDPROC
```

Chapter 7

1

```
100 DIM store(6)
120 MODE 7
140 PRINT'"How many times do you wish to"
160 INPUT'"throw the dice ",total
180 FOR count=1 TO total
200   num=RND(6)
220   store(num)=store(num)+1
240   NEXT count
260 PRINT'"Press the space bar to see the results."
280 ZZ=GET
300 FOR count=1 TO 6
320   PRINT;count;" occured ";store(count);" times."
340   NEXT count
```

2

```
100 MODE 7
120 TIME=423434
140 CLS
160 REPEAT
180   seconds=TIME DIV 100 MOD 60
200   minutes=TIME DIV 6000 MOD 60
220   hours=TIME DIV 360000 MOD 24
240   PRINT TAB(10,6):hours;"    hours"
260   PRINT TAB(10,8);minutes;"   minutes"
280   PRINT TAB(10,10):seconds;"   seconds "
300   IF minutes=11 AND seconds=0 THEN PROCmessage
320   UNTIL FALSE
340 DEF PROCmessage
360 CLS
380 FOR repeat=1 TO 3
400   FOR count=1 TO 3
420     SOUND 1,-15,RND(200),10
440     PRINT TAB(5,16):"Your appointment is due."
460     z=INKEY(50)
480     CLS
500     NEXT count
520   CLS
540   NEXT repeat
560 ENDPROC
```

3

```
100 MODE 7
120 TIME=0
140 T1=TIME
160 CLS
180 REPEAT
200   seconds=TIME DIV 100 MOD 60
220   minutes=TIME DIV 6000 MOD 60
240   hours=TIME DIV 360000 MOD 24
260   PRINT TAB(3,3);"Stop watch time "
280   PRINT TAB(10,6);hours;"    hours"
300   PRINT TAB(10,8);minutes;"   minutes"
320   PRINT TAB(10,10);seconds;"   seconds "
340   PRINT TAB(0,13);"To use the stop watch press the
      letter B"
360   Z$=INKEY$(0)
380   IF Z$="B" THEN PROCstop
400   UNTIL FALSE
420 DEF PROCstop
440 T2=TIME
460 PRINT TAB(3,15);"Stop watch time is "
480 PRINT TAB(10,18);hours;"    hours"
500 PRINT TAB(10,20);minutes;"   minutes"
520 PRINT TAB(10,22);seconds;"   seconds "
540 PRINT TAB(1,24);"To return to watch press space bar"
560 Z=GET
580 laptime=INT((T2-T1)/100)
600 PRINT TAB(10,26);"Lap time is ";laptime
620 Z=INKEY(200)
640 T1=T2
660 CLS
680 ENDPROC
```

4

```
100 MODE 1:REM MODE 5 for Model A
120 REPEAT
140   lenx=RND(600):REM side of rectangle
160   leny=RND(600):REM side of rectangle
180   col=RND(4):REM color of rectangle
200   GCOL 0,col
220   x=RND(1000):REM bottom left corner
240   y=RND(1000):REM bottom left corner
260   REM next four lines draw rectangle
280   MOVE x,y
300   MOVE x+lenx,y
320   PLOT 85,x,y+leny
340   PLOT 85,x+lenx,y+leny
360   z=INKEY(50):REM a small delay
380   UNTIL FALSE
```

Chapter 8

1

```
100 MODE 7
120 DIM x(100),y(100)
140 PROCbegin
160 PROCvalues
180 PROCdisplay
200 END
220 DEF PROCbegin
240 CLS
260 PRINT'"What is the function to be used "
280 INPUT'"Always use lower case x ",fn$
300 INPUT'"What is the lower limit of x  ",lower
320 INPUT'"What is the upper limit of x  ",upper
340 INPUT'"What is the step  ",step
360 ENDPROC
380 DEF PROCvalues
400 count=0
420 FOR x=lower TO upper STEP step
440   count=count+1
460   x(count)=x
480   y(count)=EVAL(fn$)
500   NEXT x
520 ENDPROC
540 DEF PROCdisplay
560 FOR x=1 TO count
580   PRINT TAB(1);x(x);TAB(15);y(x)
600   IF INT(x/20)=x/20 THEN PRINT''"Press space bar"':Z=GET
620   NEXT x
640 ENDPROC
```

2
```
100 MODE 7
120 PROCinput
140 REPEAT
160   PROCdigits
180   PROCanswer
200   UNTIL end
220 END
240 DEF PROCinput
260 INPUT''"Put in a 3-digit number "num
280 ENDPROC
300 DEF PROCdigits
320 right=num MOD 10
340 left=num DIV 100
360 middle=num DIV 10-10*left
380 newnum=FNdigits(left,middle,right)
400 ENDPROC
420 DEF PROCanswer
440 PRINTnewnum,
460 num=newnum
480 PRINT''"Do you want another run "
500 ans$=GET$
520 IF ans$="Y" OR ans$="y" THEN end=FALSE:GOTO580
540 IF ans$="N" OR ans$="n" THEN end=TRUE:GOTO580
560 PRINT''"Try again":GOTO 480
580 ENDPROC
600 DEF FNdigits(a,b,c)=a^2+b^2+c^2
```

Chapter 9

1
```
100 REM 5 card poker
120 MODE 7
140 DIM number$(13),suit$(4),card$(13,4),store(30)
160 PROCsetupvariables
180 PROCchoosehands
200 END
220 DEF PROCsetupvariables
240 DATA ACE,2,3,4,5,6,7,8,9,10
260 DATA JACK,QUEEN,KING
280 DATA HEARTS,CLUBS,SPADES,DIAMONDS
300 REM read card numbers
320 FOR count=1 TO 13
340   READ number$(count)
360   NEXT count
380 REM read card suits
400 FOR count=1 TO 4
420   READ suit$(count)
440   NEXT count
460 REM store cards in card$(13,4)
480 FOR count1=1 TO 4
500   FOR count2=1 TO 13
520     card$(count2,count1)=number$(count2)+"  OF  "+suit$(count1)
540     NEXT count2
560   NEXT count1
580 ENDPROC
600 DEF PROCchoosehands
620 count=0
640 REM choose 2 hands
660 FOR hands=1 TO 2
680   FOR cards=1 TO 5
700     choice=RND(52)
720     count=count+1
740     REM check if card is new
760     flag=0
780     FOR c=1 TO count
800       IF choice=store(c) THEN flag=1
820       NEXT c
```

continued

```
 840      IF flag=1 THEN 700
 860      REM end of check
 880      store(count)=choice
 900      IF choice>39 THEN suit=1:choice2=choice-39
 920      IF choice<40 AND choice>26 THEN suit=2:choice2=choice-26
 940      IF choice<27 AND choice>13 THEN suit=3:choice2=choice-13
 960      IF choice<14 THEN suit=4:choice2=choice
 980      PRINT card$(choice2,suit)
1000      NEXT cards
1020    PRINT''
1040    NEXT hands
1060 ENDPROC
```

2

```
100 DIM letter$(26),letter1$(26),vowel$(5),word$(50),loc(3)
120 MODE7
140 PROCarrays
160 PROCintro
180 PROCinput
200 IF spaces=1 THEN PROClistone ELSE PROClisttwo
220 END
240 DEF PROCarrays
260 spaces=0:word$=""
280 DATA A,B,C,D,E,F,G,H,I,J,K,L,M,N,O,P,Q,R,S,T,U,V,W,X,Y,Z
300 DATA A,E,I,O,U
320 FOR count=1 TO 26:READ letter$(count):NEXT count
340 FOR count=1 TO 5:READ vowel$(count):NEXT count
360 ENDPROC
380 DEF PROCintro
400 PRINT"              CROSSWORDS"
420 PRINT'"If you have a word with one or two"
440 PRINT"letters missing this program will help"
460 PRINT"you."
480 PRINT''''"First count the number of letters"
500 INPUT"in the word and input this  "letters
520 PRINT'''"Do you wish to include all the letters"
540 PRINT"in your list of possible solutions"
560 PRINT"or can it be confined to the vowels."
580 INPUT"Input A or V  "ans$
600 IF ans$="A" OR ans$="a" THEN num=26:GOTO660
620 IF ans$="V" OR ans$="v" THEN num=5:GOTO660
640 PRINT'"Try again.":GOTO 520
660 IF num=26 THEN PROCletters ELSE PROCvowels
680 ENDPROC
700 DEF PROCinput
720 CLS
740 PRINT"Now input the letters of the word one"
760 PRINT"at a time.  Where the letter is not "
780 PRINT"known input a dash like  -."
800 FOR count = 1 TO letters
820   letter$=GET$
840   PRINTTAB(count+15,10);letter$
860   word$=word$+letter$
880   IF letter$="-" THEN spaces=spaces+1:loc(spaces)=count
900   IF spaces>2 THEN PRINT'"Only 2 spaces. Press space
      bar.":spaces=0:Z=GET:GOTO720
```

continued

```
 920   word$(count)=letter$
 940   NEXT count
 960 PRINT TAB(3,12);"The word is  "word$
 980 INPUT"Is this correct  (Y/N) "ans$
1000 IF ans$="Y" OR ans$="y" THEN 1060
1020 IF ans$="N" OR ans$="n" THEN PRINT'"Try again.":GOTO720
1040 PRINT'"Try again.":GOTO980
1060 ENDPROC
1080 DEF PROCletters
1100 FOR count=1 TO num
1120   letter1$(count)=letter$(count)
1140   NEXT count
1160 ENDPROC
1180 DEF PROCvowels
1200 FOR count=1 TO num
1220   letter1$(count)=vowel$(count)
1240   NEXT count
1260 ENDPROC
1280 DEF PROClistone
1300 FOR count=1 TO num
1320   word$(loc(1))=letter1$(count)
1340   word1$=""
1360   FOR count1=1 TO letters
1380     word1$=word1$+word$(count1)
1400     NEXT count1
1420   PRINTword1$
1440   NEXT count
1460 ENDPROC
1480 DEF PROClisttwo
1500 FOR count=1 TO num
1520   FOR count1=1 TO num
1540     word$(loc(1))=letter1$(count1)
1560     word$(loc(2))=letter1$(count)
1580     word1$=""
1600     FOR count2=1 TO letters
1620       word1$=word1$+word$(count2)
1640       NEXT count2
1660     PRINTword1$,;
1680     NEXT count1
1700   PRINT'''"Press space bar."'':Z=GET
1720   NEXT count
```

3

```
100 DIM letter(26)
120 MODE 7
140 PROCintro
160 PROCinput
180 END
200 DEF PROCintro
220 PRINT"            LETTER COUNTER"
240 PRINT''"This program allows you to type in a"
260 PRINT'"passage of prose; it then counts the"
280 PRINT'"number of times each letter of the "
300 PRINT'"alphabet occurs.  The following codes"
320 PRINT'"are used:-"
340 PRINT''"   9...means abort the count"
360 PRINT'"   <...means delete the last entry"
380 PRINT'"   *...means the end of the input."
400 PRINT'''"      Press the space bar"
```

continued

```
 420 z=GET
 440 PRINT''''"After about 160 letters the machine"
 460 PRINT'"does an interim count so there will"
 480 PRINT'"be a short delay each time you reach"
 500 PRINT'"this number of letters."
 520 PRINT''"When the screen becomes blank"
 540 PRINT'"begin to type in your passage."
 560 PRINT''"      Press the space bar"
 580 Z=GET
 600 ENDPROC
 620 DEF PROCinput
 640 CLS
 660 passage$="":REM cumulates letters
 680 count=0:REM counts letters
 700 REPEAT
 720   letter$=GET$:REM current letter
 740   IF letter$="9" THEN PROCend:GOTO860
 760   IF letter$="<" THEN PROCremove::GOTO720
 780   IF letter$="*" THEN PROCcount:END
 800   passage$=passage$+letter$
 820   PRINT TAB(count); letter$;
 840   count=count+1
 860   IF count>160 THEN PROCcount
 880   UNTIL FALSE
 900 ENDPROC
 920 DEF PROCend
 940 CLS
 960 PRINT''"Are you sure that you wish to"
 980 INPUT'"stop at this stage (Y/N) ",ans$
1000 IF ans$="Y" OR ans$="y" THEN  END
1020 CLS
1040 PRINTpassage$;
1060 ENDPROC
1080 DEF PROCcount
1100 count=count-160
1120 len=LEN(passage$)
1140 FOR c=1 TO len
1160   c$=MID$(passage$,c,1)
1180   k=ASC(c$)
1200   IF k<64 THEN 1280:REM tests for punctuation
1220   IF k>96 THEN k=k-32
1240   k=k-64
1260   letter(k)=letter(k)+1
1280   NEXT c
1300 IF letter$="*" THEN PROCprint:END
1320 passage$=""
1340 ENDPROC
1360 DEF PROCremove
1380 len1=LEN(passage$)
1400 passage$=LEFT$(passage$,len1-1)
1420 count=count-1
1440 CLS
1460 PRINTpassage$;
1480 letter$=""
1500 ENDPROC
1520 DEF PROCprint
1540 CLS
1560 FOR k=1 TO 13
1580   PRINT TAB(5,k+5);CHR$(k+64);TAB(15,k+5);letter(k);
       TAB(25,k+5);CHR$(k+77);TAB(35,k+5);letter(k+13)
1600   NEXT k
1620 ENDPROC
```

Chapter 10

1
```
100 DIM name$(100,4),cost(100)
120 MODE 7
140 PROCintro
160 PROCenter
180 PROCcalc
200 PROCprint
220 END
240 DEF PROCintro
260 CLS
280 PRINT'"       Detailed Account"
300 PRINT''"In this program the details of a bill"
320 PRINT'"or list of items are entered."
340 PRINT'"   First the name of each item."
360 PRINT'"   Then the price of each item."
380 PRINT'"   Then the % discount (if any) on each."
400 PRINT'"   Then the number of each."
420 PRINT'''"     Press the space bar"
440 Z=GET
460 ENDPROC
480 DEF PROCenter
500 CLS
520 INPUT'"How many items are to be entered ",num
540 FOR count=1 TO num
560   PRINT'''"This is number ";count
580   INPUT''"What is the name of item ",name$(count,1)
600   name$(count,1)=LEFT$(name$(count,1),8)
620   INPUT''"What is the price of this item ",name$(count,2)
640   INPUT''"What is the % discount on this item ",name$(count,3)
660   INPUT''"How many of this item  ",name$(count,4)
680   NEXT count
700 PRINT''"That was the last item."
720 PRINT'''"     Press the space bar"
740 Z=GET
760 ENDPROC
780 DEF PROCcalc
800 FOR count=1 TO num
820   n=VAL(name$(count,2))
840   p=VAL(name$(count,3))
860   d=VAL(name$(count,4))
880   cost(count)=n*(p-p*d/100)
900   cost(count)=INT(100*cost(count)+.5)/100
920   NEXT count
940 ENDPROC
960 DEF PROCprint
980 CLS
1000 PRINT TAB(1);"Name";TAB(10);"Price";TAB(18);"Dis";
     TAB(24);"no";TAB(32);"Total"
1020 PRINT''
1040 FOR count=1 TO num
1060   PRINT TAB(1);name$(count,1);TAB(11);name$(count,2);
       TAB(18);name$(count,3);TAB(24);name$(count,4);TAB(32);
       cost(count)
1080   NEXT count
1100 ENDPROC
```

2
```
 100 DIM name$(100,4)
 120 MODE 7
 140 PROCintro
 160 DEF PROCintro
 180 CLS
 200 PRINT"              Stock control"
 220 PRINT'"Choose one of the following by"
 240 PRINT"pressing the appropriate key"
 260 PRINT''"   1....Begin a new list."
 280 PRINT'"   2....Save on tape."
 300 PRINT'"   3....Recover from tape"
 320 PRINT'"   4....Print list on screen."
 340 PRINT'"   5....Update quantities."
 360 PRINT'"   6....Finish for now."
 380 ans=GET
 400 ans=ans-48
 420 IF ans<1 OR ans>6 THEN 200
 440 IF ans=1 THEN PROCbegin:PROCintro
 460 IF ans=2 THEN PROCsave:PROCintro
 480 IF ans=3 THEN PROCrecover:PROCintro
 500 IF ans=4 THEN PROCprint:PROCintro
 520 IF ans=5 THEN PROCupdate:PROCintro
 540 IF ans=6 THEN PRINT'"Thank you for now.":END
 560 ENDPROC
 580 DEF PROCbegin
 600 CLS
 620 INPUT'"How many items  ",num
 640 FOR count=1 TO num
 660   PRINT'"This is number ";count
 680   INPUT'"Name of item  ",name$(count,1)
 700   name$(count,1)=LEFT$(name$(count,1),12)
 720   INPUT'"How many of each ",name$(count,2)
 740   INPUT'"How much is this item "name$(count,3)
 760   INPUT'"Minimum number of this before reordering   ",
       name$(count,4)
 780   NEXT count
 800 PRINT''"That was the last one."
 820 ENDPROC
 840 DEF PROCsave
 860 PRINT'"Make sure cassette is ready."
 880 INPUT'"What is the file name ",file$
 900 x=OPENOUT(file$)
 920 FOR count=1 TO num
 940   FOR count2=1 TO 4
 960     PRINT#x,name$(count,count2)
 980     NEXT count2
1000   NEXT count
1020 CLOSE#x
1040 PRINT''"Data now saved.  Press space bar."
1060 Z=GET
1080 ENDPROC
1100 DEF PROCrecover
1120 PRINT'"Make sure cassette is ready."
1140 INPUT'"What is the file name ",file$
1160 x=OPENIN(file$)
1180 count=0
1200 REPEAT
1220   count=count+1
1240   FOR count2=1 TO 4
1260     INPUT#x,name$(count,count2)
1280     NEXT count2
1300   UNTIL EOF#x
1320 PRINT''"Data now recovered.  Press space bar."
1340 Z=GET
1360 ENDPROC
```

Chapter 11

1

```
100 REM bouncing ball
120 MODE 4
140 PROCvalues
160 REPEAT
180   PROCmove
200   UNTIL FALSE
220 END
240 DEF PROCvalues
260 x=8:y=8
280 xchange=1:ychange=4
300 GCOL 0,1
320 ENDPROC
340 DEF PROCmove
360 IF y>1016 THEN ychange=-ychange
380 IF y<0 THEN ychange=-ychange
400 IF x>1270 THEN CLG:x=0
420 x=x+xchange
440 y=y+ychange
460 PLOT69,x,y
480 PLOT71,x-xchange,y-ychange
500 ENDPROC
```

2

```
100 MODE 4
120 PROCvalues
140 PROChexagon
160 END
180 DEF PROCvalues
200 CLS
220 GCOL 0,1
240 x=50:y=86.5
260 ENDPROC
280 DEF PROChexagon
300 FOR across=0 TO 3
320   FOR down=0 TO 10 STEP 2
340     MOVE (6*across+1)*x,down*y
360     DRAW 6*across*x,(down+1)*y
380     DRAW(6*across+1)*x,(down+2)*y
400     DRAW(6*across+3)*x,(down+2)*y
420     DRAW(6*across+4)*x,(down+1)*y
440     DRAW(6*across+3)*x,down*y
460     DRAW(6*across+1)*x,down*y
480     IF across=3 THEN 540
500     MOVE(6*across+4)*x,(down+1)*y
520     DRAW(6*across+6)*x,(down+1)*y
540     NEXT down
560   NEXT across
580 ENDPROC
```

3

```
100 MODE 7
120 x1=0:y1=0:total=40
140 DIM sum(4,10): REM stores numbers
160 PROCintro
180 PROCshape
200 MODE 4
220 PROCdraw
240 PROCgame
260 MODE 7
280 END
300 DEF PROCintro
320 CLS
```

continued

```
 340 PRINT'"          COUNTERS"
 360 PRINT''"A game for 2 players.  Each player"
 380 PRINT'"chooses one of the numbers 1,2 or 3"
 400 PRINT'"each time.  That number of counters"
 420 PRINT'"is then taken away from an"
 440 PRINT'"array of 40 counters.  The player"
 460 PRINT'"who takes the last counter"
 480 PRINT'"is the loser."
 500 PRINT'''"      Press the space bar"
 520 Z=GET
 540 INPUT'''''"First player's name    ",one$
 560 INPUT''''"Second player's name  ",two$
 580 ENDPROC
 600 DEF PROCshape
 620 VDU23,240, 1,3,7,127,127,127,127,127
 640 VDU23,241, 128,192,224,254,254,254,254,254
 660 VDU23,242, 63,31,15,7,1,1,1,1
 680 VDU23,243, 252,248,240,224,128,128,128,128
 700 counter$=CHR$(240)+CHR$(241)+CHR$(10)+CHR$(8)+CHR$(8)+
     CHR$(242)+CHR$(243)
 720 ENDPROC
 740 DEF PROCdraw
 760 CLS:CLG
 780 VDU5
 800 FOR y=700 TO 1000 STEP 100
 820   FOR x=100 TO 1000 STEP 100
 840     MOVE x,y
 860     PRINTcounter$
 880     NEXT x
 900   NEXT y
 920 VDU4
 940 ENDPROC
 960 DEF PROCgame
 980 count=0
1000 REPEAT
1020   count=count+1
1040   IF INT(count/2)=count/2 THEN player$=one$
       ELSE player$=two$
1060      PRINT TAB(3,20);"                                              "
1080   PRINT TAB(3,20);"Your turn          ";player$
1100   PRINT TAB(3,25);"                                    "
1120   INPUT TAB(3,25)"Enter 1,2 or 3    ",num
1140   PRINT TAB(3,28);"                            "
1160   IF num<1 OR num>3 THEN PRINT TAB(3,28);"Try again ";
       player$:GOTO1120
1180   PROCremove
1200   UNTIL total<=0
1220 CLS:CLG
1240 PRINT TAB(3,10);"Hard luck ",loser$;" you lose."
1260 PRINT TAB(10,20);"Press the space bar"
1280 Z=GET
1300 ENDPROC
1320 DEF PROCremove
1340 VDU5
1360 FOR loop= 1 TO num
1380   MOVE 100+100*x1,1000+100*(-y1)
1400   VDU9,9,127,127,9,9,10,127,127
1420   IF x1=9 THEN y1=y1+1:x1=-1
1440   x1=x1+1
1460   total=total-1
1480   IF total=0 THEN loser$=player$
1500   NEXT loop
1520 VDU4
1540 ENDPROC
```

Chapter 12

1

```
 100 MODE 7
 120 DIM pitch(30),tune(400),dur(400),tune$(400)
 140 PROCvalues
 160 PROCintro
 180 END
 200 DEF PROCvalues
 220 flag=0
 240 DATA 41,49,53,61,69,73,81,45,57,65,77,85
 260 DATA 89,97,101,109,117,121,129,93,105,113,125,133
 280 FOR count=1 TO 24
 300   READ pitch(count)
 320   NEXT count
 340 ENDPROC
 360 DEF PROCintro
 380 CLS
 400 PRINT'"         WRITING  MUSIC"
 420 PRINT''"Do you wish to:-"
 440 PRINT'"  1....Begin a new tune."
 460 PRINT'"  2....List notes on screen."
 480 PRINT'"  3....Save a tune on cassette."
 500 PRINT'"  4....Recover a tune from cassette."
 520 PRINT'"  5....Play the tune."
 540 PRINT'"  6....Change a note on tune."
 560 PRINT'"  7....Add a new note to the tune."
 580 PRINT'"  8....Finish for now."
 600 PRINT''"Choose a number.";:Z=GET
 620 Z=Z-48
 640 IF Z<1 OR Z>8 THEN 380
 660 IF Z=1 THEN PROCbegin:PROCintro
 680 IF Z=2 THEN PROClist:PROCintro
 700 IF Z=3 THEN PROCsave:PROCintro
 720 IF Z=4 THEN PROCrecover:PROCintro
 740 IF Z=5 THEN PROCplay:PROCintro
 760 IF Z=6 THEN PROCchange:PROCintro
 780 IF Z=7 THEN PROCadd:PROCintro
 800 IF Z=8 THEN PRINT'"Thank you for now.":END
 820 ENDPROC
 840 DEF PROCbegin
 860 CLS
 880 PRINT"You can choose from 2 octaves running"
 900 PRINT'"from A to G, and you can choose to"
 920 PRINT'"make each note natural or sharp."
 940 PRINT'''"When you have finished entering notes"
 960 PRINT'"put in the word  end  to stop."
 980 PRINT''"      Press the space bar."
1000 ZZ=GET
1020 PRINT"Input each note as a 3-symbol"
1040 PRINT"combination as shown below."
1060 PRINT'"A,B,C,.G  stand for the musical notes."
1080 PRINT"N means Natural.     S means Sharp."
1100 PRINT"2 means octave two.  1 means octave one."
1120 PRINT'"   G           G2N  or  G2S"
1140 PRINT"  F__________  F2N  or  F2S"
1160 PRINT"   E           E2N"
1180 PRINT"  D__________  D2N  or  D2S"
1200 PRINT"   C           C2N  or  C2S"
1220 PRINT"  B__________  B2N"
1240 PRINT"   A           A2N  or  A2S"
1260 PRINT"  G__________  G1N  or  G1S"
1280 PRINT"   F           F1N  or  F1S"
```

continued

```
1300 PRINT"  E__________     E1N"
1320 PRINT"   D              D1N  or  D1S"
1340 PRINT"  C__________     C1N  or  C1S"
1360 PRINT"   B              B1N"
1380 PRINT"  A__________     A1N  or  A1S"
1400 PRINT'"       Press the space bar"
1420 Z=GET
1440 IF flag=1 THEN 1520
1460 IF flag=2 THEN1500
1480 note=0
1500 REPEAT
1520   PRINT''"Now input a note in the 3-letter form."
1540   INPUT'"Remember to use end to stop  ";note$
1560   IF note$="end" OR note$="END" THEN end=TRUE ELSE
       end=FALSE
1580   IF end=TRUE THEN 2140
1600   l$=LEFT$(note$,1)
1620   m$=MID$(note$,2,1)
1640   r$=RIGHT$(note$,1)
1660   IF flag=1 THEN 1700
1680   note=note+1
1700   l=ASC(l$)-64
1720   IF l<1 OR l>7 THEN PRINT'"Try again.":GOTO1540
1740   m=VAL(m$)
1760   IF m<1 OR m>2 THEN PRINT'"Try again.":GOTO1540
1780   IF m=2 THEN m=15
1800   r=ASC(r$)
1820   IF r=78 THEN r=1:GOTO 1880
1840   IF r=83 THEN r=8:GOTO 1880
1860   PRINT'"Try again.":GOTO1540
1880   pitch=l+m+r-2
1900   IF flag=1 THEN tune(chan)=pitch(pitch):tune$(chan)=note$:
       GOTO 1960
1920   tune(note)=pitch(pitch)
1940   tune$(note)=note$
1960   PRINT''"Now input length of note:-"
1980   PRINT'"   16  for a semi-breve"
2000   PRINT'"    8  for a minim"
2020   PRINT'"    4  for a crotchet"
2040   PRINT'"    2  for a quaver"
2060   PRINT'"    1  for a semi-quaver"
2080   INPUT'"     ",dur
2100   IF flag=1 THEN dur(chan)=dur:GOTO 2160
2120   dur(note)=dur
2140   UNTIL end
2160 ENDPROC
2180 DEF PROClist
2200 CLS
2220 PRINT"The notes are:-"''
2240 FOR count=1 TO note
2260   PRINT;count,tune$(count),dur(count)
2280   NEXT count
2300 PRINT'"         Press the space bar."
2320 Z=GET
2340 ENDPROC
2360 DEF PROCsave
2380 CLS
2400 INPUT"What is the file name ",name$
2420 PRINT''"The tune is now being saved."
2440 x=OPENOUT(name$)
2460 FOR count=1 TO note
2480   PRINT#x,tune(count)
2500   PRINT#x,dur(count)
2520   PRINT#x,tune$(count)
```

continued

```
2540   NEXT count
2560 CLOSE#x
2580 PRINT''"The tune is now saved. Press the space bar."
2600 Z=GET
2620 ENDPROC
2640 DEF PROCrecover
2660 CLS
2680 INPUT"What is the file name ",name$
2700 PRINT''"The tune is now being recovered."
2720 x=OPENIN(name$)
2740 note=0
2760 REPEAT
2780   note=note+1
2800   INPUT#x,tune(note)
2820   INPUT#x,dur(note)
2840   INPUT#x,tune$(note)
2860   UNTIL EOF#x
2880 CLOSE#x
2900 PRINT''"The tune is now recovered. Press the space bar."
2920 Z=GET
2940 ENDPROC
2960 DEF PROCplay
2980 FOR count=1 TO note
3000   SOUND 1,-15,tune(count),dur(count)
3020   NEXT count
3040 ENDPROC
3060 DEF PROCchange
3080 CLS
3100 PRINT'"What is the number of the note"
3120 INPUT'"that you want to change "chan
3140 flag=1
3160 PROCbegin
3180 flag=0
3200 ENDPROC
3220 DEF PROCadd
3240 CLS
3260 PRINT"Remember that you must stop by"
3280 PRINT'"putting in end.  Press the space bar."
3300 Z=GET
3320 flag=2
3340 PROCbegin
3360 flag=0
3380 ENDPROC
```

Chapter 13

1

```
100 DIM  book$(3,50),aux$(5)
120 total=0
140 PROCintro
160 MODE 7:REM menu
180 PRINT"      Number of books in is  ";total
200 PRINT'"Choose one of these numbers:-"
220 PRINT'"    1...Begin a new list."
240 PRINT'"    2...Read a current list."
260 PRINT'"    3...Alphabetical order."
280 PRINT'"    4...Add a book."
300 PRINT'"    5...Delete a book."
320 PRINT'"    6...Change entry on a book."
340 PRINT'"    7...Save on tape."
360 PRINT'"    8...Recover from tape."
380 PRINT'"    9...Finish for now."
```

continued

```
 400 Z=GET:IF Z<49 OR Z>57 THEN400
 420 Z=Z-48
 440 ON Z GOTO 480,500,520,540,560,580,600,620,640
 460 GOTO 160
 480 PROCbegin:GOTO 160
 500 PROCread:GOTO 160
 520 PROCalpha:GOTO 160
 540 PROCadd:GOTO 160
 560 PROCdelete:GOTO 160
 580 PROCchange:GOTO 160
 600 PROCsave:GOTO 160
 620 PROCrecover:GOTO 160
 640 PRINT''"Thank you for now.":END
 660 DEF PROCintro
 680 CLS
 700 PRINT TAB(10,1);"BIBLIOGRAPHY"
 720 PRINT''"This program allows you to enter a"
 740 PRINT'"Bibliography, save it, recover it "
 760 PRINT'"amend it and display it."
 780 PROCholdscreen
 800 ENDPROC
 820 DEF PROCholdscreen
 840 PRINT''"      Press the space-bar."
 860 ZZ=GET
 880 ENDPROC
 900 DEF PROCbegin
 920 CLS
 940 PRINT'"When you have finished entering books"
 960 PRINT'"type in END as the name of"
 980 PRINT'"the author and the routine will end."
1000 total=0
1020 REPEAT
1040   end=0
1060   total=total+1
1080   PRINT'''"This is book number  ";total
1100   PRINT'"Enter the author's name.  Put the"
1120   INPUTLINE'"surname first  ",book$(0,total)
1140   IF book$(0,total)="END" THEN end=-1:GOTO1220
1160   INPUTLINE'"Now input name of book ",book$(1,total)
1180   INPUTLINE'"Now input name of publisher ",book$(2,total)
1200   INPUTLINE'"Now input year of publication ",book$(3,total)
1220   UNTIL end
1240 total=total-1
1260 ENDPROC
1280 DEF PROCread
1300 CLS
1320 FOR count=1 TO total
1340   PRINT'"This is number ";count
1360   FOR j=0 TO 3
1380     PRINT book$(j,count)
1400     NEXT j
1420   PROCholdscreen
1440   NEXT count
1460 PRINT''"That was the last one."
1480 PROCholdscreen
1500 ENDPROC
1520 DEF PROCalpha
1540 j=0
1560 FOR count=1 TO total-1
1580   IF book$(0,count)<=book$(0,count+1) THEN 1720
1600   FOR count2=0 TO 3
1620     aux$(count2)=book$(count2,count+1)
```

continued

```
1640      book$(count2,count+1)=book$(count2,count)
1660      book$(count2,count)=aux$(count2)
1680      NEXT count2
1700   j=j+1
1720   NEXT count
1740 IF j>0 THEN 1540
1760 PRINT''"Now in alphabetical oeder."
1780 PROCholdscreen
1800 ENDPROC
1820 DEF PROCadd
1840 CLS
1860 total=total+1
1880 INPUTLINE'"Name of author   ",book$(0,total)
1900 INPUTLINE'"Book title       ",book$(1,total)
1920 INPUTLINE'"Publisher        ",book$(2,total)
1940 INPUTLINE'"Year of publication ",book$(2,total)
1960 PROCholdscreen
1980 ENDPROC
2000 DEF PROCdelete
2020 CLS
2040 INPUTLINE'"What is the author's name ",name$
2060 FOR count=1 TO total
2080   IF book$(0,count)=name$ THEN 2160
2100   NEXT count
2120 PRINT'"This is not on the list."
2140 GOTO2360
2160 FOR count2=count TO total-1
2180   FOR count1=0 TO 3
2200     book$(count1,count2)=book$(count1,count2+1)
2220     NEXT count1
2240   NEXT count2
2260 FOR count1=0 TO 3
2280   book$(count1,total)=""
2300   NEXT count1
2320 total=total-1
2340 PRINT''"This book has now been removed."
2360 PROCholdscreen
2380 ENDPROC
2400 DEF PROCchange
2420 CLS
2440 INPUTLINE '"Name of author to be changed ",name$
2460 FOR count = 1 TO total
2480   IF book$(0,count) = name$ THEN 2560
2500   NEXT count
2520 PRINT''"Not on list."
2540 GOTO2720
2560 PRINT''"Current name is ";book$(0,count)
2580 INPUTLINE''"New name is ",book$(0,count)
2600 PRINT''"Current title is ";book$(1,count)
2620 INPUTLINE''"New title is ",book$(1,count)
2640 PRINT''"Current publisher  is ";book$(2,count)
2660 INPUTLINE''"New publisher is ",book$(2,count)
2680 PRINT''"Current year is ";book$(3,count)
2700 INPUTLINE''"New year is ",book$(3,count)
2720 PROCholdscreen
2740 ENDPROC
2760 DEF PROCsave
2780 CLS
2800 INPUT''"What name will you give the file ",file$
2820 X=OPENOUT(file$)
2840 PRINT'"Data now being stored on tape."
2860 FOR count=1 TO total
```

continued

```
2880   FOR count1=0 TO 3
2900     PRINT#X,book$(count1,count)
2920     NEXT count1
2940   NEXT count
2960 CLOSE#X
2980 PRINT'"Data now stored on tape"
3000 PROCholdscreen
3020 ENDPROC
3040 DEF PROCrecover
3060 CLS
3080 INPUT''"What is the file-name ",file$
3100 PRINT'"Move the tape to the correct position"
3120 PRINT'"and then press the PLAY key."
3140 total = 0
3160 X = OPENIN(file$)
3180 REPEAT
3200   total=total+1
3220   FOR count1=0 TO 3
3240     INPUT#X,book$(count1,total)
3260     NEXT count1
3280   UNTIL EOF#X
3300 CLOSE#X
3320 PRINT'"Data now recovered."
3340 PROCholdscreen
3360 ENDPROC
```

2

```
 100 DIM name$(100),score(100),stscore(100)
 120 total=0
 140 PROCintro
 160 MODE 7:REM menu
 180 PRINT TAB(15,1);total;" Pupils"
 200 PRINT'"Choose one of these numbers:-"
 220 PRINT'"   0...Begin again."
 240 PRINT'"   1...Read list."
 260 PRINT'"   2...Alphabetical order."
 280 PRINT'"   3...Add name to list."
 300 PRINT'"   4...Remove name from list."
 320 PRINT'"   5...Change all scores."
 340 PRINT'"   6...Change one score."
 360 PRINT'"   7...Save on tape."
 380 PRINT'"   8...Recover from tape."
 400 PRINT'"   9...Finish for now."
 420 Z=GET:IF Z<48 OR Z>57 THEN 420
 440 Z=Z-47
 460 ON Z GOTO 500,520,540,560,580,600,620,640,660,680
 480 GOTO 160
 500 PROCbegin:PROCstats:GOTO 160
 520 PROCread:GOTO160
 540 PROCalpha:GOTO160
 560 PROCadd:PROCstats:GOTO160
 580 PROCremove:PROCstats:GOTO160
 600 PROCallchange:PROCstats:GOTO160
 620 PROConechange:PROCstats:GOTO160
 640 PROCsave:PROCstats:GOTO160
 660 PROCrecover:PROCstats:GOTO160
 680 END
 700 DEF PROCintro
 720 CLS
```

continued

```
 740 PRINT"  ______________________________________"
 760 PRINT
 780 PRINT"  *********CLASS TESTS**********"
 800 PRINT
 820 PRINT"  ______________________________________"
 840 PRINT''"This program accepts the name and test"
 860 PRINT'"mark of 60 or more class members.  It"
 880 PRINT'"will then standardise the scores to"
 900 PRINT'"any given mean and standard deviation."
 920 PROCholdscreen
 940 ENDPROC
 960 DEF PROCholdscreen
 980 PRINT'"            Press the space-bar."
1000 ZZ=GET
1020 ENDPROC
1040 DEF PROCbegin
1060 CLS
1080 INPUT'"How many pupils  ",total
1100 PRINT'':FOR count=1 TO total
1120   IF count = 1 THEN 1160
1140   PRINT"Now next pupil."'
1160   INPUT"Pupil's name  "name$(count)
1180   INPUT''"Now the score  "score(count)
1200   PRINT'':NEXT count
1220 PRINT''"That was the last pupil."
1240 PROCholdscreen
1260 ENDPROC
1280 DEF PROCread
1300 CLS
1320 FOR count=1 TO total
1340   PRINTname$(count);TAB(22);score(count),INT(10*stscore
       (count)+.5)/10
1360   NEXT count
1380 PROCholdscreen
1400 ENDPROC
1420 DEF PROCalpha
1440 CLS
1460 PRINT'"Names being put into alphabetical order"
1480 j=0
1500 FOR count=1 TO total-1
1520   IF name$(count)<name$(count+1) THEN 1660
1540   x$=name$(count+1):x1=score(count+1):x2=stscore(count+1)
1560   name$(count+1)=name$(count)
1580   score(count+1)=score(count)
1600   stscore(count+1)=stscore(count)
1620   name$(count)=x$:score(count)=x1:stscore(count)=x2
1640   j=j+1
1660   NEXT count
1680 IF j>0 THEN 1480
1700 PRINT'"Now in alphabetical order."
1720 PROCholdscreen
1740 ENDPROC
1760 DEF PROCadd
1780 CLS
1800 INPUT'"Name of new student  "new$
1820 INPUT'"Score of new student  "nscore
1840 total=total+1
1860 name$(total)=new$
1880 score(total)=nscore
1900 PRINT'"New student now entered."
1920 PROCholdscreen
1940 ENDPROC
1960 DEF PROCremove
```

continued

```
1980 CLS
2000 INPUT'"Name to be removed "remove$
2020 FOR count=1 TO total
2040   IF name$(count)=remove$ THEN 2120
2060   NEXT count
2080 PRINT'"Not on list"'
2100  GOTO2460
2120  FOR j=count TO total-1
2140   name$(j)=name$(j+1):score(j)=score(j+1):stscore(j)=
       stscore(j+1)
2160   NEXT j
2180 name$(total)=" ":score(total)=0:stscore(total)=0
2200 total=total-1
2220 PRINT'"Now removed"
2240  PROCholdscreen
2260 ENDPROC
2280 DEF PROCallchange
2300 CLS
2320 PRINT'"Input new scores"
2340 FOR count=1 TO total
2360   PRINT name$(count);TAB(15);:INPUT score(count)
2380   NEXT count
2400 PRINT'"New marks now entered."
2420 PROCholdscreen
2440 ENDPROC
2460 DEF PROConechange
2480 CLS
2500 INPUT'"Name of student ",stud$
2520 FOR count=1 TO total
2540   IF stud$=name$(count) THEN 2640
2560   NEXT count
2580 PRINT''"Not on the list."
2600 PROCholdscreen
2620 GOTO 2700
2640 INPUT'"What is the new score ",score(count)
2660 count=total
2680 PROCholdscreen
2700 ENDPROC
2720 DEF PROCsave
2740 CLS
2760 X=OPENOUT"names"
2780 PRINT'"Data now being stored on tape."
2800 FOR count=1 TO total
2820   PRINT#X,name$(count)
2840   PRINT#X,score(count)
2860   PRINT#X,stscore(count)
2880   NEXT count
2900 CLOSE#X
2920 PRINT"Data now stored on tape."
2940 PROCholdscreen
2960 ENDPROC
2980 DEF PROCrecover
3000 CLS
3020 PRINT"Data now being recovered from tape."
3040 PRINT'"Move the tape to the correct position"
3060 PRINT'"and then press the PLAY key."
3080 total=0
3100 X=OPENIN"names"
3120 PRINT"Data now being recovered."
3140 REPEAT
3160   total=total+1
3180   INPUT#X,name$(total)
3200   INPUT#X,score(total)
```

continued

```
3220   INPUT#X,stscore(total)
3240   UNTIL EOF#X
3260 CLOSE#X
3280 PROCholdscreen
3300 ENDPROC
3320 DEF PROCmeanone
3340 CLS
3360 PRINT"Mean and standard dev. now "
3380 PRINT"being computed."
3400 sum=0:sumsquares=0:mean=0:variance=0:stdev=0
3420 FOR count=1 TO total
3440   sum=sum+score(count)
3460   sumsquares=sumsquares+(score(count)^2)
3480   NEXT count
3500 mean=sum/total
3520 variance=sumsquares/total-mean^2
3540 stdev=SQR(variance)
3560 mean=INT(10*mean+.5)/10
3580 stdev=INT(10*stdev+.5)/10
3600 PRINT'"The mean is           "mean
3620 PRINT'"The standard dev. is "stdev
3640 PROCholdscreen
3660 ENDPROC
3680 DEFPROCmeantwo
3700 CLS
3720 sum=0:sumsquares=0:meantwo=0:variancetwo=0:stdevtwo=0
3740 FOR count=1 TO total
3760   sum=sum+stscore(count)
3780   sumsquares=sumsquares+(stscore(count)^2)
3800   NEXT count
3820 meantwo=sum/total
3840 variancetwo=sumsquares/total-meantwo^2
3860 stdevtwo=SQR(variancetwo)
3880 meantwo=INT(10*meantwo+.5)/10
3900 stdevtwo=INT(10*stdevtwo+.5)/10
3920 PRINT'"The mean of standardised scores is "meantwo
3940 PRINT'"The standard dev. of the standardised
     scores is  "stdevtwo
3960 PROCholdscreen
3980 ENDPROC
4000 DEF PROCstd
4020 CLS
4040 INPUT'"What is the chosen mean ",meantwo
4060 INPUT'"What is the chosen stand. dev. ",stdevtwo
4080 FOR count=1 TO total
4100   stscore(count)=meantwo+((score(count)-mean)/stdev)*
       stdevtwo
4120   NEXT count
4140 PRINT'"Scores now standardised."
4160 PROCholdscreen
4180 ENDPROC
4200 DEF PROCstats
4220 PROCmeanone
4240 PROCstd
4260 PROCmeantwo
4280 PROCholdscreen
4300 ENDPROC
```

Appendix D Further reading

BASIC

Listed below is a short selection of the great many books about BASIC. Look at as many as you can and try to find one that suits your own needs.

Each of these books, with one exception, can be used as an introductory text. The exception is the one by Lien. This is an encyclopedia of the BASIC language and is a most useful reference book.

Alcock, D. Illustrating BASIC. Cambridge : Cambridge University Press, 1977.

Bishop, P. Computer Programming in BASIC. Walton-on-Thames, Surrey : Nelson, 1979.

Coan, J.S. Advanced BASIC : Applications and Problems. Rochelle Park, N.J.: Hayden Book Company, Inc., 1978.

Deitel, H.M. Introduction to Computer Programming with the BASIC Language. Englewood Cliffs, N.J. : Prentice-Hall, 1978.

Dwyer, T.A. and Crutchfield, M.A. BASIC and the Personal Computer. London : Addison Wesley, 1978.

Eagle, M.R. An Introduction to BASIC. London : Bell and Hyman, 1976.

Farina, M.V. Programming in BASIC, the Time-sharing Language. Englewood Cliffs, N.J. : Prentice-Hall, 1968.

Hubin, W.N. BASIC Programming for Scientists and Engineers. Englewood Cliffs, N.J. : Prentice-Hall, 1978.

Lien, D.A. The BASIC Handbook : An Encyclopedia of the BASIC Computer Language. San Diego, Ca. : Compusoft Publishing, 1979.

Monro, D.M. Interactive Computing with BASIC, a First Course. London : Edward Arnold, 1978.

Scott, P.E. Programming in BASIC : a Beginner's Course. London : Hodder and Stoughton, 1975

The BBC Microcomputer

This second list is specifically about the BBC Microcomputer includes books, journals and associations.

Acorn User is a journal devoted exclusively to the computers and systems produced by Acorn Computers Ltd. This includes the BBC Microcomputer, available monthly from : Addison-Wesley Publishers Ltd., Douglas Road, Tonbridge, Kent TN9 2TS.

BBC Computer Literacy Project. This makes much use of the computer and enquiries should be sent to : British Broadcasting Services, PO Box 7, London, W3 6XJ.

BEEBON. A journal published bi-monthly exclusively about the BBC Microcomputer. Available from : The Beebon, 106 The Albany, Old Hall Street, Liverpool, Merseyside, L3 9EP.

BEEBUG. Independent national User Group for the BBC Microcomputer. Produces a monthly newsletter called Beebug Newsletter. Available from : Beebug, Dept. 6, 374, Wandsworth Road, London, SW3 4TW.

LASERBUG. Independent National User Group for the BBC Microcomputer. Produces a newsletter called Laserbug. Available from : Laserbug, 10 Dawley Ride, Colnbrook, Slough, Berks., SL3 0QH.

Birnbaum,I. Assembly Language Programming for the BBC Microcomputer. London : Macmillan Press, 1982.

Coll,J. The BBC Microcomputer : User Guide. London : British Broadcasting Corporation, 1982.

Cownie,J. Creative Graphics on the BBC Microcomputer. Cambridge : Acornsoft, 1982.

Cryer,N. and Cryer,P. BASIC Programming on the BBC Microcomputer. Hemel Hempstead : Prentice Hall, 1982.

Dane,P.M. Learning to use the B.B.C. Microcomputer. London : Gower, 1982.

Deeson,E. Easy Programming for the BBC Micro. Nantwich, Cheshire : Shiva, 1982.

Hartnell,T. Let your BBC Micro Teach you to Program. London : Interface, 1982.

Hartnell,T. and Ruston,J. The Book of Listings: Fun Programs for the BBC Microcomputer. London : Interface, 1982.

Johnson-Davis,D. Practical Programs for the BBC Computer and Acorn Atom. Sussex : Sigma Technical Press, 1982.

Ruston,J. The BBC Micro Revealed. London : Interface, 1982.

Thomas,A. Further Programming for the BBC Micro. Nantwich, Cheshire : Shiva, 1983.

Ward,B.J. The BBC Microcomputer Disk System User Guide. Cambridge : Acorn Computers Ltd., 1982.

Williams,P. Programming the BBC Micro. London : Newnes Microcomputer Books, 1983.

INDEX